Studies in Economic Reform and Social Justice

HARRY GUNNISON BROWN
AN ORTHODOX ECONOMIST AND HIS CONTRIBUTIONS

T0338078

Blackwell
Publishing

The Series
Studies in Economic Reform and Social Justice

Laurence S. Moss, Series Editor

Robert V. Andelson, ed.
Land-Value Taxation Around the World

J. A. Giacalone and C. W. Cobb, eds.
The Path to Justice: Following in the Footsteps of Henry George

Christopher K. Ryan
Harry Gunnison Brown
An Orthodox Economist and His Contributions

Studies in Economic Reform and Social Justice

HARRY GUNNISON BROWN
AN ORTHODOX ECONOMIST AND HIS CONTRIBUTIONS

By

Christopher K. Ryan

Series Editor
Laurence S. Moss

Blackwell
Publishing

Blackwell Publishers, Inc.
350 Main Street
Malden, MA 02148 USA

Blackwell Publishers, Ltd.
108 Cowley Road
Oxford OX4 1JF
United Kingdom

Library of Congress Cataloging-in-Publication Data Information is located at the Library of Congress.

Includes bibliographical references and index.
ISBN 1-4051-1156-9 (case : alk. paper) — ISBN 1-4051-0864-9 (pbk.: alk. paper)

ISBN 1-4051-1156-9
ISBN 1-4051-0864-9
ISSN 0002-9246

Cover images: Image of Harry Gunnison Brown courtesy of the Robert Schalkenbach Society; image of Jesse Hall courtesy of the University of Missouri–Columbia. The University of Missouri–Columbia was founded in 1839 as the first public university west of the Mississippi River, the first state university in Thomas Jefferson's Louisiana Purchase territory.

Dedication

I would like to dedicate this book to the memory of
Elizabeth Read Brown (1902–1987)
and Will Lissner (1908–2000).

A portrait of the young Harry Gunnison Brown, courtesy of the Robert Schalkenbach Foundation, New York, NY.

A portrait of the older Harry Gunnison Brown, courtesy of the
Robert Schalkenbach Foundation, New York, NY.

Contents

Foreword

I am delighted that Harry Gunnison Brown at last has the biography that he so clearly deserves.

My close acquaintance with Professor Brown was limited to the one short academic year, 1937–38, I spent at the University of Missouri as his teaching assistant and graduate student.

I think what impressed me more than anything else about his economic thinking was its coherence, its thorough internal consistency, and its apparent sufficiency; his trust in the functioning of competitive markets wherever competition is feasible; his painstakingly analytical elaboration of the consistent economic principles for regulating markets in which competition is infeasible (a glance at my own two-volume *Economics of Regulation* will quickly show how very heavily, a full half-century later, I drew on his *Principles of Commerce* and his historic exchanges with John Bauer); his unswerving espousal of free trade; his belief in the sufficiency of monetary policy to solve the problem of macroeconomic instability; and, of course, his espousal of the tax on land values as the only method of financing government revenues most fully consistent with economic efficiency, distributive justice, and—especially considering its corollary, the removal of taxes on capital improvements and investment generally—with economic progress.

Of course all this was thoroughly classical (except for the reference to the emphasis on land value taxation—but even this was beautifully compatible with the classical model) and is subject to whatever reservations one may have about the sufficiency of that approach; but it is an admirable system of economic thinking, still highly relevant today, and Professor Brown expounded it with grace, persistence, intellectual incisiveness, and verve.

I must add that I came to have enormous affection and respect for him. He was a superb teacher and a delightful human being.

Alfred E. Kahn
Ithaca, New York
September 29, 1986

Preface and Acknowledgments
to This Edition

THIS STUDY WAS originally a 1985 Ph.D. dissertation prepared for the Department of Economics at Iowa State University in Ames, Iowa. In 1987 Westview Press of Boulder, Colorado published a thoroughly edited version of the study with its original title, *Harry Gunnison Brown: Economist.* This title was chosen to bring Brown's contributions as an economist into contemporary focus. Brown will be best remembered as one of the very few academic economists of roughly the first half of the twentieth century to champion what he saw as Henry George's greatest legacy: his land value taxation proposal. Yet it is a contention of this book that Brown's other work merits reconsideration as well.

The nature of the study has a biographical dimension that has limitations: Brown left no personal papers, diaries or correspondence. In addition, almost all the people with whom I conversed or corresponded knew him only during or after his late fifties. I did not personally know Dr. Brown. The correspondence that I reference in the study is located at the Yale University Library (Irving Fisher and James Harvey Rogers Papers) and at the University of Missouri Library in the University of Missouri Western Historical Manuscripts Collection. (Letters to and from Brown are preserved as departmental correspondence.) All other related correspondence that I have listed as "Personal Files" in the Endnotes and Bibliography will be transferred to the above collection in Columbia, Missouri.

The 1987 edition and, perhaps more so, this revision is from beginning to end a sympathetic study of Brown. I began my research with only a vague recollection of a 1939 *JPE* article by him and a skeptical reading of George's *Progress and Poverty* in a graduate course. I was influenced not only by my readings but also by the opinions of others, many of whom did not know Brown personally, either.

In retrospect my acknowledgements in the first version of this study were overly terse. I would now like to extend my list of those who aided in this work either by help or encouragement. Bobbie Horn of Tulsa University suggested the topic to me. I found that Pinkney C. Walker of Missouri University had compiled a list of Brown's publications from 1907–1951. William Spellman of Coe College shared with me an independently derived, updated bibliography, and Elizabeth Read Brown (Brown's second wife) aided the Special Collections Department of the University of Missouri Library in collecting copies of Brown's articles and pamphlets. In 1980, Paul Junk of the University of Minnesota-Duluth wrote a compelling biographical sketch of Brown in his "Preface" to *Selected Articles by Harry Gunnison Brown: The Case for Land Value Taxation*. Alfred Kahn replied to a letter of inquiry about Brown with an astoundingly acute appreciation of him. Professors Dudley Luckett and Charles Meyer of Iowa State University were sympathetic and helpful in the realization of the original version. Elizabeth Read Brown and Phillips Hamlin Brown (Brown's son) were helpful readers. Will Lissner was, I suspect, instrumental in the Westview publication, and Spencer Carr was a particularly enthusiastic editor. Mason Gaffney has been a very highly valued commentator over many years. Although I have had little or no connection with Georgist groups, I found the late Robert Clancy's review article to be a welcome source of encouragement. There remains a substantial number of economists who recognized or came to recognize Brown's worth as an economist, many of whom I have communicated with, and I once again extend my thanks for their help.

For the present edition of this study, I have attempted to expand and correct the original version and incorporate, although in limited fashion, new developments as they relate to Brown's contributions. Some of the added material was originally published in a 1997 *AJES* article titled "Harry Gunnison Brown's Advocacy: The Case He Made for Land Value Taxation 1917–1975." My principal acknowledgement for this opportunity, which I value very highly, is to the Board of Directors of the *AJES* and in particular to its editor, Laurence S. Moss. My final and most important acknowledgement is to one whom George Stigler called an "indulgent spouse." I would venture to change his adjective to "intelligent" and add her name, Helen.

Chapter 1

Introduction

PAUL SAMUELSON ONCE formulated a list of early prominent American economists born after 1860.[1] To the list consisting of W. C. Mitchell, Allyn Young, H. L. Moore, Frank Knight, Jacob Viner and Henry Schlutz he added the name of Harry Gunnison Brown. It is improbable that Brown's name has a familiar ring for contemporary students. It is possible, however, that some student may recall that the library catalog card for Irving Fisher's classic work *The Purchasing Power of Money* lists Brown as assisting Fisher in this work.

Harry Gunnison Brown was roughly of the second generation of American economists who followed the pioneering generation that included John Bates Clark, E. R. A. Seligman, Frank Taussig, Francis Walker, Simon Patten, Richard Ely, Thomas Nixon Carver, Herbert Davenport and Irving Fisher, among others. Brown studied under and taught with Fisher at Yale until 1915. He and James Harvey Rogers were said to be Fisher's favorite and ablest students.[2] Brown became a monetarist in the tradition of Fisher. Although on several occasions they differed, Brown demonstrated enduring respect for his mentor and colleague.

Another economist, Herbert J. Davenport, was held in particular regard by Brown. He joined Davenport at the University of Missouri for a year before Davenport left for Cornell. Davenport's work in refining and, at times, defending classical economic doctrine was admired by Brown. The discipline at that time struggled with the question of how much of the classical thought of the British School was to be retained as sound. Brown's position in this regard was exemplified by his self-description as "an economist unemancipated from the classical tradition." He implied by this statement that other economists had gone too far in their rejection of classical doctrine. Brown, who had read J. S. Mill before entering college, would in some respects retain strong elements of the classical approach in his writing.[3]

An element in Brown's thought that would make him stand out among academic economists was his staunch belief in and advocacy of the ideas of Henry George. In particular, Brown would argue throughout his life for tax reform along the lines espoused by George when the profession tended to dismiss George's thought as utterly fallacious. Most prominent among Brown's areas of specialization was that of taxation and especially, tax incidence. His text, *The Economics of Taxation*, stood for a time as a benchmark for texts on the subject of tax incidence.

In his chosen profession, Brown's record was exemplary during five decades of teaching at Yale, Missouri, The New School of Social Research, Mississippi and Franklin and Marshall. He wrote more than 100 articles and 10 books. He was said to be for many years the dominant influence behind Missouri's School of Business and Public Administration.[4] His dedication to teaching has been praised by his students, many of whom were to become prominent in economics and related areas.

Brown's Work

ALTHOUGH BROWN'S CONCERNS WERE DIFFUSE, I would like to emphasize three characteristics of his work: its "modernity"; its classical roots; its emphasis on welfare considerations. Through Fisher's influence, Brown was aware of developments that anticipated the direction of economics as a field of study. He displayed, if not mathematical rigor, a dedication to a clear, logical approach to economic theory as well as an appreciation of the value of statistical application to the testing of economic theories. Harold Hotelling once commented that Brown's logic was mathematical in nature.[5] On the other hand, although Brown was by definition a neoclassical economist, he tended to retain key elements of the classical approach, as seen in his selective use of Davenport's work, in his rejection of the claims of the Psychological School of Frank Fetter and in his later objections to Keynesian economics. Characteristic of Brown's work was a consistent attempt to relate economic questions to what he termed the "common welfare."

That he found inspiration in the writings of Henry George was not unusual. Brown's steadfastness in his espousal of George's proposed reform in the face of the hostility, skepticism and indifference of the profession was unusual.

As is frequently commented upon, the advance and profusion of a discipline in many regards tend to foster the "bureaucratic" phenomenon of "constructive forgetting."

Although certainly not without merit, this process stands subject to Santayana's famous dictum.[6] Arnold Harberger made this point in the following manner:

> Brown was one of a small group of economists of his era (which included Frank Knight, Irving Fisher, A. C. Pigou) who really carried the science forward by large steps. For decades, their work was neglected as the profession pursued one fad after another, but now, as economists have returned, more or less, to their mainstream, they are seeing once again the brilliance and insight of people like H. G. Brown.[7]

Milton Friedman and Kenneth Boulding have commented that they felt that Brown's work has been overlooked.[8] Thus, my proposition is to examine his work with an even treatment of his efforts, always trying to place them in the proper historical context and to render evaluatory comments where relevant.

Brown's contributions can best be examined by considering separately his work in the wide variety of topics that interested him. First, however, this chapter will present a brief biography abstracted largely from obituary and memorial statements. Chapter 2 is an attempt to set the scene of Brown's earlier years in the profession by surveying different views of a key question for Brown in economic theory. Chapter 3 treats his views on capital and interest theories. Chapter 4 combines macroeconomic considerations of business cycles, monetary policy and Brown's view of Keynesianism. Chapter 5 examines Brown's work in taxation, excluding the question of land value taxation, which is treated in Chapter 6. His early interest in railroad rates and public utility pricing are dealt with in Chapter 7. Chapter 8 examines another early interest in international trade and finance. Chapter 9 comments on his professional career as an educator and writer of textbooks. The final chapter is an attempt to evaluate and classify Brown's thought in economic and political spheres.

Harry Gunnison Brown: A Biography

HARRY GUNNISON BROWN WAS BORN in Troy, New York, on May 7, 1880.[9] His father, Milton Peers Brown, was an accountant. Harry's middle name derived from his mother's maiden name—Elizabeth H. Gunnison. At age four, he was stricken with tuberculosis of the hip, which would recur and alter his vocational possibilities. After completing high school, he worked in a factory but after one year the tuberculosis became active and forced him to spend the next year in bed. He took advantage of the situation and read extensively, including in his reading works of J. S. Mill, Herbert Spencer and Henry George. The illness, abetted undoubtedly by Brown's intellectual curiosity, led him to enroll at Williams College at the turn of the century. He graduated from Williams in 1904, which he accomplished with the financial aid of his grandfather, scholarships, part-time jobs and summer farm work. (In 1936, Williams awarded Brown an honorary L.H.D.)

Brown next attended Ohio State University in 1905–1906, where he coached debating teams, an activity he had pursued as an undergraduate. He entered Yale University the following year and completed his Ph.D. in economics in 1909. His dissertation under Irving Fisher's supervision was titled *Some Phases of Railroad Combination*. His earliest published articles date from 1907. Faculty members present at Yale mentioned by Brown (other than Fisher) were Clive Day, H. C. Emery and Fred Fairchild. Although no longer teaching economics courses, William Graham Sumner had been an early influence on Yale's teaching of political economy. Also, the acting president of Yale, Arthur Twining Hadley, had an active interest in economic questions.

Upon completion of his degree, Brown joined the faculty at Yale where he taught as an instructor until 1915. In this period, he assisted Fisher in *The Purchasing Power of Money* and began his own publishing career with Macmillan. It has been reported that he solidified his interest in Henry George and became an advocate of land value taxation before leaving Yale.[10]

Brown became an assistant professor at the University of Missouri in 1916. The Economics Department was headed by Herbert J. Davenport and counted Thorstein Veblen as a member. Missouri's economics faculty had then a reputation as one of the strongest in the country.[11] Davenport left in 1917, but the department retained a fine reputation under Brown's chairmanship as well as a close relationship with Yale. Brown became a full professor in 1918 and chaired the department with only brief respites until 1947. He also served as acting dean of the School of Business and Public Administration during the years 1934–1936 and 1942–1946. He was made professor emeritus in 1950. Brown published nine books and many articles in his 35 years at Missouri. He served as a member of the executive committee of the American Economics Association for the years 1937–1938. He was elected president of the Midwest Economics Association for 1941–1942. He became a director and member of the editorial board of the *American Journal of Economics and Sociology* and was a frequent contributor to this journal dedicated to interdisciplinary research in the social sciences.

In 1951, on the invitation of Alvin Johnson, Brown taught at the New School for Social Research and also at the Institute for Economic Inquiry in Chicago. As a visiting professor at the University of Mississippi he taught six more years. He then completed his formal teaching career at Franklin and Marshall College. While residing in Pennsylvania, he and his second wife, Elizabeth Read Brown, were active in promoting local tax reform. After his retirement he remained active by writing and lecturing on tax reform and other subjects. When he was 93, the Department of Economics at Missouri sponsored a symposium on taxation and tax reform in his honor. His death occurred in March 1975.

Brown married his first wife, Fleda Phillips, in 1911. In many of his books, he cited her aid as a proof and critical reader. She died in 1952. They had three children: Cleone Elsa, Phillips Hamlin and Richard Flint. He was married to Elizabeth Lumley Read[12] in 1953. She collaborated with him in his endeavors and continued this work until her death in February of 1987.

Notes

1. Paul Samuelson (1967). *Ten Economic Studies in the Tradition of Irving Fisher.* New York: John Wiley & Sons: 17.

2. Karl Bopp (1965). *Essays in Monetary Policy in Honor of Elmer Wood.* Ed. Pinkney Walker. Columbia, MO: University of Missouri Press: 8.

3. Paul Junk (1980). Preface. *The Selected Articles by Harry Gunnison Brown.* New York: Robert Schalkenbach Foundation: xv.

4. Pinkney Walker (1952). Preface. "Essays in Honor of Harry Gunnison Brown, Ph.D.; On the Occasion of His Retirement from the University of Missouri." *American Journal of Economics and Sociology* 11 (April): 228.

5. Will Lissner (1975). "In Memoriam: H. G. Brown 1880–1975." *American Journal of Economics and Sociology* 34 (July): 246.

6. George Santayana (1905), "Progress far from consisting in change, depends on rententiveness. . . . Those who cannot remember the past are condemned to repeat it." In *Life of Reason*, Vol. 1, *Reason in Common Sense.* New York: C. Scribner's & Sons: 284.

7. Arnold Harberger (1979). Quoted on the back cover of *The Economics of Taxation* by Harry Gunnison Brown. Chicago: University of Chicago Press.

8. Milton Friedman (October 6,1984), letter to author. Personal files, Iowa City, IA. Kenneth Boulding (December 10, 1984), letter to author. Personal files, Iowa City, IA.

9. This biography is based primarily on the material cited in Notes 3, 4 and 5 and on *The National Cyclopedia of American Biography*, v. 58, Clifton, NJ: James T. White and Company, 1979: 43–44.

10. Lissner (1975): 246.

11. Frank Fletcher Stevens (1962). *A History of the University of Missouri.* Columbia, MO: University of Missouri Press: 419.

12. See Will Lissner (1987) "In Memoriam: Elizabeth Read Brown." *American Journal of Economics and Sociology* 46 (3): 383–384.
Christopher K. Ryan (2000). "Elizabeth Read Brown (1902–87)." *A Biographical Dictionary of Women Economists.* Eds. Robert W. Dimand, Mary Ann Dimand and Evelyn L. Forget. Cheltenham, UK and Northampton, MA: Edward Elgar: 89–91.

Chapter 2

Land as a Factor of Production

Introduction

A BRIEF SURVEY OF CONTEMPORARY INTRODUCTORY TEXTBOOKS in economics indicates that the classification of the factors of production utilized by classical political economists has been retained. To land, labor and capital these texts occasionally add entrepreneurship. The returns to the factors—rent, wages and interest (as well as profit)—are explained in rough accordance to usage of more than 100 years. When more advanced texts in microeconomic theory are examined, however, the accordance disappears.

In the March 1928 issue of the *American Economic Review*, Clark Warburton examined prominent textbooks of the time, comparing and contrasting the economic terminology employed to describe the factors of production and the distributive shares. Taking the terminology used by John Stuart Mill as a model, Warburton found a wide divergence in the usage of the terms and noted a tendency to retain the tripartite grouping of the factors while recognizing that it was both vague and misleading.[1] One of the inherent problems that accounted for the wide differences in approach was that there were differing views of capital and interest. Another problem was the question of the relationship of land to capital. Although these questions are clearly interrelated, I will discuss the narrower question in the following manner: Is land an independent factor of production? Should the terminological distinction between land and capital be retained for analytical purposes? Is the distinction important for welfare considerations?

The position of land in theories of value and distribution had been debated for many years prior to Harry Gunnison Brown's entrance into economic studies. The questions noted previously had generated an interesting distribution of opinion among the political economists who preceded Brown as well as among his contemporaries. Because for Brown these questions and their various answers constituted an important element in his thought and work, I will survey this distribution, arbitrarily beginning with Alfred Marshall and concluding with Brown's American colleagues. In reviewing these opinions, I will attempt to point out relevant tendencies in the arguments without critiquing individual positions in detail.

Views of English and Continental Political Economists

ALFRED MARSHALL'S SOMEWHAT EQUIVOCAL POSITION is familiar. His statement that the rent of land is the "leading species of a large genus"[2] breaks away from Ricardo's thought. Yet, he modified this statement with "though, indeed, it has peculiarities of its own which are vital from the point of theory as well as practice"[3] and in the same article said, "And even there in a new country land must be regarded as a thing by itself from the ethical point of view."[4] Marshall's views on land and rent were challenged by several economists, some of whom will be noted later. Francis Edgeworth followed Marshall's lead and viewed land as a form of capital to the individual but not to society.[5]

However, Edwin Cannan traced the usage of three "requisites of production" in English political economy and argued that by 1848 the triad "was not quite firmly established."[6] He identified the origin of the terminology with Adam Smith but noted that Smith's successors varied considerably in their approaches. James Mill, for example, identified only labor and capital as "requisites." Later in Cannan's *A Review of Economic Theory*, he maintained that the attempt to distinguish land from other forms of property was futile.[7] Philip Wicksteed, despite a lifelong sympathy for land nationalization programs as well as a friendship with George, viewed land as a "tool" co-ordinate with other factors in the determination of distribution and, as Mark Blaug has pointed out, appeared to overlook the relative fixity of the supply of land.[8] Mason Gaffney has argued Wicksteed's contribution was simply a "mathematical insight" which should not be taken as proof that

Wicksteed did not view land as fundamentally different in the Ricardian fashion.[9]

Knut Wicksell discussed the question of whether land should be included with capital. He concluded that the tripartite division of the factors was justifiable.[10] Wicksell approved of Henry Seager's definition of capital as the produced means of further production. This, for Wicksell, distinguished capital from land and labor *a priori* as they are not "produced" in the same sense as is capital. Furthermore, he viewed interest as an organic growth out of capital in contrast to wages and rent; although rent may be expressed as a percentage, like interest, this was "something derivative and secondary."[11]

In a similar manner, Gustav Cassel defended the traditional classification. He noted the assertion that the classification was due to particular social conditions in England wherein the classical theory evolved but stated that "this classification is without doubt in complete accord with requirements of a theory of pricing, and that its place in theoretical economics is fully justified."[12] Cassel distinguished between natural and "produced" land and argued that the price of the former is a secondary result of the pricing process, in that rent is capitalized with respect to the current rate of interest.

George Stigler, in discussing the theorists of the Austrian school, noted that only Eugen Böhm-Bawerk trenchantly defended the traditional classification of land as an independent factor.[13] Although Böhm-Bawerk saw justification for including land with capital as "acquisitive instruments," he maintained that it was preferable to retain the distinction. He argued that land's distinguishing factors included immobility, fixity of supply and a difference in origin as well as having societal implications.[14] On terminological grounds, he noted that the distinction accords roughly with common usage, and the proposal to lump it with capital would leave us without a convenient term for the produced means of "acquisition."[15]

Menger, again following Stigler, criticized the classical division of factors but conceded that the relative immobility of land had economic significance.[16] Wieser analyzed the returns to what Stigler termed the "holy trinity," and found the appropriation via taxation of "unearned" urban rents to be justifiable.[17] Perhaps more significantly, Menger's assumed static case made the distinction irrelevant, because all "factors" were fixed. Thus, for purposes of analysis land was treated as capital.

In the Walrasian system, all factors or resources are fixed or given such that the supposed unique attribute of land is assumed for all factors.[18] Walras did consider important the aspect of "extension" with respect to land, in that land could not be produced or destroyed, but land played at most a minor role in his analysis of production. Vilfredo Pareto's position was similar in that he argued "land capital" had no precedence over other capital.[19] However, he did concede that distinguishing land from capital was of possible political importance. Pantaleoni's treatment of land as one of many "instrumental commodities"[20] demonstrates Menger's influence. James M. Buchanan has suggested that Pareto's as well as Pantaleoni's rejection of Ricardian rent theory was inspired by the earlier work of Francesco Ferrara who interpreted rent as accruing to all factors of superior productivity.[21]

Views of American Economists

Pre-1900 Writers

Early American writers on political economy reacted negatively to Ricardo's theory of rent. Frank Fetter commented in the introduction to J. R. Turner's *The Ricardian Rent Theory in Early American Economics* that, "They denied, with almost as close approach to unanimity, the 'orthodox' contrast between land and capital in the sense of artificial agents."[22] Henry Carey and Francis Bowen argued that land was capital and that Ricardo's theory was formulated with respect to England's "peculiar social conditions."[23] Arthur L. Perry, who taught at Williams, maintained that all land value was due to human effort with only minor exceptions (unusual fertility or location).[24] In contrast, Francis Walker followed the classical treatment of land as a distinct agent in production.[25] However, the influential Simon N. Patten argued that the social imperatives no longer applied so that incomes no longer should be separated out as in the classical construct.[26]

At the turn of the century, American political economists were heterodox in their approaches to economic theory. Several had studied in Europe, especially at German universities.[27] Doctorate programs were developing that permitted a greater specialization in economic theory. Professional journals were established, and the publication of texts in economics expanded rapidly, frequently with "Principles" as a title. American scholars were achieving increasing recognition in the older centers of study.

John Bates Clark, who studied at Heidelberg under Karl Knies and later taught at Columbia University, is considered by several commentators to be the first prominent American economic theorist. Clark's definition of capital denied land a separate role. He argued that the traditional treatment of land was based on its absolute fixity as opposed to other factors as well as on the differential nature of its return.[28] His analysis fixed all "instruments," or resources, and illustrated that the distributive shares were determined in a differential fashion. Marshall once wrote to Clark: "I have been looking a little at your *Distribution of Wealth* recently again. I am always struck by its power and freshness. But it does not lead me to yield an inch on the controverted distinction between interest and rent proper."[29] Three other important theorists of this era were Frank Fetter, Irving Fisher and Herbert J. Davenport. Although they debated frequently and at length with one another as well as with Clark, they were unified in their rejection of the traditional approach.

Fetter, Fisher and Davenport

The debate on the significance of land in economic theory was enlivened with the publication of Clark's *The Distribution of Wealth* in 1899 and Fetter's articles in the *Publications of the American Economics Association* and the *Quarterly Journal of Economics*.[30] Economists who applied the "traditional" classification seemed driven in their attempts to defend it against the "modern" view. Fetter's arguments were more detailed and emphatic than those of previous authors. He challenged Böhm-Bawerk's reasons for viewing land as separate from capital. After refuting his arguments one by one, Fetter concluded that Böhm-Bawerk was influenced by a labor theory of value that perceived land as a gift of nature and capital as the result of nature.[31] During the same year, Fetter argued that Marshall had mixed individual versus societal and "static" versus "dynamic" views in distinguishing land from capital.[32] Essentially, Fetter felt that land should be considered augmentable under dynamic conditions in a manner commensurate with capital. Furthermore, he argued that a distinction based on a societal rather than an individual viewpoint relied upon a "real cost" concept of rent. Whereas Marshall had found that the property of extension (situation) led to "true rent" even in a "new country," Fetter maintained that from a static view, no such distinction could be made between incomes from a property of a factor and the income of the factor itself. Marshall's response in the 1907 edition of his *Principles of Economics* was that extension was the chief property of land and thus justified consideration of "true rent"; he added that other properties as well worked to codetermine the composite value of land.[33] Fetter's own classificatory system differed radically from previous usage.[34] In another article, he stressed the impossibility of a practical division between land and capital.

> The notion that it is a simple matter to distinguish between the yield of natural agents and that of improvements is fanciful and confusing. . . . The objective classification of land and capital as natural and artificial agents is a task that always must transcend the human power of discrimination.[35]

From another standpoint, Fetter was concerned (as were other economists of the time) with the terminological differences between academic and business usage of terms. He pointed out that the distinction between land and capital was of little importance for practical businessmen. (Many years later Fetter would be criticized by an otherwise sympathetic commentator, Murray Rothbard, for having "completely misunderstood" the distinction between land and capital goods. In Rothbard's interpretation of Austrian economics the "permanence" or "non-reproducibility" of a resource distinguishes it from other goods.[36])

Irving Fisher's definition of capital consistently included land. In *Elementary Principles of Economics*, he pointed out that other authors limit the concept but that "such a limitation, however, is not only difficult to make, but cripples the usefulness of the concept in economic analysis."[37] However, he conceded the importance of land as a special category of capital as well as the significance of land's relative fixity for purposes of taxation.[38] In reviewing Fisher's 1906 *The Nature of Capital and Income*, John Commons grouped Fisher with Clark and Fetter as developing the theory of what he termed "business economy" as opposed to political economy. Commons said:

> The issue is now clear. The older political economists were working on a serious social problem—that of earned and unearned incomes. They carried everything back into terms of cost, effort, enterprise, sacrifice, abstinence, and distinguished the income that corresponded to cost from that which came as a surplus above cost. They were political economists.[39]

Herbert J. Davenport, Brown's colleague at Missouri, investigated the separation of land from capital in more detail than Fisher, although Davenport agreed in large part with Fisher's view of capital. In the preface to *Value and Distribution* in 1908, he listed the doctrines he would eliminate from economic theory. Last on the list was the tripartite classification of the productive factors. Denying that a clear distinction could be made on technological grounds, he suggested that as many factors could be distinguished as were pertinent although they may be myriad.[40] As to the relative fixity or perceived inelasticity of the supply of land, Davenport pointed out that this view involved conjecture or prophecy and as such should not be admissible in rigorous theory.[41] Although he was convinced on technical grounds that no distinction was tenable, he examined the influences behind the tradition and remarked, "With these spatial qualities of land are more or less closely associated certain legal, jurisdictional and territorial aspects possessing great social significance."[42] He indicated that the English common-law distinction between realty and personalty is parallel to and interrelated with the traditional division of the factors. For Davenport, separating land from capital was valid in "a larger social, historical and philosophical view,"[43] and invalid for competitive analysis. What he may have been referring to in the first case was his Veblen-like views of "capitalized privilege and predation" in which he included land ownership.[44]

Other American Views

In a publication of the American Economics Association in 1902 titled "Rent in Modern Economic Theory," Alvin S. Johnson, one of J. B. Clark's students, included a long chapter on land as an independent factor in production. Johnson began with the proposition that only if land has distinct characteristics of true economic significance can rent from land be treated as a distinct class of income. He discounted the "origins" or "gifts of nature" as inadequate or metaphysical. Where Alfred Marshall and John Commons had found situation or extension a distinguishing element, Johnson denied that this was substantial enough to make the distinction meaningful. He also dismissed the argument that the value of capital will tend to equal "cost" while the value of land will exceed its "costs"; Johnson thought the argument relied upon unreal assumptions made with regard to the capital market, that is, perfect competition with perfect knowledge or insurance. He further found economic land to be augmentable but added, "The laws that govern the increase in land are not identical with those which cause capital to increase."[45] Ultimately he accepted land as a factor for the dynamic analysis of price and income movements.

At least 11 members of the American Economics Association were given an opportunity to respond to a paper by Fetter presented at the Association's meeting in 1903.[46] Their response was not only to Fetter's position given previously, but also, in part, to the well-known views of J. B. Clark on the subject of land's relationship to capital. Although the responses were largely critical, they did contain concessions to the newer approaches. Thomas Nixon Carver maintained that a clear distinction between income from land and other incomes existed in the particular sense that "rent does not enter into cost or into price."[47] He also believed that "production would be quite as efficient as it now is even if no one were allowed rent as a personal income."[48] Carver conceded, however, that for a functional view of distribution (rather than a personal view), the distinction was unimportant. Carver's remarks were rebutted by Fetter who argued that land rent is necessary to maintain the supply of land's productive qualities as well as to induce their expansion.

Among the other dissenting discussants were Jacob H. Hollander, Richard T. Ely, James E. LeRossignol and W. G. Langworthy Taylor. Hollander provided a defense along the lines of Marshall, arguing that land (as opposed to capital) would be available for "normal, long-time" production only in diminishing efficiency with respect to extensive use. Ely contented, in this instance, that Fetter's approach underestimated the "inseparable conditions of land." Ely's position in later writings emphasized that he viewed land as differing from capital in degree only: "Land in any usable shape had normally and regularly to be produced."[49] LeRossignol stressed the difference between goods that are reproducible and those that are not. Finally, Taylor emphasized, in the dynamic view, land's greater inherent scarcity.

Henry Seager in a review of Clark's *The Distribution of Wealth* commented

> From the point of view of economic dynamics the fact that land is a gift of nature while other instruments are themselves the products of human industry attaches to the former an interest which the latter are without.[50]

Charles Tuttle presented a similar critique of this aspect of Clark's book.[51]

John Commons maintained that for social and ethical reasons land should be viewed as distinct from capital. He acknowledged that soil is capital but situation per se is not, as it neither produces nor is it produced. Land in the sense of its situation was, for Commons, a "social relation." He argued, "If there is a difference between patent right and capital, there is a similar difference between land and capital."[52]

Frank T. Carlton's article, "The Rent Concept, Narrowed and Broadened," published in the *Quarterly Journal of Economics* 1907–1908, was illustrative of the strategic retreat taken by many writers in their defense of land as a separate factor. Reacting primarily to Clark and Johnson, Carlton pointed to the rapid growth of urban lands wherein the capital and site values may be distinguished more easily than in the case of agriculture. He follows Commons by defining land as only that which "furnishes standing room and situation with regard to markets."[53] He proceeded to broaden the concept of rent by including special privileges or special relations to markets that cannot be duplicated or physically depreciated.

Harvard's Frank Taussig retained the classical division of the factors while admitting to the practical difficulty of distinguishing land from capital; he employed the term "natural capital" to designate land and other "natural agents." Making a number of qualifications, he argued that there was a broad margin toward which the return to capital would tend while no such tendency governed the return to "natural capital."[54] For Taussig, truly permanent improvements embodied in land should be treated as land and their return as rent.[55]

E. R. A. Seligman closely followed Marshall's approach to the classification of factors by alternatively using a two, three, or four breakdown, whichever was appropriate. For example, if capital were a fund, then land would be a sub-category. Seligman's justification for the separation of land from capital was that he found "peculiar consequences" in the law of diminishing returns when applied to land.[56]

It is noteworthy that in 1928 Paul Douglas and Charles Cobb concluded their famous article by saying:

> We should ultimately look forward to including the third factor of natural resources in our equations and seeing to what degree this modifies our conclusions and what light it throws upon the theory of rent.[57]

Brown's Position

Harry Gunnison Brown's position reflected portions of earlier conceptions. He accepted the narrower view of the rent concept in defining land as "land space," thereby excluding all improvements associated with land. As did other economists, he included (but without great emphasis) mineral and water resources in his concept of land. The return to "land space" was thus a situation rent very similar to Marshall's true or ground rent. Brown's primary defense of the continued distinction was based on the nonreproducibility of land space as a key property distinguishing it from ordinary goods.

He admitted that this property was not unique to land space because works of art, genius and so on have a like characteristic. The reproducibility of land was physically improbable and entailed prohibitively high marginal costs in all but exceptional circumstances.[58] Brown attempted to integrate his distinction between land and capital into a theory of value and distribution, by establishing that the return to land space was only superficially similar to the return to "made capital." The essential difference, in his view, rested on the mode of land and capital's valuations and the belief that capital was a derivative factor.[59] These arguments will be elaborated on in the succeeding chapter as they bear directly on Brown's part in controversies dealing with capital and interest theories.

Later Commentary

WHEN BROWN BEGAN HIS ACADEMIC CAREER, the question of the place of land in economic theory was far from resolved. Several more contributions to the debate were yet to be made, usually in connection with capital theory, methodology, or simply terminology. The exchanges of Knight and Kaldor may be noted as one example. Knight contended that

> land is capital merely; defined in any realistic way, it presents an infinite variety of conditions as to maintenance and replacements, and possibilities for increase in supply, as does any other general class of capital instruments.[60]

He also remarked,

> The notion that what are called "natural agents" are not produced is false and reflects a false conception of production.[61]

For Kaldor,

> Even if the distinction between "permanent" and "non-permanent" resources or between "original" and "produced" is untenable or irrelevant, there is still a distinction to be drawn between "producible" and "non-producible" resources.[62]

As late as 1937 L. M. Fraser commented,

> The truth is that economists have not as a whole clearly made up their minds what to mean by "land"—much less, how important a part it should play in their expositions of value theory.[63]

However, from the 1928 date of Warburton's article forward one must look ever more closely to find expressions relevant to the question of the role of land in economic theory.[64] It was certainly not the central point of contention in the later capital theory debates alluded to above. The scrutiny required to find such relevant references might well be indicated by Mason Gaffney's mention of a footnote to the chapter, "A Digression on Rent," in Joan Robinson's 1933 *The Economics of Imperfect Competition*, wherein she wrote: "From the point of view of society, land, by definition, is provided free, and the whole rent is a surplus and none of it is a real cost."[65] More representative of the sparse commentary is the 1951 resolutory statement, also found by Gaffney, of Tibor Scitovsky in his well-known text *Welfare and Competition*: "there is no logical reason for treating land as a separate factor because, from the economist's point of view, it is similar in all essentials to produced factors. This is why we propose to regard land as a capital good."[66] Later microeconomic texts such as those of C. E. Ferguson and Henderson and Quandt did not find it necessary to even provide the explanation found in Scitovsky's note/appendix.

That this has become the modern view is seen by Blaug as the "final nail in George's coffin."[67] However, the proposition that, in Blaug's terms, "a line between land and capital" *should* be drawn is argued extensively in two contemporary studies: indirectly, using a study of the history of the rent concept in Terence Dwyer's 1980 Ph.D. thesis; and directly, in Mason Gaffney's chapter, "Land as a Distinctive Factor of Production," in *Land and Taxation* of 1994.[68]

Concluding Comments

SOME GENERAL TRENDS IN THE EARLIER DISCUSSION can be discerned. Marshallian theory retained the usage of land but reduced its theoretical importance. Marshall's justifications, although more precise than Ricardo's "original and indestructible powers," were open to question. Modes of analysis, especially the general equilibrium approaches of Walras and Pareto, facilitated the exclusion of land in the sense that their assumptions attributed to any "factor" that property thought to be representative of land alone. Also, the growing concentration on price theory, as reflected in Clark, Fetter, Fisher, Davenport and others, found consideration of land as a factor redundant given their definitions of capital.

Given the strengths of these variations of neoclassical economics as well as emerging statistical studies that indicated that a surprisingly small share of income accrued in the form of rent,[69] it would appear that an explanation for the continued reference to land as a factor of production in contemporary introductory textbooks would be in order. One must bear in mind the strength of tradition in economic thought. Marshall's thought on the subject "marginalized" land but retained it as well. His treatment left open a limited acceptance of the views of Ricardo and J. S. Mill. Thus, the followers of Marshall, such as A. C. Pigou, tended to carry forward variations of his ideas.[70] As I have noted previously, many of the justifications for retaining land as an independent factor draw implicitly on Marshall. Other prominent theorists, such as Wicksell and Böhm-Bawerk, undoubtedly had a like influence on their readers.

This explanation for the continued usage of land must be supplemented with sociopolitical considerations. Political economists of the late nineteenth century were uniformly concerned with social questions of land and land ownership. This may be seen in those arguments that presented social or ethical reasons for the retention of land as a factor. This reasoning, of course, had its origin in the connection between social class and a particular type of income. The connection surely was eroding in most European countries and, perhaps, was never perceived as strongly in this country. Yet many political economists gave currency to the classification of incomes as "earned" and "unearned." For them the rent of land and monopoly profits were prime examples of "unearned" incomes. In addition, toward the end of the century, economists became keenly interested in both the practical and theoretical questions of taxation and tax reform. In this respect, the work of John Stuart Mill and Henry George was important because most students of economics of the time were likely to have read both. In his work, Mill advocated, with qualifications, greater taxation of land, as had earlier English reformers. The influence of George (although academic reaction to his theories was largely negative[71]) was widespread and profound as his teachings brought forth both a positive, renewed vitality to the study of the dismal science,[72] and a "negative" determination to undermine the theoretical relevancy of his proposal.[73] Of George's ideas at the time of his death only the single tax idea survived in active academic debate. The underlying principles of his proposal gathered wide support among many economists even if its implementation tended not to.

The peculiarities of land so often mentioned by the economists cited here also motivated the retention of land as a concept in economic theory when stronger currents of thought found little or no use for it. Some of these peculiarities became the focus of special fields of study, such as land economics, aspects of urban economics, and, more recently, resource economics.

The reasons for the abandonment of land as an unique or special factor in economic theory stem clearly from the negative reactions to Ricardian rent theory and its modifications by J. S. Mill and Marshall, but most strikingly to Henry George's proposal to tax away, in its entirety, the rent of land.[74] This proposal and Brown's analysis and advocacy of it are the subject of Chapter 6 so I will defer further discussion.

Harry Gunnison Brown in his efforts to emphasize the concept of land and integrate it into economic theory would find increasingly fewer colleagues with a like interest. His advocacy of land value taxation played a double role in his theoretical defense of land as an independent factor. First, if land were to be treated exactly like capital, economic arguments for its special taxation in effect would be erased. Second, even if land were treated as a subcategory of capital, the effect would be to diminish the weight and clarity of the arguments for land value taxation. However, in surveying the views of the early neoclassical economists and his notable contemporaries, Brown could not have anticipated that his position on the role of land in economic theory would be, before long, found to be outside of the discipline's orthodoxy.

Notes

1. Clark Warburton (1928). "Economic Terminology: Factors of Production and Distributive Shares." *American Economic Review* 18 (March): 73.

2. Alfred Marshall (1893). "On Rent." *Economic Journal* 3: 76.

3. *Ibid.*

4. *Ibid.*: 77.

5. Francis Y. Edgeworth (1925). *Collected Papers Relating to Political Economy*, Vol. 1. New York: Burt Franklin: 33–35.

6. Edwin Cannan (1967[1894]). *A History of the Theories of Production and Distribution in English Political Economy 1776–1848*. London: Rivington; reprint ed., New York: Augustus Kelly: 33–35.

7. Edwin Cannan (1967[1930]). *A Review of Economic Theory*. London: P.S. King & Son; reprint ed., New York: Augustus Kelly: 241–249.

8. Charles Albro Barker (1955). *Henry George*. New York: Oxford University Press: 381–382, 392.
Mark Blaug (1985). *Economic Theory in Retrospect*. 4th ed. Cambridge: Cambridge University Press: 492–493.

9. Mason Gaffney (1994). "Neo-Classical Economics as a Strategem against Henry George." *The Corruption of Economics*. Eds. Mason Gaffney and Fred Harrison. London: Shepeard-Walwyn: 63–65.

10. Knut Wicksell (1967[1934]). *Lectures on Political Economy*, Vol. 1. New York: Macmillan & Co.; reprint ed., New York: Augustus Kelly: 85.

11. *Ibid.*: 145.

12. Gustav Cassel (1932). *The Theory of Social Economy*. New York: Harcourt Brace & Co.: 167.

13. George J. Stigler (1968). *Production and Distribution Theories*. New York: Agathon Press: 192–193.

14. Eugen V. Böhm-Bawerk (1923). *The Positive Theory of Capital*. New York: G. E. Stechert & Co.: 55.

15. *Ibid.*: 56.

16. Stigler (1968): 154–155.

17. Wieser, Frederich von (1927). *Social Economics*. New York: Greenburg: 345.

18. See Athanassios Skouras (1980) "Land and Taxation as Issues in Economic Theory." *American Journal of Economics and Sociology* 39 (October): 378.

19. Vilfredo Pareto (1971). *Manual of Political Economy*. New York: Augustus Kelly: 321.

20. Maffeo Pantaleoni (1898). *Pure Economics*. London: Macmillian and Co.: 264–265.

21. James M. Buchanan (1960). *Fiscal Theory and Political Economy: Selected Essays*. Chapel Hill, NC: The University of North Carolina Press: 27–30.

22. John Roscoe Turner (1921). *The Ricardian Rent Theory in Early American Economics*. New York: New York University Press: xii.

23. *Ibid.*: 146–147.

24. *Ibid.*: 184–185.

25. Francis Amasa Walker (1988). *Political Economy*. New York: Henry Holt & Co.: 34, 61.

26. Simon N. Patten (1902). *Theory of Prosperity*. New York: Macmillan Co.: 5.

27. John Parrish (1967). "The Rise of Economics as an Academic Discipline: The Formative Years to 1900," *Southern Economic Journal* 34 (July): 1–17.

28. John Bates Clark (1899). *The Distribution of Wealth*. New York: Macmillan Co.: 388.

29. A. C. Pigou, ed. (1925). *Memorials of Alfred Marshall*. London: Macmillan and Co.: 413.

30. Frank Fetter (1900). "Recent Discussion of the Capital Concept." *Quarterly Journal of Economics* 15 (November): 1–45.

———. (1901). "The Passing of the Old Rent Concept." *Quarterly Journal of Economics* 15 (May): 416–455.

———. (1904). "The Relations Between Rent and Interest." *Publications of the American Economics Association* 5, ser. 3, February: 176–240.

31. Fetter (1900): 34–37.

32. Fetter (1901): 421–423.

33. Alfred Marshall (1907). *Principles of Economics*, 8th ed. New York: Macmillan & Co.: 442.

34. Frank Fetter (1904). *The Principles of Economics* New York: Century Co.: 257–264.

35. Fetter (1904): 189–190.

36. Murray Rothbard (1977). Introduction. *Capital, Interest and Rent: Essays in the Theory of Distribution By Frank A. Fetter*. Kansas City: Sheed Andrews and McMeel, Inc.: 6.

37. Irving Fisher (1911). *Elementary Principles of Economics*. New York: Macmillan Co.: 34.

38. *Ibid.*: 390.

39. John R. Commons (1907). "Political Economy and Business Economy: Comments on Fisher's Capital and Income." *Quarterly Journal of Economics* 22 (Nov): 120.

Fisher's reply to Commons came in the *Quarterly Journal of Economics* 23 (May) 1909. Fisher noted: "The truth is that market valuation seldom, if ever, exactly registers utility to society." He argued then: "The proper place for a study of social pathology and therapeutics seems to me to be at the end and not at the beginning of economic analysis. We shall reach sounder conclusions in regard to the best remedies to be applied to social conditions if first we study those conditions exactly as they are and not as we should prefer to have them. Our analysis should be as complete and as faithful to the facts as possible." This is all quite reasonable as long as the "facts" are not in dispute.

40. Herbert J. Davenport (1908). *Value and Distribution.* Chicago: University of Chicago Press: 128.

41. Davenport pointed out that food may become in the future wholly a laboratory product without agricultural application.

42. Davenport (1908): 133.

43. Herbert J. Davenport (1910). "Social Productivity versus Private Acquisition." *Quarterly Journal of Economics* 25 (November): 104.

44. Herbert J. Davenport (1911). "The Extent and Significance of the Unearned Increment." *Publications of the American Economic Association* 11 (April): 322–331.

45. Alvin S. Johnson (1902). "Rent in Modern Economic Theory." *Publications of the American Economic Association* 3, ser. 3 (February): 920.

46. Supporting Fetter's views were Winthrop Daniels and Franklin Giddings in the published proceedings.

47. Thomas Nixon Carver (1903): 200. Discussant of Fetter's (1901) paper.

48. *Ibid.*: 201.

49. Richard T. Ely (1928). "Land Income." *Political Science Quarterly* 43 (September): 423.

50. Henry Seager (1900). "Review of J. B. Clark's *The Distribution of Wealth.*" *Annals of the American Academy of Political and Social Sciences* 16 (September): 127.

51. Charles Tuttle (1902). "Review of J. B. Clark's *The Distribution of Wealth.*" *Yale Review* 11 (August): 179.

52. John Commons (1900). "Review of John Hobson's *The Economic of Distribution.*" *Annals of the American Academy of Political and Social Sciences* 16 (July): 135.

53. Frank T. Carlton (1907–1908). "The Rent Concept Narrowed and Broadened." *Quarterly Journal of Economics* 22 (November): 53.

54. Frank Taussig (1926). *Principles of Economics*, Vol. 1. New York: Macmillan & Co.:128.

55. *Ibid.*: 93.

56. E. R. A. Seligman (1926). *Principles of Economics*. New York: Longman, Green & Co.: 306–307.

57. Charles W. Cobb and Paul H. Douglas (1928). "A Theory of Production." *American Economic Review* 18 (March): 165.

58. Harry Gunnison Brown (1931). *Economic Science and the Common Welfare*. Columbia, MO: Lucas Brothers: 266–267.

59. *Ibid.*: 53.

60. Frank Knight (1956). *On the History and Method of Economics: Selected Essays*. Chicago: University of Chicago Press: 54.

61. *Ibid.*: 53

62. Nicolas Kaldor (1960). *Essays on Value and Distribution*. Glencoe, IL: Free Press of Glencoe, Illinois: 174.

63. L. M. Fraser (1937). *Economic Thought and Language*. London: A. & C. Black: 386.

64. Two significant, but rarely mentioned, exceptions to this trend are Carl Rollinson Bye's *Developments and Issues in the Theory of Rent* (New York: Morningside Heights, Columbia University Press, 1940) and Dean A. Worcester's 1946 article "A Reconsideration of Rent Theory" (*American Economic Journal* 36[3]: 258–277). The former study is not without merit, but tends to be more descriptive than analytical. The latter should be reread today as it brings out the idea of "Paretian rent" in a admirable fashion. However, its conclusions do not, in my judgment, follow from the writer's analysis. I should point out that both the Dwyer (endnote n. 67) and Feder theses referenced in Chapter 6 give due consideration to Worcester's contribution.

65. Joan Robinson (1933). *The Economics of Imperfect Competition*. London: Macmillan: 107.
Mason Gaffney (1994a). "Neo-classical Economics as a Strategem against Henry George." *The Corruption of Economics*. Eds. Gaffney and Harrison. London: Shepheard-Walwyn: 114.

66. Tibor Scitovsky (1951). *Welfare and Competition: The Economics of a Fully Employed Economy*. Chicago: Richard D. Irwin, Inc. : 227–228.
Gaffney (1994a): 59.

67. Mark Blaug (2000). "Henry George: Rebel with a Cause." *European Journal of the History of Economic Thought* 7 (2): 282.

68. Terence M. Dwyer (1980). *A History of Land-Value Taxation*. Diss. Harvard University. Ann Arbor, MI: UMI (1990): 4–94.
Mason Gaffney (1994b). "Land as a Distinctive Factor of Production." *Land and Taxation*. Ed. Nicolaus Tideman. London: Shepheard-Walwyn: 39–102.

69. W. I. King (1915). *The Wealth and Income of the People of the United States*. New York: Macmillan Co.

70. Lionel Robbins, decidedly not a follower of Marshall, in 1930 commented on Marshall's well-known elaboration of his views in a letter to Edgeworth: "it is *wisest not* to say that rent does not enter into the cost of production, for that will confuse many people. But it is *wicked* to say that rent does enter into cost of production, because that is *sure* to be applied in such a way as to lead to the denial of subtle truths, which in spite of their being subtle, are of the very highest importance scientifically, and also in relation to the practical well-being of the world." (*Memorials*: 436)

Robbins's comment was: "It is improbable that at the present day there would be found many economists who would regard it as '*wicked*' to say that rent does enter into costs of production. But it is true that, if we are contemplating a stationary equilibrium of the kind conceived by the classics, the proposition that it does not, does imply, even if it does not state correctly, subtle truths which we should be ill advised to lose sight of. And it is significant that those who have urged most strongly for its retention have been those who have learnt their analysis from classical sources whereas those who have opposed it have been very largely under the influence of Clark." ("On a Certain Ambiguity in the Conception of Stationary Equilibrium," *Economic Journal* 40 (June)1930: 211.)

71. See Robert V. Andelson, ed. (1979). *Critics of Henry George*. Rutherford, NJ: Fairleigh Dickinson University Press.

72. To pick only one example of many, Frank Fetter was reported by Dorfman to have become interested in political economy through the reading of George, yet Fetter became a stern opponent of George's reform.

73. See Gaffney (1994a).

74. Besides Gaffney *ibid* and Skouras (1980), see Ben Fine (1983), "The Historical Approach to Rent and Price Theory Reconsidered," *Australian Economic Papers* 22 (June): 137–143 and Mark Blaug (2000): 270–288.

Chapter 3

Capital and Interest Theories

Introduction

HARRY GUNNISON BROWN IN HIS YEARS as an instructor at Yale (1910–1916) is said to have solidified his interest in Henry George's proposal to tax land rent. As was argued in the previous chapter, the defense of the distinctiveness of land space from capital was a key to the Georgist proposal. Brown would object to theoretical treatments of interest rate determination in which this distinction played no role. Although Brown never tried to justify Henry George's interest rate theory, he came to oppose the pure time preference theory as espoused by Frank Fetter and he never reconciled his own views with those of Irving Fisher.

The Fisher-Seager Exchange

IN THE YEARS OF BROWN'S EDUCATION, questions on capital and interest were among the most, if not the most, difficult subjects of economic theory. Böhm-Bawerk and Fisher both attested to their intricacy. Moreover, numerous debates and exchanges in journals attracted wide interest, especially in this country. The longest and perhaps best known of these exchanges was between Böhm-Bawerk and John Bates Clark concerning (among other points) the concept of capital. Böhm-Bawerk's theories had greatly influenced the thinking of American economists; however, his theory of interest was received unevenly. Some economists, such as Fetter, Patten and Taussig, were inclined to accept it in part and to emphasize Böhm-Bawerk's "time preference" explanation of interest rates. Others, such as Seligman and Seager, tended to reject the theory for explanations of interest rates that emphasized the "productivity" of capital along the lines of Clark. Irving Fisher's 1907 book, *The Rate of Interest,* took an intermediate position. In an article in *Scientia*[1] and later in his *Elementary Principles of Economics*, Fisher reiterated his theory in simplified form and introduced the term "impatience" to distinguish his view from Böhm-Bawerk's "agio" theory and to replace the term "time preference" that Fisher had employed earlier. Fisher saw the term "impatience" as expressing the "real basis of interest"[2] as well as constituting "a fundamental attribute of human nature."[3]

In 1912, Henry Seager[4] initiated an exchange that ultimately involved Fetter and Brown as well as Fisher.[5] Seager attacked Fisher's "principles" treatment of capital and interest. Fisher later would counter that this was unfair, as his more complete statements were ignored. As mentioned in the previous chapter, Seager took issue with a definition of capital that incorporated land, unlike Böhm-Bawerk's formulation. Moreover, Seager felt that Fisher, in rejecting Böhm-Bawerk's third explanation for interest or the "technical superiority of present over future goods," had denied a role to the productivity of capital in determining interest rate levels. Seager implied that Fisher's theory was methodologically incapable of serving as a theory of production and distribution. Fisher, in his first approximation, had taken income as a given but then had relaxed the assumption in his second approximation in *The Rate of Interest*. Fisher also countered that he already had given special emphasis to the role of productivity in his theory (if not explicitly in his textbook) and felt that his contribution in this regard was the most original and difficult of the undertaking.[6]

Seager went on to criticize Fisher's refutation of productivity-related theories. Böhm-Bawerk, among others, had found a *petitio principii* fallacy in using the productivity of capital as an explanation for interest wherein implicitly an existing interest rate was presupposed in the valuation of capital via the discounting of future income from it. To Fisher's reiteration of this charge, Seager gave a somewhat oblique defense. He first charged Fisher with using land to represent capital, thereby obscuring the role of the "expenses" of production in the determination of value in exchange. Fisher had used a hypothetical example of an orchard whose physical productivity doubled while the value of its products remained unchanged; the return or interest would remain the same while the value of the orchard would double.[7] Seager agreed in this case that the rate of interest would remain the same, but for a different reason. He viewed the orchard as consisting of reproducible machines or tools and argued that these tools would be multiplied under competitive conditions so as eventually to eliminate in large part a rise in the value of the tools. Yet, the greater returns to the tools would have insufficient impact on the capital market to significantly alter interest rates. Seager clearly felt that Fisher had obscured the issue by adopting the not-so-easily reproducible orchard for his example. Also, inadvertently or not, the orchard example tended to identify productivity theorists with older discredited theories that attempted to find in the productivity of nature a cause for interest.

Fisher recognized that his first example was insufficient and altered the proposition to that of a universal doubling of capital's productivity. He argued,

> It is true that doubling the productivity of the world's capital would not be entirely without effect upon the rate of interest; but this would not be in the simple ratio supposed. Indeed, an increase in the productivity of capital would probably result in a decrease, instead of an increase, of the rate of interest.[8]

He added that the value of capital would be at least doubled. For Seager, this result was unimaginable, and he argued as before that

> time being allowed for an adjustment to the new conditions, the values of produced means to further production will be brought into conformity to the expense of producing them.[9]

Thus for Seager, some large increase in the interest rate, if not a doubling, was inevitable. In Fisher's reply to Seager, he expanded his argument by considering effects upon the prices of capital's products and the costs of producing capital. He maintained that product prices should fall while costs should rise, thereby mitigating a substantial rise in the return to capital. Further, the ultimate effect would be a lowering of the interest rate as the lower rates of impatience to which interest rates must eventually adjust.[10] Seager was unconvinced by Fisher's rebuttal and replied: "He fails to comprehend clearly the way in which productivity and time discount operate in the determination of the current rate of interest in any given time period."[11]

Brown's Intervention

BROWN, THEN FISHER'S COLLEAGUE AT YALE, was similarly unconvinced. He had been cited, along with a fellow student of Fisher's, J. H. Parmelee, "for valuable aid in proof-reading, including many keen and fruitful suggestions" in the Preface to *The Rate of Interest.*[12] Brown wrote an article in 1913 titled "The Marginal Productivity Versus the Impatience Theory of Interest."[13] The article was clearly inspired by that of Seager and was supportive, in part, of Seager's objections. Brown's stated position and the attempt of the paper was to show

> that productivity and impatience are coordinate determinants, i.e., that productivity is as direct a determinant as is impatience, and that productivity may be, in a modern community, the more important determinant.[14]

Brown stated in several instances that he was an earlier adherent of "time preference" theories of interest; thus, Seager's paper may have been influential in an uncharacteristic change in opinion by Brown.

Brown's dissent from Fisher's theory rested on the observation that Fisher failed to admit that productivity had a *direct* rather than an indirect influence on the rate of interest through its effect on impatience rates. Brown acknowledged that the productivity of waiting[15] could in Cassel's terms affect the individual rates of impatience and thus interest rates but wished to establish that the productivity of waiting could directly influence these rates. Here Brown was facing the problem with which Böhm-Bawerk and others had struggled. In addition, Brown would have to meet Fisher's refutation of Böhm-Bawerk's arguments.

Brown began by assuming that "indirect" production could be extended indefinitely without reducing the reward of marginal waiting to less than 10 percent. He then proceeded to explain how this would influence both the supply and demand for present goods. In terms of demand, he argued that any rate of exchange (of present versus future goods) less than 10 percent will result in an excess demand for present goods. To show that this excess demand need not necessarily be due to "impatience," he presented the simple case of a person needing a certain amount of present goods that he can procure either through direct production or by borrowing these goods and thereby undertaking roundabout production. The decision, Brown maintained, would not be based on the desire to provide for present goods out of future abundance; rather, the decision would be the result of comparing the outcomes of the options. Brown was perhaps drawing on Böhm-Bawerk[16] when he stated: "He is comparing two futures, rather than a present and a future."[17] Davenport, in a review of Frank Fetter's *Principles of Economics* in 1916, accepted Brown's point as relevant.

> It is, however, not true that interest can emerge where present consumables are inadequate for present need, or where, through substitution for future purposes, they are made less than adequate. The interest contract may present nothing more or other than a choice between future incomes, no question of present enjoyment of incomes possibly entering the case.[18]

Fisher had criticized Böhm-Bawerk's demonstration of the "technical superiority of present goods" by showing that when the first two grounds for explaining interest were absent,

> the only reason anyone would prefer the product of a month's labor invested today to the product of a month's labor invested next year is that today's investment will mature earlier than next year's investment.[19]

By insisting that a *present* comparison of options was the relevant view, Brown was making a strong point with respect to the limits of a pure preference approach to interest determination, but was he successfully defending the "technical superiority of present goods" as an independent determinant of the interest rate?

On the supply side, Brown showed, with same assumption, that the supply of present goods would be decreased if the rate of exchange were anything less than the assumed productivity of "waiting" because the supplier chose to adopt roundabout methods to attain a greater final product. Brown again argued that "impatience" was not decisive in this case but that "nature or invention, or more properly both"[20] is what gives people the option of receiving more for present effort. As to the issue between Fisher and Seager on the hypothetical doubling of productivity, Brown agreed with Seager, so long as the productivity increase was defined as the increase in the surplus marginal product of indirect or direct production. He conceded, however, to Fisher that an increase in wealth could eventually reduce impatience and further the extension of indirect production such that a lower marginal product of waiting could result.

Another significant difference in Fisher's and Brown's views was Brown's insistence that capital's value, unlike that of land, was not necessarily due only to its expected future earnings and a discount rate determined by impatience.

> We may say that a person's valuation of capital, along with the valuations of other persons in a like situation, is less the direct result of a previously existing market rate of interest, than it is, by affecting his or their attitude toward the market, a determinant of the rate of interest.[21]

In emphasizing the difference between land and capital (that in large land has no cost of production), Brown argued that the given surplus obtainable from the use of capital will have the effect of fixing not only the rate of discount but also the rates of impatience.

He then altered the assumption to that of a constant marginal product of waiting with respect to any indefinite *decrease* of roundabout production; he proceeded to show how the demand for and supply of present goods would be affected by the superiority of roundabout production so as to hold interest rates down to this assumed level. Finally, Brown reversed the assumption by taking a constant natural rate of impatience invariant with respect to changes in the income stream with the marginal productivity of waiting declining as indirect production is extended. In this case, the marginal productivity would adjust to the impatience rate via the extension or reduction of indirect production. Brown concluded that in the real world adjustment would take place in both rates but that impatience was not the fundamental cause of modern interest or even a cause through which all other causes must operate, but that it is one of two coordinate causes and is also to some extent a joint consequence, with interest, of the other cause, the superiority of indirect production.[22]

He clearly felt marginal productivity did not only influence the demand for present goods and that impatience did not only limit the supply of present goods.

Fetter and Brown

IN 1914 FRANK FETTER PRESENTED AN ARTICLE responding to Brown's article as well as to Seager's and to the response by Fisher.[23] Fetter's well-known position was that of a pure time preference theory of interest; accordingly, he referred to himself as a capitalization theorist. In the article, he was particularly concerned with Fisher's partial concessions to productivity influences in interest rate determination. Moreover, Fetter sought to show that time valuation was a prerequisite to the determination of interest rates, that such a valuation did not imply a preexisting money interest, and that Fisher's charge of circular reasoning was mistaken. Fetter called Brown's theory "eclectic," presumably because it lacked a single unambiguous cause for interest, and he raised three specific objections. First, Fetter maintained that those examples that assumed a rate of productivity begged the question and failed to establish technical productivity as a cause of interest. Second, he argued that Brown's perspective was oriented toward the enterpriser or middleman and thereby ignored the ultimate influences and motives of the consumer. Finally, Fetter rejected Brown's distinction between land and capital where the cost of production concept was used to support the distinction.

Brown replied in the next issue of the journal to Fetter's criticisms as well as to Fetter's time-preference or psychological theory of interest. He described this theory in the following manner:

> Not only do the time-preference theorists explain the value of all capital by the discount process, but they explain cost-of-production in the same way. The expense of hiring labor to construct capital is said to be fixed by the discounted value of the future benefits constructed. The

cost of raw materials and machinery and, further back, the wages of labor employed to produce these, likewise depend, directly, only upon the far future benefits to be yielded.[24]

Brown clearly felt that the "pure" theory was unrealistic and, in an elaborate example, tried to show that the cost of production of capital must play a role in its valuation along with time preference. As in his previous article, he used quantities of goods to form his rate of productivity instead of employing value terms to avoid the circular reasoning charge. Fetter pointed out in a rejoinder that this constituted a present good standard that disguised an implied value relation.[25] Fisher later indicated in the 1930 version of *The Rate of Interest* that Brown's conclusions followed, given his conditions.[26] However, in Brown's Crusoe-type example he repeated an argument to which both Fetter and Fisher objected. Brown posited two coexistent methods of producing the same good; one was direct and the other roundabout. Fetter saw this as only a temporary possibility in that it could occur only in a competitive economy when the rate corresponding to the "gain" from the roundabout process was coincident with the rate of time preference. Otherwise, one of the two processes would be uneconomic. In Fetter's words, "Time preference dominated the choice of techniques."[27] Although Fisher rejected this view as too narrow in that it ignored at any moment in time "the opportunity of choosing among many income streams,"[28] he later faulted Brown for trying to prove too much with the example.

Brown's "Capital Valuation and the Psychological School'"

IN A 1929 ARTICLE, "Capital Valuation and the 'Psychological School,'" Brown made clearer his divergence with current thought on the valuation of capital and its relation to the causes of interest.

> It may be noted that the idea that the productivity (or the net gain from roundabout production) has *direct* effect on the interest rate, and not merely an indirect effect, goes logically with idea that cost has a *direct* effect on capital value. On the other hand, the idea that capital value is determined only *through* discounting is part and parcel of the idea that the interest rate is affected only through time preference.[29]

The "indirect effects" of cost on capital that Brown referred to were those of discounted future repair costs and changes in the present costs that alter the perceived value of its future services. The direct influence that he wished to emphasize was to operate via opportunity cost on the demand for as well as the supply of capital goods. He added to the normal considerations of long-run demand and supply the possibility of a demander becoming a supplier and vice versa. Following Davenport, he defined the cost of production as "the amount of other goods which the same effort and sacrifice would produce."[30] Thus, he argued that, in this sense long-run supply and demand for capital depends on the present cost of production and that therefore the value of capital is influenced directly by its cost of production. He illustrated this view with the following example:

> Nowell is a fisherman. His usual catch is $40 worth of fish a week. His boat, a necessity of his business, is wearing out. He needs a new one very soon. He is a pretty good carpenter. He can build himself, a satisfactory boat in a week's time. Kelleher, a dealer, offers to sell him a boat for $100. Nowell and other fishermen similarly situated refuse to pay such a price. Thus, the demand for Kelleher's boat is affected by the opportunity cost to Nowell and others of building their own boats. Nowell refuses to pay Kelleher $100 for the boat.[31]

Brown believed that

> in equilibrium we should ordinarily have a value of capital (assuming it to be worth constructing and not yet depreciated) which would be the same as its marginal cost and also the same as the discounted value of its future services. . . .
>
> For if capital, which has its value directly (and not indirectly) controlled by opportunity cost, is able to add to production, in its lifetime, goods in excess of those which measure its costs (on an opportunity cost basis), then its productivity influences the interest rate directly and not merely through first affecting the distribution of income over time and thereby affecting time preference.[32]

Brown, then, as in the previously cited article, applied his ideas to the distinction between land and capital. The value of land apart from its improvements is arrived at solely by discounting prospective net income at the current rate of interest, while the value of capital is directly affected by the present costs of production or duplication. Land or land space not practically reproducible earns, for Brown, a situation rent best seen as "an absolute amount measured and determined by the surplus over production at the margin."[33] Thus, the similarity between interest and rent viewed as a percentage of values of capital and land respectively is only a superficial likeness.

There were two responses to Brown's article.[34] William W. Hewett of the University of Cincinnati accepted Brown's arguments in general but wished to expand them by applying Marshall's concept of the short and long run—this is to a period where a market disturbance has led to a disequilibrium and a period where there is a general tendency toward equilibrium. For Hewett, in the short run the value of capital tends to equal the discounted prospective income and in a long run, the cost of reproducing the capital. Hewett's major criticism was that "the option to reproduce capital can be instantly effective,"[35] and thus he suggested that Marshall's concept of a quasi-rent be utilized to describe the return to capital in the short run. The other response, from Edwin Cannon, dealt primarily with the arguments Brown had used to separate land from capital. Cannon noted that Brown avoided Ricardo's inclusion of fertility as part of land and that situation value "in the useful sense of relative accessibility is altered by human efforts everyday."[36]

Brown replied to both comments.[37] He made a partial concession to Hewett in admitting that the alternative opportunity of switching to the production of a good temporarily in excess demand may well be a practical impossibility for many buyers. However, Brown maintained that as long as the opportunity was available to some, the effect would be immediate and tend to reduce the effects of the supposed scarcity, although the short-run price of capital would tend to exceed the long-run price. Hewett replied that his perception of the extent of the alternatives was much more limited than Brown's.

To the first of Cannan's points, Brown replied that he had always maintained that the value of land due to the maintenance or enhancement of its fertility be considered apart from land's situation value as capital. He argued that the situation or site value of land may well have been humanly produced but this, in all but exceptional cases, did not bear weight against his point. A reasonable duplication of a site whose value rests on advantages in transportation, communication or location with respect to population and so on is a practical consideration only to a mammoth corporation or a collective action by some institution. Brown argued that such decisions were not commonly found in the current situation. However, he did admit to the existence of borderline cases, such as the founding of Gary, Indiana. Brown found such cases inadequate to support the theory that the cost of reproduction or duplication could to any significant degree influence land's site value.

Fisher and Brown

IN 1928 FISHER WROTE BROWN as he was preparing a revised version of *The Rate of Interest*. He indicated in the letter than only he and Brown were in agreement as to the essentials of a theory of interest: "you have essentially the same idea and both of us have been voices crying in the wilderness. . . ."[38] Fisher also said he felt that the "productivity" side of his theory was an original contribution, although he found that Brown's references to Jevons and Davenport cast some doubt on this. Fisher said of *The Rate of Interest*,

> I have found no other writers except you who agrees with me! And I only know of a half a dozen others who agree with me—namely all students who have read my book! I doubt if many more have read it, including the Appendix. This book, *The Rate of Interest*, is the only serious work of mine the reception of which has been a profound disappointment and it is a great humiliation now to find the only other writer who agrees doesn't realize it! It must very largely be my fault.[39]

Fisher went on to request that Brown criticize, "on a business basis," the manuscript in detail.

However, along with Fisher's flattery and expression of humbleness he added a none too subtle implication that Brown, especially in his long treatment of interest in the third edition of his text *Economic Science and the Common Welfare*, was plagiarizing

Fisher's productivity treatment. He commented in the letter: "Of course, I'm delighted that you rediscovered my theory." Brown made notes in preparation to answer Fisher. (The actual letter has not been found either in the Yale or Missouri archives.) These notes clearly indicate his distress over Fisher's implicit charge. "I realize full well how much I owe you as my former teacher. I regret most sincerely having been the occasion of adding to your discouragement over the reception of your book which surely deserves more attention by scholars than it has had."[40] Despite this Brown goes on to make a case for essential differences in his and Fisher's presentations of interest rate theory. He reminds Fisher of criticisms he made as a proofreader of *The Rate of Interest* and maintained that his differences were "a matter of slow growth." He compliments Fisher for introducing the clarifying concept of the income stream and for the precision achieved by specifying the conditions in equation by which interest is determined. However, he adds: "But just as a law of correlations is not necessarily a law of causation, so equations which must be fulfilled by the interest rate, e.g., that the interest rate must equal the time preference rate and must equal the productivity rate, indicate nothing as to whether the productivity rate causes the time preference rate or vice versa. . . . In short one might agree with you on the significance of all your equations and upon the importance of the income concept and yet believe that the logical (or shall I say psychological) lines of causation are not quite as you *seem* to indicate and as, in some passages, I believe you definitely assert them to be."[41] Avi Cohen in a forthcoming book on capital theory points to Brown providing a "decisive rebuttal" to one of Fisher's, at times, exaggerated claims.[42] The rebuttal was to his assertion that "impatience" is the only reason for preferring labor today over labor tomorrow.[43] In arguing that the mathematical solutions do not sufficiently explain causality or the "sequence of causality," he was, intentionally or not, harking back to Böhm-Bawerk's 1912 criticism of Fisher's model. Whereas many commentators found his argument to betray a lack of understanding of the nature of simultaneous solution to multiple equations, Cohen (*supra*) has defended Böhm-Bawerk against this charge.[44] Brown concluded his preparatory letter by indicating that he felt his differences with

Fisher to be substantive and that he doubted that Fisher would accept his emendations.

Fisher wrote Brown in October of 1929:

> I want to thank you for the time and effort which you devoted to the reading and criticism of the manuscript of *The Theory of Interest.* In spite of your pessimistic forebodings as to the effect of your criticisms on my book, I am sure from the stimulus I have received from your emphatic objections that they have helped rather than hindered the forceful treatment of my theory.
>
> It has been interesting to read in your criticisms what appears to you to be a difference of opinion between us when I find myself in agreement with the position which your criticism takes. I have a feeling that we are perhaps closer together on the main principles of interest theory than either of us is to any other writer.[45]

Fisher thanked Brown for his criticism of his "opportunity principle" in his preface to *The Theory of Interest*.[46] In a chapter titled "Objections Considered," Fisher addressed his continuing disagreements with Brown and in particular his 1929 article. Fisher reproduced a more detailed version of Brown's example[47] and then stated,

> I accept all of Professor Brown's reasoning and conclusion except his application to me. His contention that the cost of duplicating existing capital will influence the value of capital is perfectly correct, but so is the discount formula.[48]

Fisher pointed out that Brown's example was an isolated or nonmarginal case and that when "Nowell" made a marginal decision in a "perfect" market, he would choose the income stream that maximizes at the market rate of interest his present worth. Turning to a brief consideration of the cost concept, Fisher alluded to Davenport's view as generally correct. Fisher maintained that future costs with respect to capitalization enter on the same footing as does future income but that past costs only influence present valuations indirectly as they affect future expected income or cost. This indirect influence of cost would be through the limiting of supply, which alters the quantity and value of future services.

Brown apparently was never willing to concede these arguments to Fisher and repeated his ideas in several later articles and succeeding editions of his textbook. Brown may have thought that his argument respecting the opportunity cost influence on the demand for capital had not adequately addressed by Fisher. Also, one might speculate that Brown did not consider Fisher's identification of "past" costs to be descriptive of what Brown saw to be "present" opportunity costs.

Later Articles

IN THE AFTERMATH OF THE ABOVE EXCHANGES, Brown contributed a somewhat obscure comment to the *American Economic Review.* His stated purpose was to

> merely show that such an attack as Marshall levels against the opportunity cost theory as applied to rent has neither less nor more validity against the opportunity cost theory as applied to wages or interest.[49]

Although Brown did not mention it, his attention was probably drawn to the question by an exchange initiated in the *Economic Journal* by F. W. Ogilvie in the previous year.[50] Ogilvie had questioned the continued service of Marshall's thought on rent. Specifically, Marshall was criticized for failing to note, when he argued the "inexpediency" of saying that the rent of land does not enter into the price of its product, that it would be similarly inexpedient to say that the wages of labor do not enter into the price of what it produces. Brown simply expanded upon this point by illustrating that like the no-rent margin for land, one could conceive of a "no-wage" margin for labor and a "no-interest" margin for capital. Perhaps due to Brown's earlier articles he was challenged by R. W. Souter for having suggested that those who deny the distinction between land and capital do so on the basis of the doctrine of opportunity cost.[51] Souter also classified Brown as a "repressed utopian." Souter's interpretation appears to rely heavily on imputation (Brown's other writings on land value taxation) and is not substantiated by what Brown actually wrote in the comment.

In 1944, Brown published an article, "An Off-Line Switch in the Theory of Value and Distribution," wherein he suggested that Böhm-Bawerk had erred on two counts and misled those who elaborated on his theory. First, Brown felt that Böhm-Bawerk's concept of direct production, which involved only the "naked fist," was misleading. Brown proposed an alternative concept to distinguish direct from roundabout methods of production: immediacy of the end product regardless of the mixture of capital, labor and land utilized in the process. Thus, Brown would broaden the alternatives of a worker in the sense that his (or her) minimum offer price for one's labor would be set by the augmented opportunities available in "direct" production or the production of "present" (immediately consumable or nearly so) goods. Assuming some general degree of possible substitution in the production of "present" versus capital goods, Brown maintained that the marginal cost of the production of capital goods was the "present" goods that the factors producing capital might produce instead. In this manner then, Brown argued for a direct influence of the cost of production on the value of capital as in his earlier writing. In a 1962 article, Brown noted the current acceptance, if not dominance, of Fisherian interest theory and took the occasion to reiterate his dissent.[52]

Conclusion

IN SUMMARIZING BROWN'S CONTRIBUTIONS to this area of economic thought, especially in the years 1913 to 1931, his influence on Fisher's revision of *The Rate of Interest* is of the greatest interest. Fisher commented in the book that anything new he offered in his revision "was chiefly on the objective side";[53] he cited only Brown's text *Economic Science and the Common Welfare* as a "somewhat similar treatment"[54] in a nonmathematical form. Gottfried Haberler commented in his review that Fisher was at great pains to clarify the role of productivity in interest determination but that his explanation still left doubts.[55] The emphasis Brown wished to lend to the role of productivity in interest rate determination was greater in Fisher's revision; however, it was less than that desired by Brown. As noted previously, Brown saw productivity as having a direct effect on interest rates coordinate with time preference but for practical purposes dominating time preference.

Brown's disagreements with Fisher stem, I believe, from the following considerations. First, Brown was unable, as was Böhm-Bawerk, to convince Fisher of an independent influence of productivity on interest rates. Second, Brown's arguments, that employed the broad opportunity cost concepts of Jevons and Davenport, were not accepted by Fisher. Brown's attempt to portray a supply and demand interdependency in the capital market received no comment from Fisher or any other critic. Although conceivable, the possibility was, and still is, viewed as having a negligible effect, at least under competitive conditions. Third, Brown as well as Seager found Fisher's and even more so Fetter's emphasis on time preference to be deficient as a realistic explanation for interest rate determination and capital evaluation.[56] This may be due in part to their strong assumption of perfect foreknowledge. Lastly, although it does not appear in their published arguments or correspondence, Fisher and Brown were mutually aware of a basic disagreement exemplified by Fisher's comment in a 1930 letter to Dennis Robertson: "Interest and rent are different ways of measuring."[57] Of course, for Brown this was not true.

Subsequent capital theory debates would reformulate these questions and find a more persuasive influence of productivity in interest rate determination, yet Brown never alluded to these presentations and certainly would not have supported the positions taken by Knight or Hayek. Brown could have found in later writing on capital theory a welcome reconsideration of "waiting" as factor of production in Robert Dorfman[58] and Leland Yeager.[59] He may also have noted that Paul Samuelson has at least hinted that the omission of land as a consideration in theories of capital and interest is not justifiable.[60]

In his time the position taken by Brown appeared to be representative of a not-uncommon attitude, despite inadequacies in its presentation, that the role of physical productivity was not then being accorded its rightful place in explanation of interest.[61] A contemporary commentator on the state of economic theory, Daniel H. Hausman, pointed out continuing difficulties with capital theory in the following manner:

Economists do not understand the phenomena of capital and interest. They do not understand why the rate of interest is generally positive (and thus how it is that capitalism can work).[62]

Notes

1. Irving Fisher (1911). "The Impatience Theory of Interest." *Scientia* 9: 380-401.
2. Irving Fisher (1911). *Elementary Principles of Economics*. New York: Macmillan and Co.: 386.
3. *Ibid.*: 387.
4. Henry Rogers Seager (1870-1930) studied at Halle in Berlin and at Vienna. He favored the approach of the Austrians to that of the German historical school. He received his doctorate from the University of Pennsylvania working with Simon Patten. See *Labor and Other Economic Essays* (New York: Harper & Brothers, 1931) and in particular the introduction by Wesley Claire Mitchell.
5. Henry Seager (1912). "The Impatience Theory of Interest." *American Economic Review* 2 (September): 834-851.
6. Irving Fisher (1913). "The Impatience Theory of Interest." *American Economic Review* 3 (September): 610-618.
7. Irving Fisher (1907). *The Rate of Interest*. New York: Macmillan Co.: 15-16.
8. *Ibid.*
9. Seager (1912): 487
10. Fisher (1907): 16.
11. Henry Seager (1913). "Comment on the Impatience Theory of Interest." *American Economic Review* 3 (September): 618-619.
12. Irving Fisher (1907): ix.
13. Harry Gunnison Brown (1913). "The Marginal Productivity Theory Versus the Impatience Theory of Interest." *Quarterly Journal of Economics* 3 (August): 630-650.
14. *Ibid.*: 634.
15. Although Brown followed Cassel's treatment of "waiting" as a factor of production, he used the term as roughly synonymous with capital.
16. See Eugen Böhm-Bawerk (1959). *Capital and Interest*. Vol. 3. South Holland, IL: Libertarian Press: 178-179, 238.
17. Brown (1913): 637.
18. Herbert J. Davenport (1916). "Fetter's *Principles*." *Journal of Political Economy* 24: 347.
19. Fisher (1907): 70-71.
20. Brown (1913): 641.
21. *Ibid.*: 644.
22. *Ibid.*: 649-650.

23. Frank Fetter (1914). "Interest Theories, Old and New." *American Economic Review* 4 (March) : 68-92.

24. Harry Gunnison Brown (1914). "The Discount Versus the Cost of Production Theory of Capital Valuation." *American Economic Review* June: 342.

25. Frank Fetter (1914). "Capitalization Versus Productivity Rejoinder." *American Economic Review* 4 (December) : 856-859.

26. Irving Fisher (1965[1930]). *The Theory of Interest.* New York: Macmillan and Co.; reprint ed., New York: Augustus Kelly: 192-194.

27. Fetter (1914): 848.

28. Fisher (1930): 469.

29. Harry Gunnison Brown (1929). "Capital Valuation and the 'Psychological School.'" *American Economic Review* 19 (September): 360.

30. Harry Gunnison Brown (1931). *Economic Science and the Common Welfare.* Columbia, MO: Lucas Brothers: 249.

31. Brown (1929): 358.

32. *Ibid.*

33. *Ibid*: 362.

34. William W. Hewett (1929). "Capital Value Once More." *American Economic Review* 19 (December): 646-648.
Edwin Cannon (1930). "Land and Capital." *American Economic Review* 20 (March): 78-79.

35. Hewett (1929): 648.

36. Cannon (1930): 79.

37. Harry Gunnison Brown (1930). "Land, Capital and Opportunity Cost: A Reply." *American Economic Review* 20 (June): 248-251.

38. Irving Fisher to Harry Gunnison Brown (May 10, 1928). Joint Collection, University of Missouri Western Historical Manuscript Collection, Columbia, MO. The letter in its entirety reads:

> My dear Mr. Brown:
>   This is a reply to yours of January 17th to Dr. Meeker! I have just read carefully your two excellent chapters on interest. Not only do I agree with you in all essentials (unless some of what I think non-essentials are, in your mind, essentials) but such agreement is definitely implied in my book! You will find almost no one else who agrees with me! And I only know half a dozen others who agree with me, namely all students who have read my book! I doubt if many more have read it, including the Appendix. This book, the Rate of Interest, is the only serious work of mine the reception of which has been a profound disappointment and it is a great humiliation now to find that the only other writer who agrees doesn't realize it! It must be very largely my fault. Of course I'm delighted that you rediscovered my theory. I believe it to be original, although your references to Jevons and Davenport make me wonder if they really anticipated me. I made the mistake of youth in not blowing my own horn, expecting others to discover my merits and fall all over themselves in admiring them. Instead they have not even read the book. Even Seager who reviewed it confessed he had

never read it but instead read the condensation of it in my Elementary Principles of Economics to save himself the trouble! The condensation left out my especial contribution as being too technical. I merely referred to it in a paragraph. I then realized that I had made a tactical blunder of not finding and shouting out a slogan. The phrase "rate of return on sacrifice" was too long. I did, after the Rate of Interest was published, but before I realized that it had fallen flat, find and advertise the word "impatience." I did this to help the elementary student who balked at "time-preference" as a hard word and not self-explanatory. It worked and the word has gotten into the literature. But it has put technical economists off the track more than ever as to their understanding of the theory. It led them to two mistakes (1) that I claim in that new word an original idea; and (2) that I overlook "productivity." The "impatience" side is not original except in form of presentation. The productivity side is original. So for some years, in my advanced classes, I have launched another slogan "opportunity" and am thinking of entitling my revision "The Impatience and Opportunity Theory of Interest," or "The Rate of Interest as Determined by Impatience to Spend and Opportunity to Invest." I shall try this time to give no ground for thinking that the latter factor is less vital than the former. I am also determined to put the idea across. As you have essentially the same idea and both of us have been voices crying in the wilderness I am wondering if you would care, on a business basis, to criticise my manuscript by making such detailed suggested emendations of every sentence which you think still vulnerable. The final manuscript is due before July 1st. Please wire me if you would be interested. I would gladly pay for the havoc wrought in your plans!

Sincerely, [signed Irving Fisher]

39. *Ibid.*

40. Brown (1928-9). Notes, Joint Collection, Columbia, MO. (no date is given)

41. *Ibid.*

42. Cohen, Avi (forthcoming). *A Century of Capital Controversy: Scarcity, Production, Equilibrium and Time from Böhm-Bawerk to Bliss.* Chapter 4, "Is Equilibrium Enough? The Böhm-Bawerk / Fisher Controversy."

43. Fisher (1907): 70-71.

44. Cohen (forthcoming). Chapter 4, subsection "The controversy over simultaneous equations."

45. Fisher (October 1, 1929), Letter to Brown (Date on letter is incorrectly given as 1922). Yale University Library, New Haven CT: 1.

46. Fisher (1930): xi.

47. *Ibid.*: 463-464.

48. *Ibid.*: 464.

49. Harry Gunnison Brown (1931). "Opportunity Cost: Marshall's Criticism of Jevons." *American Economic Review* 21 (September): 498-500.

50. F. W. Ogilvie (1930). "Marshall on Rent." *Economic Journal* 40 (March): 1-24.

51. R. W. Souter (1932). "Land, Capital and Opportunity Cost." *American Economic Journal* 22 (June): 207.

52. Harry Gunnison Brown (1962). "An Oversight in the Dominant Theory of Interest." *American Journal of Economics and Sociology* 21 (April): 203-207.

53. Fisher (1930):183.

54. *Ibid.*: 182.

55. Gottfried Haberler (1931). "Irving Fisher's *Theory of Interest.*" *Quarterly Journal of Economics* 45 (May): 499-526.

56. Modern Austrian economists beginning with Murray Rothbard (1977) in his Introduction to *Capital, Interest and Rent* by Frank A. Fetter have rediscovered Fetter's original pure time preference theory of interest. Both Ingo Pellengahr (1986) in *Lecture Notes in Economics and Mathematical Systems: Studies in Austrian Capital Theory, Investment and Time* (ed. Malte Faber) and Israel Kirzner (1993) in *The Meaning of Ludwig von Mises: Contributions in Economics, Sociology, Epistemology, and Political Philosophy* (ed. Jeffrey Herbener) make mention of one of Brown's arguments in their articles which attempt to clarify Fetter's pure time preference theory.

57. Fisher, Irving (August 13, 1930), letter to Dennis Robertson. *The Works of Irving Fisher: Volume* 9 (1997). Ed. William J. Barber. London: Pichering & Chatto: 4.

58. Dorfman, Robert (1959). "Waiting and the Period of Production." *Quarterly Journal of Economics* 73 (August): 351-368.

59. Yeager, Leland (1979). "Capital Paradoxes and the Concept of Waiting." *Time, Uncertainty and Disequilibrium*: 187-214.

60. Samuelson, Paul (1979). "Land and the Rate of Interest." *Theory for Economic Efficiency: Essays in Honor of Abba P. Lerner.* Eds. B. I. Greenfield, A. M. Levenson, W. Hamovitch and E. Rotwein. Cambridge: MIT Press: 664-682.

———. (2001). "A Modern Post-Mortem on Böhm's Capital Theory: Its Vital Normative Flaw Shared by PreSraffian Mainstream Capital Theory." *Journal of the History of Economic Thought* 23 (3): 301-317.

61. H. A. Millis, a reviewer of Fetter's *Principles of Economics*, made this point in the *Quarterly Journal of Economics* 45 (May) 1916: 564.

62. Daniel H. Hausman (1981). *Capital, Profits and Prices.* New York: Columbia University Press: 191.

Chapter 4

Monetary Economics

Introduction

AS ONE WOULD ANTICIPATE, Harry Gunnison Brown was a strong and life-long adherent of the monetary approach of Irving Fisher. Brown began his career when such views were considered orthodox, saw the eclipse during the 1930s, and witnessed their revival in part in his later years. Joseph Dorfman, in *The Economic Mind in American Civilization*, characterized Brown as a monetary specialist. This is not strictly true because his concentration produced only four articles along with the relevant sections of his texts prior to 1940. But the characterization is accurate insofar as Brown did collaborate with Fisher in *The Purchasing Power of Money* and in later years would write articles on macroeconomic issues, some of which were critical of Keynesian views. Brown also read and commented on the manuscripts of other books by Fisher, such as *Booms and Depressions*. As Paul Junk noted, in 1935 Fisher called Brown one of eleven economists in the United States "who understood the real significance of money."[1] Milton Friedman has commented favorably on Brown's work in the area of money.[2] W. W. Hutt in *The Keynesian Episode* ranked Brown with such economists as Wicksell, Cannan, Mints, Hayek, Viner, Kemmerer and Benjamin Anderson as leaders in the pre-Keynesian thought on money.[3] Leland Yeager and James Dorn have identified Brown as part of the tradition of the "theory of monetary disequilibrium."[4]

Brown's exact role in *The Purchasing Power of Money* is impossible to determine. Robert W. Dimand has recently provided an analysis of Brown's "contribution" to the study.[5] Fisher felt that Brown's efforts were so extensive that they deserved acknowledgment on the title page. As Fisher stated in his preface,

There are two persons to whom I am more indebted than to any others. These are my brother, M. Herbert W. Fisher and my colleague, Dr. Harry G. Brown.... My thanks are due ... to Brown for his general criticism and suggestions as well as detailed work throughout. In recognition of Mr. Brown's assistance, I have placed his name on the title page.[6]

What can clearly be discerned is that Brown took advantage of this experience and wrote several texts of his own within a few years.

Early Articles

BROWN PUBLISHED THREE ARTICLES ON MONETARY TOPICS while still an instructor at Yale; all three were cited by Fisher in *The Purchasing Power of Money*. The first, "A Problem in Deferred Payments and the Tabular Standard," considered the problems of price indexing set forth by Correa Walsh and Fisher.[7] Brown explained how the stated purpose of the tabular standard (that of ensuring that contracting parties receive or pay back with interest purchasing power over an equivalent amount of goods) was complicated by the type of good to be chosen as a standard: capital or consumption goods. Brown saw no solution but that of a practical compromise, which was to

> weigh the price change of each kind of good in proportion to neither an existing stock nor to consumption during any period, but in proportion to the value of the "exchanges" of that kind of goods during the period.[8]

R. A. Jones has credited Brown with having "convincingly demonstrated that the linking of payments to a price index could not generally eliminate all price risk for both payer and recipient."[9]

Brown's second article was primarily a description of the role of commercial banks in financial intermediation and emphasized the part played by banks in interest rate determination.[10] This short article is quite farsighted in that Brown remarks on the efficiency aspects of financial intermediation and its contribution to economic growth. In addition, Brown noted in 1909 that banks and trusts were beginning to pay interest on demand deposits. He reasoned that the convenience return to depositors and the competition among banks were not sufficient to attract deposits adequate to meet loan demands.

The third article, "Typical Commercial Crises Versus a Money Panic," appeared in the *Yale Review* in 1910.[11] In it, Brown attempted to describe a typical credit cycle that culminated in a speculation crisis. The key factor in the cycle was the lagging adjustment of nominal interest rates to unanticipated changes in the price level. Charles Kindleberger in his *Manias, Panics and Crashes* would later refer to this as the "Fisher-Brown" thesis.[12] The credit cycle would feature alternating periods of speculative prosperity and depression, even with a sound banking system. (Brown appears to be drawing primarily on the early work of Fisher and Wicksell.[13]) However, with a less than sound banking system, a loss of confidence would tend to precipitate a money panic. The panic period, according to Brown, typically would feature plentiful currency followed by sudden scarcity, which would drive rates abruptly upward. He then tried to identify those crises in the United States since 1873 that displayed these characteristics, taking into account those that were due, at least in part, to other, nonmonetary causes. Using what he admitted to be inadequate data, Brown examined the crises of 1873, 1882–1884, 1890, 1893 and 1907. He found indications that in most of these crises low real (virtual) rates of interest may have stimulated credit expansion, which led to a high ratio of deposits to reserves, and precipitated a crisis that featured falling prices and a rapid rise in nominal interest rates.

The Business Cycle

BROWN ORIGINALLY PUBLISHED HIS PRINCIPLES TEXT, *Economic Science and the Common Welfare*, in 1923. It underwent several editions; in 1942 the title was changed, and subsequent editions retain the title *The Basic Principles of Economics*.[14] In three early chapters, he dealt with the relationships of money, commercial banking and business cycles to prices. His statement and explanation of the equation of exchange followed that of Fisher. Brown maintained that despite other influences "the effect of an increase of money is to make prices higher than they would be if the quantity of money did not increase."[15] He also emphasized "the evils of a fluctuating price level." In regard to banking and prices, Brown's 1942 edition put greater emphasis on open market operations and indicated a greater confidence in the Federal Reserve System's ability to control the level of prices than did the 1931 edition. In the same section, he entertained the question of whether demands for higher wages could raise the level of prices and concluded that

> We can ... more reasonably think of wages and price changes as being, in the main, joint effects of a common cause, than as being, either, the cause of the other.[16]

In the chapter "Depression, Prosperity and Prices," Brown analyzed the business cycle along the lines of Mitchell, Fisher and Davenport. Mitchell's *Business Cycles* may have convinced Brown to abandon Fisher's earlier emphasis on the lagging adjustment of nominal interest rates as the key explanation for cycles. Also, as Dorfman pointed out, Brown introduced qualifications of his own. Dorfman singled out his emphasis on propensities to spend. Brown said that

> No theory of prices can be accepted as perfect and complete which makes the price level depend upon the quantity of money and bank deposits without reference to the general readiness to spend or hesitancy in spending[17]

Brown further emphasized this point:

> But from one phase of the business cycle to another phase of the same cycle, changes in the readiness to spend are perhaps of equal and possibly greater significance (than changes affecting the supply of money).[18]

In the case of a depression, Brown noted that a general unwillingness to spend was of particular importance in the case of businesses, as this would imply an unwillingness to borrow, despite low or falling interest rates. This unwillingness was explained in part by the reluctance of businessmen to accept lower prices for their goods as well as that of labor to accept lower nominal wages. Revival from a depression should be accompanied, if not preceded, by an expansion of credit. However, just as important for

Brown was a positive change in business sentiment. Increased buying and hiring by businesses would be facilitated by an increase in credit, and for a time the general price level would not be increased as businesses and workers would accept the existing lower prices and wages respectively. Leland Yeager has noted that Brown's emphasis on the inability of the price system to respond quickly to a monetary disturbance was similar to the emphasis of Clower, Leijonhufvud and Alchian on informational difficulties.[19] Yeager in a later essay on the significance of monetary disequilibrium quotes and interprets Brown as pointing to the "who-goes-first" problem in a declining economy.[20]

In discussing the crisis and ensuing depression, Brown felt that one of the many symptoms of a slowing prosperity was "the condition of bank reserves and the policy of the controlling banking system."[21] Speculative buying, unevenness of demand, or maladjustment of production may arise during the course of prosperity, but these in and of themselves should not cause a crisis. He looked to the condition of banks for indication of a turnaround. Banks whose loans had grown relative to their reserves may raise their rates or arbitrarily limit further credit. The perceived deficiency of reserves also could be due to restrictive central bank policies. Higher rates and restricted credit would affect the demand for goods and services as well as alter purchasing plans due to the expectation that prices will cease to rise at past rates. As one firm finds credit more difficult to obtain, it will begin to limit the credit it extends to customers. As prices begin to fall, a further incentive to postpone purchases becomes a part of the cumulative process. For Brown, there was "doubtless *some* level of prices, wages, etc., low enough so that, even with greatly diminished spending, business would be active."[22] Yet he recognized that the process of readjustment may well last a long period of time and entail great waste of capital and manpower as well as extensive social costs. Yeager, in his 1973 article, used Brown's explanation of a business depression as one example of a positive contribution by a quantity theorist to the process of integrating monetary theory and disequilibrium theory.[23]

Brown averred that at least a mitigation of the severity of crises and depressions was possible. A panic (which he defined as "a

disorderly process of attempted liquidation"[24]) could be checked
by the ability of the Federal Reserve to issue an unlimited volume
of Federal Reserve notes. The mitigation of the swings in the business cycle would require continuing Federal Reserve stabilization
policies.

He chose to show in his text the fallaciousness of the "oversav-
ings" hypothesis of business depression. He argued that the hypothesis depended on the assumption that the savings of the
capitalist-employers somehow prevents them from buying. He
maintained that this group could: spend on immediately consumable goods, spend on durable or investment goods, hoard its
earnings, throw its earnings into the sea.[25] The first two alternatives, if taken, should result in no deficiency in effective demand.
In the latter cases, Brown argued that the temporary or permanent
reduction of money in circulation must result in a lower price
level. He concluded,

> It is no answer to the argument presented above, to say that de-
> creased money in circulation, together with a general disinclination to
> accept reduced prices, wages, etc., may lead to a depression. For to say
> this is to admit that the problem is a monetary and credit problem and
> is to give away the whole case for "all-around over-production."[26]

In 1973, a year and a half before his death at age 95, Brown
wrote Leland Yeager to thank him for sending a reprint of his
"Keynesian Diversion" article. In it he expressed his pleasure to
find that the article recognized the contributions of Clark Warburton which Brown had made use of in the later years of his
teaching and those of Herbert J. Davenport who is referred to as
his "very good friend."[27]

The Great Depression

IN MARCH OF 1933 Brown presented his only published statement
on the causes of the Depression. In "Nonsense and Sense in
Dealing with the Depression," published in the *Beta Gamma
Sigma Exchange* (a business student honorary society publica-
tion), he strongly faulted the actions of the Federal Reserve. He, as
Dorfman noted, felt no qualms about abandoning the gold stan-

dard if ultimately it interfered with the means to bring about a re-covery.[28] Lester Chandler in his *American Monetary Policy 1928–1941* commented:

> one group of economists urged the Federal Reserve to take vigorous actions to expand the supply of money and believed that such policies would make an important contribution to economic recovery. Prominent among these were such "quantity theorists" as Professors Irving Fisher, James H. Rogers, Wilford I. King, Harry G. Brown and John R. Commons.[29]

Although Brown's views were similar to those of Cassel, Fisher and James Harvey Rogers,[30] some important differences may be noted. Also, as Frank Steindl in a recent appraisal of Brown's article pointed out, Brown's expressed views may reflect in part his discussions with two of his colleagues at Missouri, Elmer Wood and Karl Bopp, both of whom were students of central banking.[31]

Brown began the article by attacking several contemporary proposals as inimical to the goal of recovery. He mentioned the proposed sales tax, the proposed payment for holding agricultural land out of production, the proposed relaxation of antitrust laws and proposals from the "uncompromising deflation theorists." Thomas M. Humphrey in a 1971 article, "Role of Non-Chicago Economists in the Evolution of the Quantity Theory in America 1930–1950," stated that Brown, along with Fisher and W. I. King, were critical of the Federal Reserve policies but did not hold the Reserve "largely responsible for the initial turndown in business activity."[32] Brown, on the occasion of his (admittedly obscure) paper and in his correspondence, did make such a charge.

> A major cause of the depression—in my opinion the outstanding cause as far as the United States is concerned—is an inept policy of those in charge of our Federal Reserve system.[33]

He felt that those in charge were not aware of the extent of their ability to affect business prosperity. Specifically, he argued that the Federal Reserve in 1928 and in 1929 had been unduly restrictive in both open market and discount rate policies. He thought that the reversal of policy in early 1931 was too late and too restrictive to have been effective, given the existing conditions. When even the "heavy buying" of United States securities in 1932 was seen to be futile, Brown's view was that a yet-stronger policy must be pursued. (Here Steindl notes that although Brown hypothesized a one-third reduction in the money supply as defined by Fisher, he did not provide an empirical basis for the money supply behavior and interpreted the deflation for this purpose on a *prima facie* basis.)[34] To remedy this situation Brown proposed collaboration between the Treasury and the Federal Reserve wherein the government would borrow extensively from banks and spend these newly created monies in public works projects. Brown considered this a permissible unbalancing of the budget, especially because the bonds could be sold at low rates. Brown appears to have only taken this uncharacteristic position as an emergency response to the intransigence of the Federal Reserve System. Although he understood the widespread tendency for banks to hoard reserves just as other businesses were reluctant to invest, he appeared to be confident that a resolute policy on the part of the Federal Reserve could overcome these tendencies. He went on to suggest that Federal Reserve Board members had been influenced by sound banking principles in their actions and did not fully realize that these principles were not applicable to central bank policy making.

With regard to international financial considerations, Brown posited that it should be possible to restore prosperity and maintain stability at a higher price level, although he anticipated that the gold outflow might necessitate a presidential embargo on gold exports. He believed that gold holdings were sufficient in 1933 to support credit demands and maintain the gold standard domestically. His feeling was that the gold standard had become a "sacred cow" in American monetary policy. His opinion on longer-run policy was that

> it would be better to stabilize the general price level by open market purchases and sales of eligible securities as well as gold and not be dependent upon any need to interfere with the importation and exportation of gold.[35]

As to the effects of a "world-wide scramble for gold," he reasoned, "we had been not so much sinned against as sinning."[36] His views seemed to have been that this country must suffer the consequences of repercussions from abroad, which may well have been the result, at least in part, of errors in American monetary policy.

Other than in this article, Brown's views on the Great Depression may be examined in his correspondence with James Harvey Rogers. Rogers served on national committees designated to investigate the causes of and remedies for the economic crisis. However, he was best known for his work as financial advisor to President Roosevelt.[37] Brown corresponded frequently with Rogers, expressing opinions and at times urging Rogers to support certain policies. In his letters Brown showed support for the Goldborough Bill that Fisher, among others, had worked on.[38] Brown also noted in support of the Bill that he had recently learned that Wicksell had advocated price stabilization utilizing credit control, which included open market operations and international cooperation. Rogers predicted that, despite his own kindly feelings for the Bill, it ultimately would be vetoed by President Hoover and that some less objectionable approach be followed.[39]

In a November 1933 letter to Rogers, Brown stressed that the key to recovery was a monetary policy that sought to increase purchasing power as a first priority over attempts to control exchange and maintain the price of gold. Citing the investigations of his colleagues at Missouri, Elmer Wood and Karl Bopp, Brown defended attempts to use open market operations to bring about a stimulus for recovery. He noted the reluctance to lend or invest in all but government securities, but he pointed out that even these purchases would prove stimulatory. He suggested that the large excess reserves held by banks was linked in part to vacillation in Federal Reserve policy and that a stronger policy would induce banks to reduce their idle holdings. Brown also commented on the monetary critics of a managed currency in the press and in academia.[40] He felt that they could be overcome should the policy he advocated experience some measure of success. He expressed pessimism with regard to the behavior of the Board of Governors and inquired of Rogers if there was reason to hope for a change of policy. Rogers, in his reply, stated fundamental agreement with

Brown's views, but cited political difficulties he was unable, for reasons of discretion, to explain completely.[41]

Brown wrote the Committee for the Nation expressing his dissent from the President's gold purchasing program in late 1933.[42] Although Brown supported a system that allowed for change in the price of gold, he objected that gold purchases made with 90-day Reconstruction Finance Corporation (RFC) debentures were not likely to result in an increase in the money supply, which in existing conditions would be sufficient. He went on to suggest that in the face of the Federal Reserve's recalcitrance on open market policy that some separate commission be formed with power to force compliance by the Board of Governors.

Brown urged Rogers on several occasions to publicly support a petition originated by agricultural economists F. L. Thompson and O. R. Johnson and others, which had been revised in response to comments by Commons, Fisher and Rogers.[43] Brown was aware that the unanimity found among economists in opposition to tariff restrictions would not be forthcoming on questions of monetary policy. The petition itself was an attempt to emphasize the plight of agriculture and to strongly advocate a truly stimulatory monetary policy for the benefit of agriculture as well as industrial recovery. Brown was anxious to have the petition presented to Congress in light of what he called "the one presented by our conservative brother economists with its low obeisance to the sacred gold standard."[44] Although Fisher had encouraged Rogers to work on the "inside," Brown questioned the effectiveness of this strategy for Rogers as he was in the main advising officials whose philosophy on monetary and banking matters was inimical to his own. Brown stressed to Rogers the plight of the Midwest and concluded his letter by saying,

> There is a fabled center of spirit life which is said to be paved with good intentions. Stupidity in the direction of our national economic affairs when it leads to such consequences is not too harshly to be judged as criminal.[45]

In 1937, fears of an inflationary movement arising from a massive inflow of gold and the announced scheme to pay for the gold with new government securities prompted Brown to write to

Fisher.[46] Brown argued that these additions to the national debt, especially if they were large, would greatly increase the interest charge on the debt. He suggested an alternative embedded in the Agricultural Adjustment Act of 1933, which would allow the Secretary of the Treasury to refuse to buy gold at the parity level of $35 per ounce and, thereby, to allow gold's price to fall. Brown felt that this alternative in the face of a massive gold inflow should be considered, despite the legal provisions for the maintenance of parity. Fisher, in his notes made on the letter, indicated his agreement and his intention to bring the matter up in Washington.

Brown, in a later edition of his text, argued that the stability of the price level would be enhanced if the general monetary policy of the Federal Reserve and the government could be anticipated reliably. He seemed to have felt that anticipation of price movements by the public would tend to speed recovery as well as slow excessive spending in an upturn. He never expressed a view on the advisability of "money rules," but the foregoing might indicate his qualified support. He also stressed that monopolistic conditions contributed to the adversity of a depression and counseled continued enforcement of existing antitrust legislation.

100% Money

IRVING FISHER'S 1920 BOOK, *Stabilizing the Dollar,* mentioned Brown in the preface as one of several unpublished "anticipators" of his ideas.[47] Indeed, Brown evinced support of Fisher's general principles, if not acceptance of his specific program, as did many other economists of the era. In the mid-1930s several arguments were presented to the discipline in advocacy of what was then known as the 100 Percent Plan or the Chicago Plan. A. G. Hart, Henry Simons and Lauchlin Currie[48] contributed to the proposal, and it was accepted by Irving Fisher, who presented his own version in *100% Money* in 1935. Several articles appeared that were critical of some aspects of the plan but were supportive of it in general. (It should be noted that Fisher's version attempted to link the plan with overall price stabilization, unlike earlier versions.) In 1940, Brown published an article that was wholly critical of the plan.[49] In it, he brought up objections he judged to be both im-

portant and generally overlooked. The objections he presented
were intentionally general in order to respond to the various versions of the plan. He argued that the advantages gained from the
intermediary role of banks would be reduced under the plan. Specifically, the implicit convenience return to depositors would have
to fall with the requirement of 100 percent backing of demand
deposits. He objected to a proposed subsidization of deposit
banking that would allow banks to continue to offer free or low
service charges on checking accounts. He feared the possible in-
cursion of political influence as well as the creation of an economic distortion. Were subsidization linked to national debt retirement as had been suggested by Fisher,[50] Brown argued, the
concept of the debt would undergo distortion and eventually lead
to a perpetual government obligation of unknown proportions.

Brown then challenged what appeared to be the fundamental or
underlying premise of the proposal (in Frank D. Graham's words):
"One hundred per cent reserves will stop the private manufacture
of money and nothing short of this will serve."[51] Graham said this
in rebuttal to Brown's article. Two quite distinct perceptions of a
proper banking system can be noted. For Graham and others ad-
vocating this reform, the banking system should be restrained
from offering liquidity with interest on its accounts. He stated that
such practice "is responsible for most of the financial crises of
history."[52] Brown felt that the existing system was adequate if effective central banking principles were followed. Brown asked
why 100 percent was a sacred figure and why other means could
not be found to make deposit banking adequately safe and stable.
He also pointed out that other institutions may prosper by offering
accounts than can be withdrawn on short notice. Such near
money might become an attractive alternative to demand deposits,
and movements in these accounts would have effects similar to
the effects the plan was intended to arrest. Additional legal attempts to separate or isolate demand deposits from other assets
would so deprive individuals of options that such legislation
would be unlikely to find support. Brown concluded that less
radical changes in the monetary and banking system should be
examined to attain the desired stability. In a private letter to Dr.
John K. Towles of the Chase National Bank he referred to his arti-

cle and commented sardonically: "and certainly I should not wish to turn to Father Coughlin for the working out of a plan to control our monetary and banking system. . . ."[53] (It is worthy of note that Brown as well as the proponents of the plan demonstrated little confidence in the recently formed Federal Deposit Insurance Corporation's ability to avoid bank failures. This may be explained by the low levels of insurance offered by this institution in its early years.)

Comments on Macroeconomic Policies

WHILE IN HIS 60S AND 70S, Brown wrote several articles on topics in macroeconomic policy. His principal concerns were wartime price controls and subsidies, the growth of the national debt and the Keynesian "revolution." All but one of these articles were published in the *American Journal of Economics and Sociology*. In one article, Brown reflected on the New Deal legislation and found much that was ill-advised if not contradictory to the stated purpose of the acts.[54] He attacked provisions of the Agricultural Adjustment Acts of 1933 and 1938 that intended to limit agricultural supplies so as to raise prices; he pointed out that the general effects of the programs only benefited a privileged group of grower-owners and were detrimental to farm labor, renters of farm land and consumers. He further argued that the Federal Fair Standards Act of 1938, which fixed minimum wages for certain occupations, tended to result in greater unemployment in these occupations and lower wages in occupations not covered by the act. In a similar fashion, he attacked the "fair trade" legislation of the period.

Writing in 1942, Brown was critical of the decision to employ wartime price controls, but he recognized exceptions and suggested alternatives.[55] He felt that the difficulties, inefficiencies and injustices of a necessarily piecemeal approach to price controls rendered this method inferior to a program of heavy taxation of incomes to assist in meeting wartime expenses. However, he recognized that wartime priorities could necessitate emergency production priorities and rationing of certain goods, especially as the revamping of the tax system would take time and the result would not be adequate in all respects. He also saw price regulation and rationing as temporary necessities to avoid panic buying and hoarding, which, however, would be lessened if inflationary pressures were not so severe. In addition, he found redundant the idea that government subsidization of certain lines of industry would somehow serve to keep down or reduce prices in these lines.[56]

Brown's views about proper war financing were closely related to his objections to the increasing national debt. He maintained that the New Deal policies promoting business revival and stemming inflationary pressures added to the debt. Those instances in which the government borrowed from banks, as opposed to individuals and businesses, in order to finance public works projects caused the debt to increase. To the extent that the gold inflow to the Treasury was sterilized through the sale of government bonds, the debt grew as well. Brown saw the acceptance by economists of these increases as insufficiently critical. His objection was that unrestrained increases in the debt would necessitate future taxation to pay the interest on the debt and that this may in turn inhibit incentives that promote productive efficiency. He pointed out that although an internally held debt imposed no necessary intergenerational burden, this was not relevant to the question of the consequences he foresaw. Brown's view of the tax system was that it unnecessarily inhibited incentives for productive efficiency, and he assumed that a rapidly increasing debt would or could result in a heightening of the disincentives. In addition to future disincentives, he felt that a large and growing debt would provide further incentive for the government to adopt inflationary policies.[57] Although he did not attempt to predict when these negative influences would become economically significant, he argued that alternatives to the growth of the debt could and should be found.[58]

Brown appeared to be reflecting on his wartime thinking in his last article in the *American Economic Review* in 1952, "Cost of Production, Price Control and Subsidies: An Economic Nightmare."[59] He observed the growing tendency in the discipline to define costs with respect to the individual outlays of the firm. He felt that this tendency was responsible for erroneous support for the program of subsidies during the war and in the postwar era. He suggested that a broader view of cost—that is, as the alternative opportunities available to each factor of production—was the more useful view. The argument for subsidization was that prices could be held down or reduced by payment of subsidies to "high-cost" firms only, with the loss to the taxpayers exceeded by the gain to consumers. He argued that theoretically one could not distinguish a "high-cost" firm because any firm is likely to contain both high- and low-cost elements. Thus, for Brown, subsidies would have to be paid to the factors of production with high opportunity costs, which are no more productive than factors with lower opportunity costs. The subsidy program would be unfair, would be administratively difficult to apply and would deprive a factor with low opportunity costs the protection to its returns afforded by the existence of factors with higher opportunity costs, which could and would change their occupation should returns fall.

Views on Keynesianism

IN 1940 BROWN COMMENTED IN A LETTER to his ex-student, Lester Chandler, that he did not feel that the approach of Keynes need necessarily be followed "in order to make use of a demand and supply analysis in relation to money."[60] Brown argued that the Fisher equation for money and bank credit could be interpreted for this purpose. However, he did not follow up on his own suggestion.

Brown as a monetarist was not taken with the rise of Keynesian ideas. Keynes's growing influence on the discipline was apparent by the late 1930s. Joel Dirlam, a former student of Brown, reported in 1939 that the graduate orals at Yale included several questions on Keynes. He also mentioned that James Harvey Rogers believed that Keynes had thought everything out clearly first and then had consciously mixed it up when he set it down.[61] Brown made no mention of Keynes's ideas until 1948 when he wrote "Two Decades of Decadence in Economic Theorizing." His view was that Keynesianism was a fad and, moreover, a rather unproductive one. He began his article with a defense of the monetarist interpretation of the Depression.

The truth probably is that central banking policy has more to do with the alternation of prosperity and depression, and that central banking policy affects business activity through affecting the volume of circulating medium of which bank deposits subject to check are, at any rate in English-speaking countries, the major part.[62]

Brown, like other earlier critics of Keynes,[63] questioned whether there was anything new or even useful in the *General Theory*. He pointed out that the concept of the multiplier was not new and had been adequately understood in terms of the "velocity of circulation." He also argued at length that "liquidity preference" could not cause a depression. Brown included a "reluctance to spend or lend" in the contributing factors in the length and severity of a depression. However, he felt that there was no evidence that a depression was initiated by liquidity preference considerations, which were manifested "independently of any adverse banking or general monetary policy."[64] Citing Keynes as saying, "The concept of hoarding may be regarded as a first approximation to the concept of liquidity preference,"[65] Brown contended that the desire for liquidity in a depression could be overcome with wise monetary policy.

In the same article, Brown criticized statements made by Lloyd A. Metzler and Alvin Hansen. In a 1946 article, Metzler noted the demise of Say's Law of Markets and posited that, as a result, general overproduction in the economy was a theoretical possibility. Brown felt that Metzler failed to adequately qualify his argument and maintained that there would be no overproduction even with price rigidities unless a sufficient expansion in the money supply to the "currently produced goods" market was *not* effectuated. Brown also criticized Hansen's book, *Fiscal Policy and Business Cycles*.

Brown considered without merit Hansen's hypothesis that a slowing population growth rate was in part responsible for the Depression. Brown thought that Hansen's argument contained an untenable assumption—that the diminished demand for housing would result in a similarly diminished demand for goods in general. Hansen had also emphasized the relative decline in new industries in the depression years, which Brown rejected as a causative factor, arguing that Hansen had not shown how aggregate demand must fall as a result of this lack of new industry. In reply to Hansen's assertion that the supply of money and its rate of utilization would "adjust themselves to the demands of the underlying real factors," Brown argued that this assumed a monetary policy somehow attuned to the changes in these "real" factors in the economy. For Brown, the search for explanations for the depression need not go beyond institutional mismanagement of the money supply combined with the price, wage and interest rigidities in the economy. He cited the work of Henry Simons as an effective critique of the "new" economics.

Several years later (at age 79), Brown reiterated his objections to the ideas of Keynes and Hansen.[66] For statistical support, he referred to the work of Clark Warburton.[67] Brown chided the Keynesian economists for not considering land value taxation as a partial remedy for the supposed difficulties of periodically low marginal efficiency of capital. He maintained that with land value taxation, taxes on capital could be reduced, thereby raising the expected return on capital investments.

Concluding Observations

BROWN'S OPINIONS AND PRESCRIPTIONS as a long-time monetarist are certainly of interest. He sought, as had Fisher, the means by which an economy could thrive with a reasonably stable price level. Brown often stated that he would despair for the future of the price system if the government proved incapable of taking the necessary stabilizing measures.

Frank Steindl has identified Brown as constituting along with Fisher and Rogers a "Yale School" of monetary thought.[68] I would stress, instead, the possible historic importance of the Yale-Missouri connection. As students of Fisher, Brown and Rogers largely based their monetary expositions on Fisher's thought. However, in Brown's case he had never evinced support for Fisher's compensated dollar proposals and, as seen above, came to openly oppose the 100 percent reserve plan. Notably, Brown made no reference to Fisher's publications subsequent to *Booms and Depressions* and his textbook discussions of depression phe-

nomena drew on sources other than Fisher. Yet at the same time
he clearly felt that citation of Fisher was unnecessary or even redundant given the general closeness of their perspectives. He indicated in a letter to Fisher that he sought not to emphasize his
differences. The Yale-Missouri connection resulted in several Missouri students completing their doctorates at Yale. Up until and
even beyond (his text was used for several years) Brown's retirement in 1950, Missouri students (like it or not) were presented a
monetarist viewpoint when versions of Keynesianism were com-
ing to dominate most economics faculties. Student reactions, of
course, varied. Beryl W. Sprinkel, who may be taken as one type
of example, commented:

> He was a great inspiration to me and perhaps the kindest thing I
> could say is that I did not have to "unlearn" anything he taught me
> when I reached Graduate School at the University of Chicago.[69]

Others, such as Lester Chandler, would adopt Keynesian viewpoints, but retain a debt to the Missouri-Yale instruction in money
and banking. In this regard Milton Friedman stated in a letter:

> I have been impressed at the number of times in which I have come
> across people who had a real interest in economics and understanding
> of it, who trace it back to their studies with Harry Brown at the Univer-
> sity of Missouri. . . . You will find I am sure a great many people at UCLA
> with whose economic approach and development you will be highly
> sympathetic. Armen Alchian, Jack Hirshleifer, Axel Leijonhufvod, and a
> number of others there are very much in the kind of economic tradition
> that Brown represented.[70]

Although the "Chicago School" would become most closely associated with the monetarist revival, Robert W. Dimand has pointed
out its ties to Fisher and other earlier quantity theorists.[71] One may
also note that the only monetarist-leaning Federal Reserve District
Bank for many years, that of St. Louis, had as its president Darryl
Francis, a one- time student of Brown. Thus while never a specialist in monetary theory nor making any claim for original contributions to it, Brown's participation was noteworthy. As he did
not find adequate Henry George's thought in this area of eco-

nomics he provided an alternative to modern Georgists that he believed to be compatible with George's economic philosophy.

Notes

1. Paul E. Junk (1980). Preface. *Selected Articles by Harry Gunnison Brown*. New York: Robert Schalkenbach Foundation: x.

2. Beryl W. Sprinkel (December 16, 1981), letter to author. Personal Files. Iowa City, IA.

3. W. W. Hutt (1979). *The Keynesian Episode*. Indianapolis: Liberty Press: 4.

4. Leland Yeager (1973). "The Keynesian Diversion." *Western Economic Journal* 11 (June): 162
James A. Dorn (1983). "Introduction: A Historical Perspective on the Importance of Stable Money." *Cato Journal* 3 (Spring): 3.

5. Robert W. Dimand (1999). "Irving Fisher's Monetary Macroeconomics." *The Economics of Irving Fisher: Reviewing the Scientific Work of a Great Economist*. Eds. Hans-E. Loef and Hans G. Monissen. Cheltenham UK & Northampton, MA: Edward Elgar: 49–50. Notably, in Dimand's extensive studies on Fisher, he has adopted the practice of adding to Fisher's authorship a parenthetical "assisted by H. G. Brown" that seems to be in accord with Fisher's intention.

6. Irving Fisher (1911). *The Purchasing Power of Money*. New York: Macmillan & Co.: xi.

7. Harry Gunnison Brown (1909). "A Problem in Deferred Payments and the Tabular Standard." *Quarterly Journal of Economics* 23 (August): 714–718.
Correa Walsh (1901). *The Measurement of General Exchange-Value*. New York: Macmillan & Co.
Irving Fisher (1907). *The Nature of Capital and Income*. New York: Macmillan & Co.

8. Brown (1909): 718.

9. R. A. Jones (1980). "Which Price Index for Escalating Debts?" *Economic Inquiry* 18 (April): 222.

10. Harry Gunnison Brown (1910). "Commercial Banking and the Rate of Interest." *Quarterly Journal of Economics* 24 (August): 743–749.

11. Harry Gunnison Brown (1910). "Typical Commercial Crises Versus a Money Panic." *Yale Review* 19 (August): 168–175.

12. Charles Kindleberger (1978). *Manias, Panics, and Crashes*. New York: Basic Books: 30, 217.

13. Irving Fisher (1907). *The Rate of Interest*. New York: Macmillan & Co.
Knut Wicksell (1897). "Der Bankzins als Regulator de Warenpreise." *Jahrbucher für National-Okonomie und Statistik* 13 (February): 228–248.

14. I would like to note that I have worked primarily with the 1931 edition of *Economic Science and the Common Welfare* published by Lucas Brothers of Columbia, Missouri, and the 1942 edition of *The Basic Principles of Economics*, also published by Lucas Brothers. Although the two editions are quite similar, the later edition is longer by about 60 pages due to additions. The 1923 or original text was 273 pages in length, while the later editions exceed 500 pages. In this chapter I will cite the 1942 edition as *Basic Principles*.

15. Brown (1942). *Basic Principles*. Columbia, MO: Lucas Brothers: 51.

16. *Ibid.*: 89.

17. *Ibid.* : 89–90.

18. *Ibid.*: 94.

19. Yeager (1973): 160.

20. Leland Yeager (1986). "The Significance of Monetary Disequilibrium." *Cato Journal* 6 (2): 374.

21. Brown (1942) *Basic Principles*: 105.

22. *Ibid.*: 109.

23. Yeager (1973). "The Keynesian Diversion."162.

24. Brown (1942). *Basic Principles*: 110.

25. I failed to note in my 1987 Westview version that I had made use of Leland Yeager's ("The Keynesian Diversion." 161) reduction of Brown's lengthy discussion of the alternatives to four, numbered and accurate descriptive phrases. My apologies.

26. Brown (1942): 129.

27. Harry Gunnison Brown (September 18, 1973), letter to Leland Yeager. Personal files.

28. Joseph Dorfman (1959). *The Economic Mind in American Civilization*. Vol. 4. New York: Viking Press.

29. Lester V. Chandler (1971). *American Monetary Policy 1928–1941*. New York: Harper & Row Publishers: 117.

30. Gustav Cassel (1928). Testimony Before the Banking and Currency Committee of the House of Representatives. May.
Irving Fisher (1932). *Booms and Depressions*. New York: Adelphi Co.
James Harvey Rogers (1931). *America Weighs Her Gold*. New Haven: Yale University Press.

31. Frank G. Steindl (1995). "Yale and the Monetary Interpretation." *Monetary Interpretations of the Great Depression: A Review Essay*. Ann Arbor: University of Michigan Press: 110–115.
See and compare Karl R. Bopp (1932). "Two Notes on the Federal Reserve System." *Journal of Political Economy* 40 (June): 379–391.

32. Thomas M. Humphrey (1971). "Role of the Non-Chicago Economists in the Evolution of the Quantity Theory in America." *Southern Economic Journal* 38: 15.

33. Harry Gunnison Brown (1933). "Nonsense and Sense in Dealing with the Depression." *Beta Sigma Gamma Exchange* Spring: 99.

34. Steindl (1995): 111–112.

35. Brown (1933):106.

36. *Ibid.*

37. "Obituary for James Harvey Rogers." *American Economic Review* 29 (December) 1939: 913–914.

38. Harry Gunnison Brown (May, 1932). Letter to James Harvey Rogers. Rogers Papers, Yale University Library, New Haven, CT.

39. James Harvey Rogers (May, 1932). Letter to Harry Gunnison Brown. Rogers Papers, Yale University Library, New Haven, CT.

40. Harry Gunnison Brown (November, 1933). Letter to James Harvey Rogers. Rogers Papers, Yale University Library, New Haven,1 CT.

41. James Harvey Rogers (November, 1933). Letter to Harry Gunnison Brown. Rogers Papers, Yale University Library, New Haven, CT.

42. Harry Gunnison Brown (December 14, 1933). Letter to the Committee for the Nation. Rogers Papers, Yale University Library, New Haven, CT.

43. Harry Gunnison Brown (January 21, 1933) Letter to James Harvey Rogers. Rogers Papers, Yale University Library, New Haven, CT: 1

44. *Ibid.*

45. *Ibid.*: 2.

46. Harry Gunnison Brown (February 6, 1937). Letter to Irving Fisher. Fisher Papers, Yale University Library, New Haven, CT.

47. Irving Fisher (1920). *Stabilizing the Dollar*. New York: Macmillan Co.

48. A. G. Hart (1934/35). "The Chicago Plan for Banking Reform." *Review of Economic Studies* 2: 104–117.
Henry Simons (1936). "Rules Versus Authorities in Monetary Policy." *Journal of Political Economy* 44 (February): 1–30.

49. Harry Gunnison Brown (1940). "Objections to the 100% Reserve Plan." *American Economic Review* 30 (June): 309–314.

50. Irving Fisher (1935). *100% Money*. New York: Adelphi Co.: 206–207.

51. Frank D. Graham (1941). "100 Per Cent Reserves: Comment." *American Economic Review* June: 339.

52. *Ibid.*

53. Harry Gunnison Brown (September 30, 1940). Letter to John K. Towles. Joint Collection University of Missouri Western Historical Manuscript Collection, Columbia, MO.

54. Harry Gunnison Brown (1941). "The System of Free Enterprise and Its Caricature." *American Journal of Economics and Sociology* 1 (October): 87–98.

55. Harry Gunnison Brown (1942). "Fiscal Policy and War-Time Price Control." *American Journal of Economics and Sociology* 2 (October): 1–14.

56. Harry Gunnison Brown (1943). "Subsidies and War-Time Price Control." *American Journal of Economics and Sociology* 3 (June): 453–457.

57. Harry Gunnison Brown (1943). "The Danger in the Mounting National Debt." *American Journal of Economics and Sociology* 3 (October): 1–14.

58. Harry Gunnison Brown (1951). "The Size of the National Debt." *American Journal of Economics and Sociology* 11 (October): 55–60.

59. Harry Gunnison Brown (1952). "Cost of Production, Price Control and Subsidies: An Economic Nightmare." *American Economic Review* 42 (March): 126–134.

60. Harry Gunnison Brown (October 4, 1940). Letter to Lester Chandler. Joint Collection, University of Missouri Western Historical Manuscript Collection, Columbia, MO.

61. Joel Dirlam (April 29, 1939). Letter to Harry Gunnison Brown. Joint Collection, University of Missouri Western Historical Manuscript Collection, Columbia, MO.

62. Harry Gunnison Brown (1948). "Two Decades of Decadence in Economic Theorizing." *American Journal of Economics and Sociology* 7 (January): 149.

63. A. C. Pigou, Frank Knight, Gottfried Haberler, Gustav Cassel and Jacob Viner were some of the earlier critics of the *General Theory*.

64. Brown (1948): 165.

65. John Maynard Keynes (1936). *The General Theory of Employment, Interest and Money*. New York: Harcourt, Brace & Co.: 174.

66. Harry Gunnison Brown (1959). "The Keynes-Hansen 'Demand for Labor' Notion." *American Journal of Economics and Sociology* 18 (January): 149–156.
Harry Gunnison Brown (1959). "Monetary and Fiscal Counter-Depression Policy." *American Journal of Economics and Sociology* 18 (July): 337–351.

67. Brown cited Clark Warburton's (1948) "Monetary Velocity and Monetary Policy" in the *Review of Economics and Statistics* 30 (November): 304–314 and Warburton's (1948) "Bank Reserves and Business Fluctuations" in the *Journal of the American Statistical Association* 3 (December): 542–558.

68. Frank G.Steindl (1993). "Yale and the Monetary Interpretation of the Great Depression." *Quarterly Review of Economics and Finance* 33 (Winter): 305–323.

69. Beryl W. Sprinkel (December 19, 1981). Letter to author.

70. Milton Friedman (February 19, 1969). Letter to Mr. David J. Byrnes. Joint Collection University of Missouri Western Historical Manuscript Collection, Columbia, MO.

71. Robert W. Dimand (1998). "The Fall and Rise of Irving Fisher's Macroeconomics." *Journal of the History of Economic Thought* 20 (2): 195–196.

Chapter 5

Taxation

The Economics of Taxation

IN BROWN'S EARLY YEARS AT THE UNIVERSITY OF MISSOURI, he taught the advanced undergraduate course in what was then titled "Public Revenues." As not infrequently occurs, years of interaction with students in a particular subject coupled with the publication of several articles dealing with the same subject culminated in the writing of a textbook. In Brown's case the decision to develop a specialization in the field of public finance was clearly motivated by its close relation to his advocacy of land value taxation. In 1924 *The Economics of Taxation* was published by Henry Holt and Co. The book was reprinted in 1938 by Lucas Brothers and in 1979 by the University of Chicago Press (Midway Reprints). The initial reviews by Henry Simons, Frank Knight and Fred Rogers Fairchild were favorable; however, each reviewer expressed certain objections.[1] Simons concluded,

> Professor Brown has contributed a great deal of acute analysis to a more or less specific field of inquiry in which most the stuff that is written and preached is of exceedingly unattractive quality.[2]

Knight noted, "the economic analysis is at all points careful, thorough and competent, and is stated with admirable lucidity."[3] Fairchild, a successful author of textbooks, had similar praise for the book. Overseas the book was praised by W. Twerdocleboff, a Russian professor of the University of Leningrad, in a review article as one of the most important of recent publications.[4] Aside from this single reference there is no evidence of awareness of *The Economics of Taxation* outside of North America.[5] Several of the contributions of Brown's text were to be noted only many years later. In 1979, Arnold Harberger in a publisher's blurb for the reprint stated, "This is truly a classic."[6]

Preface and Comments

Brown's preface to the text was a noteworthy comment on contemporary approaches to the study and instruction of economics. He argued that with few exceptions advanced or intermediate courses in economics were less rigorous in terms of theory than the introductory "principles" courses. The tendency was to elaborate on an area of economics, such as public finance, in a narrative or descriptive fashion rather than attempt to deepen the student's theoretical grasp of the economic principles involved. Brown objected: "Only a thorough study of the cause and effect relations in taxation can, in fact, make one a competent leader of opinion on tax problems."[7] Thus, Brown's approach was to present ten chapters dealing primarily with tax shifting and incidence. This was done without the usual historical background found in McCulloch, Bastable, or Seligman. Brown generalized about the type of tax to be discussed. For example, he treated the incidences of taxes on capital and land in lieu of examining the effects of a property tax per se. A tax on labor income would be studied prior to considering income taxes. This prompted Fairchild to object: "This book deals exclusively with abstract theory, telling us virtually nothing of the relation of these theories to the facts of present day problems."[8]

That at least a part of this criticism was anticipated by Brown is evident in his preface. He believed it was unwieldy to deal with specific tax forms as opposed to basic taxation, whether realistic or not, of commodities, labor, land and capital. He felt that the development of general principles of taxation would be better served in this way. Moreover, he recognized and regretted the lack of inductive or empirical verification of the theory he presented. While welcoming empirical studies along the lines of Fisher and Mitchell, Brown argued that those who would criticize the book for being too theoretical were likely to be ignorant of the difficulty of the required statistical analysis.[9]

In his introductory chapter, Brown placed the study of taxation within the broader area of public finance. He thought that questions of taxation, and especially of its incidence, could be most fruitfully explored with economic analysis and that this could be done objectively. Knight pointed out that Brown did not deal with the "objectives of taxation, the canons of justice or administrative problems."[10] Brown maintained that knowledge of tax incidence was a necessary prerequisite to any discussion of proper policy. His stated intent was

> to keep the problems of policy in the background, and devote attention to the discovery and explanation of economic laws as such, leaving it to the readers to make such application of the conclusion reached as may seem to be proper.[11]

By this time he was a recognized advocate of land value taxation, yet none of the reviewers (and in particular Knight) found Brown's personal bias reflected in the book.

The benchmark of scholarship on taxation at that time was set by E. R. A. Seligman. The breadth of Seligman's work in the field of taxation was unparalleled. His major works, *The Shifting and Incidence of Taxation, Essays on Taxation and The Income Tax* clearly established him as the leading American authority on the subject. The first two books went through over ten editions and were clearly the dominant texts in the field for much of the first half of the century. Brown frequently referred to Seligman, although often to dissent from his views. Of the eleven times Brown cited Seligman, seven were to criticize his analysis. In Brown's correspondence he ventured the opinion that Seligman was "fearfully vulnerable on basic principles."[12] There is a similarity between Brown's and Seligman's works. Both attempted to synthesize past thought on the subject, thereby rendering the determination of original contributions difficult.

Brown's methodological approach to the determination of tax incidence is hard to classify in modern terms. He proposed first that the effects of a tax be examined by analyzing "the conditions of supply and demand insofar as they are significant for our purposes."[13] Further, his approach was nominally that of partial equilibrium analysis. However, as a student of Fisher, Brown was aware of the deficiencies in applying such analysis across the board. Therefore, in most instances, he extended the theoretical analysis toward a general equilibrium approach without the aid of a formal model. Simons noted this in saying in his review: "Especially noteworthy is the emphasis upon the extent of the diffusion process and precise definitions of its limits."[14] Brown did not specifically employ balanced-budget incidence; rather, he implied that the governmental expenditures from tax revenues would have minor or neutral effects, although he was aware of complications arising from this source. Nor can his approach be described as one of differential incidence, as he did not utilize a basis of comparison such as a proportional income tax. He would introduce a tax, analyze its incidence in the hypothetically simplest case and then extend the analysis to what he saw as relevant variations in each case. These variations might be long- versus short-run incidence, differing cost conditions, general versus specific taxation and so on.

Monetary Inflation as Taxation and the Incidence of Government Borrowing

Brown's first two chapters were unorthodox in that first he treated monetary inflation as a type of taxation and second he discussed the incidence of government borrowing. He wished to emphasize that governmental issue of inconvertible paper money in effect was taxation. He proceeded to show the effects of an increase in paper money in two cases. First, where the new issue serves primarily to displace metallic money via the workings of Gresham's Law, he argued that there would be no special burden on the issuing country's residents. He assumed no barriers to trade, gold as the medium of international exchange and government spending the new money on domestic goods and services. The initial rise in prices is modified as purchases from abroad increase with gold as payment. Thus, in roughly equivalent terms, the public loses goods to the government and replaces them with foreign goods. Then, if the paper money remains an acceptable substitute for the metallic money, no significant burden falls on the public.

Brown's second case was one in which the paper issue is continued beyond the point where metallic money ceases to circulate. Here the government in effect bids away a portion of the goods and services initially corresponding to the percentage increase in the money supply. For this result to hold, he employed several simplifying assumptions. First, the price rise could not be moderated by increased importation, as there would be no international reserves and the paper money would depreciate so as to check any increase in imports unless there was foreign speculation in this currency. The velocity of circulation was assumed to be unchanged. (However, Brown felt that it would increase with a rapid inflation, citing the cases of Germany and Austria.) Finally, for proportionality to hold, he assumed that the second-round effects of the new money spent by the government were not yet realized. With money incomes as well as prices proportionately higher, the burden of this "taxation" was "the wealth and services abstracted from them by the government when the new money was first put into circulation."[15]

Brown then discussed the distribution effects of this induced inflation. In the most simple cases—with prices all rising at the same rate—the burden was distributed according to the proportion of purchases, thus resembling, at least nominally, a general sales tax. He noted that in practice, prices and incomes do not rise to the same extent or at the same rate, thus causing the burden to be shared unequally. Brown emphasized the role of expectations in the process, whereby some gain and others lose as a result of inflation. He concluded with the admonition that such induced inflation must be recognized as taxation and should be seen by enlightened politicians as an undesirable alternative to direct taxation, despite the political difficulty of doing so. He further condemned the tendency of conservatives to find scapegoats for inflation in organized labor on one hand and radicals to find scapegoats in profiteering capitalists on the other.

A recent article by Ephraim Kleiman investigating "early inflation tax theory" sheds some light on what may have prompted Brown to present his analysis of inflation as a tax.[16] Kleiman noted that neither Jevons, Marshall, nor Fisher make mention of an "inflation tax," but that J. S. Mill had presented the basic idea without using the term "inflation."[17] J. M. Keynes is credited by Kleiman as presenting the "first full exposition of the inflation tax" in 1922 in an article titled "Inflation as a Method of Taxation" in a supplement to the *Manchester Guardian Commercial*, which was reproduced in Keynes's 1923 *Tract on Monetary Reform*. Kleiman goes on to show that Hugh Dalton, Keynes's one-time student, drew on Keynes's writing in his 1923 presentation of the idea in the first edition of his popular text, *Public Finance*. Brown made no reference to either Keynes or Dalton in his text and it is highly unlikely that he had read either Keynes or Dalton. However, Kleiman notes that Foster and Catchings' 1923 *Money*, which was the second in a series of books published by Houghton Mifflin's Riverside Press for the Pollak Foundation for Economic Research, spoke in a brief section of "inflation as indirect taxation," and in a separate section referred to another of Keynes's *Manchester Guardian* articles which reported on the Soviet inflation. Brown was much more likely, despite the tight timing, to have been aware of this publication as Irving Fisher's *The Making of Index Numbers* was the first in this series.[18] Yet it would appear more likely, as Kleiman suggests, "The occasional reference to it suggests that rather than have been forgotten, the notion of inflation as a tax was being taken for granted."[19] If indeed Brown did have a precursor in his presentation of the idea, it seems most likely to have been Mill, who he had read in his youth.

Brown began his discussion of government borrowing with some general comments related to wartime finance. He referred to the exchange between T. N. Carver and H. J. Davenport that took place during and after World War I. Brown examined bond issuance and higher taxation for their economic consequences, and he emphasized the similarity between the two since both redirect economic resources from the private to the public sector. He felt that subtle and unpredictable differences may arise with regard to saving and investment behavior.

> Discouragement to business or charitable contributions can only result if the tax method takes a larger proportion of the funds secured than does the bond-issue or borrowing method, from the particular persons who are inclined to business investment or to charity.[20]

Brown felt that the bond issuance was more likely to draw funds from those having a greater tendency to save and invest. He was not specific as to how the taxes were to be raised, but appeared to be thinking of a proportional income tax.

He had reservations about government borrowing, even for wartime revenue, which he recognized as politically expedient. However, he did not subscribe to the idea that such borrowing imposed a burden on posterity, where the borrowing is from the country's own citizens. He demonstrated that a person hypothetically could buy a bond and end up repaying the interest and principal through tax payments. Brown then showed that the much more likely case would involve intra- and intergenerational transfers but that later generations as a whole would not be burdened. He did note, however, that discriminatory tax schemes and extensive immigration would alter this conclusion somewhat in practice. He briefly considered Davenport's idea that war finance was "a mortgage of the masses to the classes."[21] This was a possibility when the bond issue was sold primarily to wealthier citizens, Brown admitted, but he pointed out that the incidence and effects of the total tax system would have to be considered to support this contention.

Brown's prime reservation about government borrowing lay in its inflationary tendencies. Only if there were a reduction in private spending commensurate with the increased purchasing power lent to the government through bond sales would the process not be inflationary. Especially under conditions of war, Brown thought that this was unlikely. Banks would tend to lower reserve requirements, purchase government bonds themselves with extended credit in the form of checking accounts or bank notes and allow as collateral government bonds on private loans In addition, this would to some degree extend the borrowing needs of the government as prices rose, depending upon the elasticities of supplies. Brown formally offered no opinion on the desirability of a restrictive policy regarding bank behavior sufficient to stem inflationary tendencies. However, in reacting to the growth of the national debt during World War II, he adamantly opposed what he considered to be an unwise growth in debt financing.[22]

Taxes on Competitively Produced Goods

In the remainder of the book, Brown considered several forms of government finance that were not taxes in disguise. He treated taxes on competitively produced goods and taxes on monopolistically produced goods. The two chapters (consisting of some 80 pages) represent a summation of the then-current views in microeconomics; Brown drew most heavily on Marshall, Seligman and Davenport. Having written well before the concepts of imperfect competition were elaborated by Robinson and Chamberlin, Brown anticipated some of these developments in theory, as will be shown later. The theory of firm he utilized lacked the precision of later presentations, and this, on at least one occasion, led Brown to err. One of the earliest economists to incorporate imperfect competition conditions and a more detailed theory of the firm into studies of incidence was John F. Due in his *The Theory of Incidence of Sales Taxation* (1942).[23] Due cited Brown more frequently than any other author and, with few exceptions, more favorably. This was due in part to Brown's 1939 article "The Incidence of a General Output or General Sales Tax," which added significantly to and amended his text's chapters on the taxation of commodities.

Brown first tested the case of a tax on the production of goods in a perfectly competitive industry where constant costs prevail over the relevant range. Assuming that all producers in the industry are marginal in the sense that any lower return would force them to cease production of the good, then this tax would be shifted in its entirety to the consumers of the good. Brown recognized the likelihood of there being inframarginal producers in the industry, but he treated this incidence under that of increasing costs.

Brown next turned to the consideration of the effect of commodity taxation on the general price level and was criticized severely for the attempt by Simons. Brown found that a tax on a particular commodity produced under constant costs would not alter the general price level. The tax would result in the price of the taxed good rising by almost the amount of the tax and all other prices falling slightly so as to leave the general price level substantially unchanged. He assumed no international trade effects, an unchanged money supply and a constant velocity of circulation. Simons felt that the treatment was an oversimplification, but he did not elaborate on his preferred approach. He said that the argument "appears to presuppose an altogether mysterious disappearance of effective demand."[24] Brown very briefly extended his argument to a tax on all goods, maintaining that the effect would be to lower all money incomes in relation to the prices of these goods. The 1939 article elaborated and modified this conclusion.

Brown next examined the case of increasing cost of production for the competitive industry. He felt this to be the normal or inevitable case as extension of production would eventually tend to encounter rising costs. He noted the factors of production may differ in their likely contributions to increasing costs. A tax in this case would be partially shifted to consumers but also would burden the factors of production in all but the extreme instance of a totally inelastic demand for the good. Brown's reasoning was that the incomplete shifting of the tax would drive from the industry those factors that were marginal between this and other industries and reduce industry supply. Further diffusion effects of the tax would operate either through the higher price of the taxed good or the altered factor supplies. The higher price may reduce spending on other goods or the addition to the factor supplies of other industries may lead to lower prices and money income there, however slightly. Brown saw no general or average effect on prices unless efficiency was lessened by the changes wrought by the tax. He illustrated his general point with examples and graphs.

His emphasis on the possibility of changes in factor prices was unusual at that time; Due noted that this possibility "has been for the most part ignored despite the fact that in terms of orthodox value analysis the incidence would be modified significantly by changes along these lines."[25] Due also pointed out that Brown's further treatment of short- as well as long-run incidence was an early contribution.[26] Brown maintained that the industry's short-run supply was likely to be less elastic than in the long run, due to the existence of specialized factors—especially capital and labor. Thus, the extent of the shifting of the tax to consumers would be less in the short run, as would be the rise in price. In the long run, the competitive conditions would dictate an almost complete shifting to consumers of the good unless elements taken as exogenous (such as tastes or technology) change.

With respect to the case of decreasing costs, Brown said, "It would seem, then, only doubtfully worthwhile to discuss the incidence of a competitive industry operating under decreasing cost."[27] Knight, in his review, concurred that in general the case is of "doubtful occurrence," but he noted that this view was considered unorthodox.[28] Brown argued that the external economies to an industry resulted in no advantage to a single management but only operated as an inducement to larger scale production in the area where the economies were effective. Were all producers marginal, a tax on production would result in a higher price by the amount of the tax plus the increased cost to the firms of producing a smaller quantity. He also pointed out that where no external economies were present, internal economies may not lead to a monopoly situation. This could be true where no one plant is capable of providing all the product demanded; thus, increasing or constant cost conditions arise. Brown recognized that unless cost conditions changed in transition, no Marshallian stable equilibrium was possible, and the inevitable result would be monopoly. The tax therefore would have an uncertain incidence depending largely on the pricing strategies of the competing firms and their capacities of supply with regard to total market demand. The extremes of incidence in this transitory state were between no shifting and a complete shifting of the tax.

Finally, in this chapter Brown noted a further effect of a commodity tax that he termed a net loss in utilities to the community. This appears to be his term for excess burden. He suggested that if the product taxed were considered injurious, the net effect of the tax may be beneficial to the community.

Taxes on Monopolistically Produced Goods

Cournot was the first to analyze the possible effects of a tax on a monopoly's product. Brown's treatment, some 86 years later, was described by Due as the most complete of the then more recent analyses.[29] Brown began by noting that the monopolistically de-termined price after the imposition of the tax could stay the same, rise by more than the amount of the tax, or rise by less. He dis-cussed the different demand conditions and, following Marshall, illustrated the first and second possibilities where constant costs prevail.[30] The tax would not be shifted when a small rise in the price greatly diminished the quantity demanded, assuming the pretax price to be at or near a point on the demand curve where it becomes more elastic. Here Brown suggested that the most profit-able alternative for the monopolist may be to absorb the tax. A tax may be shifted where the monopolist faces a demand that be-comes much more inelastic above the current price due to the ex-istence of two distinct classes of buyers in the market. Thus, he made use of what would later be known as "kinked" demand curves. (Brown's usage in the no-shifting case was, I believe, a clarification and acceptance of Seligman's analysis, to which Edgeworth had objected.)[31] (See Appendix 5A.) Finally, Brown utilized a geometrical proof to show that a linear demand would result in a price increase of one-half of the amount of the tax.

Where the monopolist operates with increasing costs,[32] Brown argued that the increase in price and the shifting would be less than in the case of constant costs in all of the foregoing demand conditions. He stated simply that "the gain from raising the price, when the tax is levied, is sooner offset by the loss of cutting off some of its former business."[33] In the case of decreasing costs or of a "natural" monopoly, he found the distinction between the short and long run to be significant. His reasoning was that in the short run (except where the tax resulted in the abandonment of the business), the monopolist would only consider operating costs that would be largely unchanged. However, this would not be true in the long run, and the monopolist would tend to raise the price by more than he would in the case of constant costs. Brown dem-onstrated this by using the same demand for both constant and decreasing cost conditions in examples using graphs and tables. Brown rationalized his conclusion in the following manner:

> For by raising its price it gains as much on each unit of business still done as if operated under conditions of constant cost; while its loss on

the business cut off is less since the cost of this business (except for marginal units) is greater than in the case of constant cost.[34]

Brown's conclusion was the opposite of the earlier views of Seligman and H. C. Adams but in accord with that of Edgeworth.[35] Brown concluded by noting that a tax on monopoly's net profit could not be shifted.

Brown was aware that imperfect information on the part of the monopolist and governmental regulation of monopolies would render uncertain his conclusions. Also, he mentioned the difficulties of deciding whether monopolistic or competitive conditions tended to prevail in a given case. "What shall we say, for instance, of a tax on entertainments in towns and cities having one, two or three movie theaters?"[36]

In a footnote, Brown entertained the somewhat minor but illustrative question of how a specific or per unit tax would differ in its effects from one that was ad valorem. The question is illustrative in that it shows how his approach could lead to errors or at least to some confusion. Brown was concerned with how a specific tax and an ad valorem tax would alter final prices in the competitive and monopolistic cases. He found in the competitive case no fundamental difference in the effects of these methods of taxation. He reasoned that, in general, in the monopoly case, the ad valorem tax on gross revenues would not tend to raise the price as much as would a specific tax. He was aware that this was not always true, but he felt that this was due to the difficulties of making the comparison. He presented in tabular form two different models of comparison—one of equal yields and one of equal initial burden. Although the second comparison bore out his reasoning, he failed to discover the reason for exceptions arising in his examples. Richard Musgrave later explained that had Brown assumed linearity of cost and revenue schedules as well as tax rates at or below the maximum yield, his reasoning "would have admitted no exceptions."[37]

Taxes on Labor

Brown's next two chapters dealt with taxes on labor. He divided his brief treatment into three cases: taxes on wages in general;

taxes on wages in a given line of work; and taxes on "surplus" labor incomes. A then largely hypothetical tax on wages had for Brown long-run effects that depended primarily on how population was affected. That the revenues from such a tax may be used to benefit wage-earners was not ignored, but he pointed out that this may not be the case and that nominal incomes were lowered regardless of other sources of income. The effect of such a tax on population growth was seen as uncertain, although a sufficiently large tax probably would reduce this rate of growth and thereby tend to raise future wage rates. He further argued that should the rate of population growth fall, the landowning class definitely would find its income reduced as the Physiocrats had maintained. However, he saw this only as a possibility contingent on many factors, as he viewed an increased birth rate as a conceivable consequence of lower living standards.

Otto von Mering, in his text *The Shifting and Incidence of Taxation* (1942), referred frequently to Brown's treatment of a wage on a particular line of work or occupation.[38] Brown saw wages in the taxed line of work eventually rising to their original position relative to other lines of work and thus putting downward pressure on other wage rates. Mering objected to Brown's implication that labor and labor alone would bear the burden of the tax.[39] Furthermore, Mering noted that this was not compatible with Brown's view of the effect of a particular commodity tax. Mering was correct in part. However, Brown had qualified his position by pointing out that his conclusion required a redistribution of workers out of the taxed area, which may occur slowly and incompletely because of a lack of substitutability in employment, tastes in work, or the existence of rents in highly specialized areas of work. Mering's point as to compatibility remained, yet Brown had indicated an awareness of the problem:

> we have to reopen for possible qualification of our conclusion, the case of taxes on commodities. For although such taxes may seem to be shifted, in large part, on consumers, in the first instance, it is possible that in the long run some or all of the consumers (in our present problem, the wage earners) will find the burden again shifted upon the shoulders of some other class or classes.[40]

Brown's last case was the incidence of taxes on surplus or un-usually high labor incomes. He described the present system of income taxes as a discriminatory tax where it applied to labor in-comes. He concluded that such a tax would not be likely to reduce the numbers in these high-paying areas because advancement toward them would remain relatively unimpeded as long as lower incomes were not taxed at the same rate.

In an article published two years earlier and included in his text, Brown considered the incidence of compulsory insurance of workers.[41] The article was probably inspired by his dissent from the then common opinion that the incidence of such a tax would ultimately lie with the consumers of the goods produced by in-sured workers. Brown cited Taussig[42] as holding in general the correct view and in the article Brown expanded and refined this view. Compulsory insurance programs were under consideration in this country, while Germany in 1884, Great Britain in 1897 and the state of California in 1916 had implemented insurance pro-grams.[43] Brown examined in succession the cases where the in-surance was general (paid by all employers) and where only high-risk industries were made to pay. Brown took into consideration the advantages of compensation for employees. He maintained (with Taussig) that in the first case the long-run effect would fall on wage earners alone with only minor qualifications. By the early 1930s unemployment insurance schemes were topical and studies would cite Brown's analysis, such as Dale Yoder's 1931 *Quarterly Journal of Economics* article: "Ultimately, wages tend to be re-duced by the amount of the tax and employment to return to its former level. Professor Brown has described this result and the manner in which this readjustment takes place with care and clar-ity."[44] J. A. Brittain has pointed out that Brown assumed in addition to a fixed labor supply that "the tax would not increase the money supply and have little effect on aggregate demand."[45] In their text *Public Finance*, Earl Rolph and George Break referred to Brown's article as the original one to treat this subject.[46] As late as 1997 a political scientist would attribute, somewhat incorrectly, the inci-dence of Social Security taxation to Brown and Brittain.[47] E. H. Downing, in his posthumous *Workmen's Compensation*, argued (as noted by Dorfman) that Brown had taken the marginal productivity doctrine to extremes in order to reach his conclusion.[48] Downing, an advocate of such insurance, mistook Brown's position and implied that he did not favor compulsory insurance when he actually did.

Where insurance was required in only certain lines of work and the workers fully valued the certainty of accident compensation, the result, as Brown saw it, was ultimately a reduction in the demand for insured labor on the part of the firms and an increase in the supply of labor to the insuring firms. Thus, employment should remain the same at a wage lowered by the amount of the premium. He then considered the situation wherein workers impute no value to the insurance and demand for the industry's product is inelastic. Workers, at least those who are marginal between their present and other employment, will resist wage reduction, which normally would result in higher prices. With an inelastic demand, consumers would tend to buy less of other goods, which in turn would bring about lower wages and prices in other industries, with no net effect upon the returns to capital and land. However when noninsured workers are diverted to the insured lines, the burden would be shared more equally by all workers. Where the demand is elastic, the result is the same, but the impact of labor leaving the insured industry would be greater than the effect of redirection of spending on the part of the consumers.

Brown mentioned several qualifications to his argument, such as possible efficiency losses, special cost and competitive situations and population effects. He wished to emphasize that his was a long-run view and that actual adoption of such programs would appropriately burden employers initially. Also, if premiums were made to depend, for example, on safety conditions at individual plants, the incentives created for employers would have desirable consequences.

Taxes on Capital and Profits

Brown's treatment of the incidence of taxes on capital and capital incomes is similar in some respects to the early work of Arnold Harberger. Brown considered the incidence of a tax on capital used in some but not all industries. This is comparable to Harberger's corporate and non-corporate division of the economy. It also is applicable to the question of the incidence of a tax on urban property, as was noted by Herbert A. Simon in a 1943 article.[49] Simon therein indicated that conceptually a tax on urban property could be separated into a tax on site value and a tax on improvements—that is, housing.[50]

Once again, Brown used the competitive case and noted that little or no shifting of the tax may take place in the short run. This would be the case were the taxed capital durable and specialized. The owners of such capital would bear the burden of the tax. However, in the long run Brown maintained that capital would tend to leave these industries, which would result in a higher relative price for their products. He rejects at this point a possible imputation of incidence as superficial. For Brown, neither consumers of these goods nor workers in these industries were likely to bear the ultimate burden of the tax. Lower prices of the goods produced with the nontaxed capital should compensate consumers, on the average. In the case of labor, should the lowered productivity not be compensated with higher prices, migration to other industries should leave the wage level as before. Brown concluded that:

> the burden of the tax on some capital is finally (assuming that it does not tend to decrease the aggregate volume of capital) distributed upon the owners of all capital in the taxed community. The marginal product of labor in general is not less. The demand for labor is not reduced. The assumed tax is not on commodities and does not rest with the consumers. It is not on wages and does not rest on wage-earners. It is not on land rent and does not rest on landowners.
>
> It does not rest exclusively on the owners of capital in the industry or industries taxed, since capital tends to be driven to some extent from such industry or industries into others. It does rest on the income of capital-in-general including capital in the industries not taxed as well as in the industries taxed.[51]

He implied that this "distribution" would tend to burden what he called the "more strongly competitive capital."[52] Jen Peter Jensen's thorough 1931 study, *Property Taxation in the United States,* found Brown's view to be "tentatively correct."[53] Simon noted in his article that

> It is Brown's contribution to have shown that this change [a lowering of the return to capital], though small, when multiplied by the total of the amount of capital supplied may significantly affect the total amount of interest paid. The point is a subtle one, but one not all uncommon in the realm of mathematics.[54]

And

> Professor Brown has performed a very valuable service, however, in pointing out that a tax upon a particular use of capital has repercussions upon income from capital in general. He has supplied an important corrective to the classical analysis which ignores these repercussions, and has shown that earlier theory is valid only if the demand for houses is entirely inelastic and independent of the demand for other commodities.[55]

Simons's "however" refers to his criticism of Brown's methodology, especially in that he made no explicit assumption about the elasticity of demand for capital goods (housing) relative to that of other goods which would determine the extend to which Brown's conclusion would hold.

Peter Mieszkowski, as early as 1969, recognized the import of Brown's insight.[56] Mieszkowski with George Zodrow found applications for what they referred to as the "Brown proposition." They interpreted this "general proposition" in the following manner:

> taxes on perfectly mobile capital, even when imposed in relatively small sectors of the economy, tend to be borne by all capital throughout the nation due to general equilibrium effects.[57]

Mieszkowski also credited Brown with an early recognition of the close similarity of a general property tax (where the tax is at the same rate taxing all income-producing wealth) and a general profits tax.[58] Mieszkowski and Zodrow in a 1989 survey article in the *Journal of Economic Literature* recount not only their own applications of the Brown proposition, but those of Courant and Rubenfield and of Wildasin.[59] They also note that David Bradford in 1978 had applied Brown's reasoning to a broader application in the following way:

The assumption that actions of a given economic unit do not affect prices elsewhere in the system of which the unit forms a part, is one of the most useful approximations in economic analysis. ..The approximation is clearly justified when the unit in question is small in a well-defined way relative to the larger system and the larger system allows a certain scope for substitutability.

It may not be widely understood that the superficially similar assumption under the same circumstances, that the *products* of prices and quantities elsewhere in the system can safely be treated as a constant, may well not be justified.[(1)60]

Bradford footnoted this statement as follows:

(1) This idea is, however, not new. As has been pointed out to me by Wallace Oates, an analysis similar in spirit to the present one was given by Herbert A. Simon in 1943, who attributed the idea to Harry Gunnison Brown (1924), who attributed it in turn to yet earlier contributors. [See Appendix 5B.]

The David E. Wildasin article applied the proposition to "The Non-negligible Impact of a Small Project." Interestingly, Wildasin drew on a different section of Brown's than had the other authors—that of the case of the incidence of a tax on bricklayers where the resulting slight reduction in all other workers' wages would equal the total tax collected.[61] Wildasin in 2000 showed how the proposition could be interpreted in case of local taxes with international factor mobility in the European Union.[62] William C. Wheaton provided yet another application wherein state taxation with a mobile capital tax base can lead to a "higher national cost of investment" and a subsequent underprovision of welfare.[63]

Brown in concluding his discussion of a tax on some capital pointed out that the federal income tax of the time, to the degree it taxed capital income but exempted state, local and Federal Farm Loan Act bonds, "illustrates the tendency of a tax on some capital to affect the rate of return on other capital."[64] Brown's treatments of a tax on some capital, a line of work, or an "income" tax on some capital all represent departures from partial equilibrium analysis. All are in need of further refinement to bring forth definite conclusions of which Brown was generally aware. Yet despite their consistency, Brown did not seem fully aware of the generality of his treatments and more specifically of the idea of very small changes affecting a very large number as having significant economic effects. The citations of Brown made by the writers mentioned above beginning with Simon are not specific in nature and can be categorized as reasonable interpretations. (Even Wildasin's quite specific reference utilizes an interpretation of what Brown actually wrote.)[65] In all cases it appears that Simon's insightful interpretation (principally via Peter Mieszkowski or Wallace Oates) influenced later readers to the extent that it may be proper to rename the "proposition" the Brown-Simon proposition.

Turning to the case where all capital is taxed, Brown argued that the effect of the tax on the aggregate supply of capital would determine the tax's incidence. He pointed out that with an open economy such a tax may reduce foreign investment in the taxing country and increase overseas investment, but he did not pursue this argument. He felt that the effect of the tax on aggregate savings was a complex question. He could not find deductively a satisfactory relationship between rates of interest and savings levels. He felt that the common supposition that savings will decrease as rates of return are diminished by the tax could not be regarded as a certainty. He pointed out that the tax may be shifted in part via higher interest rates to all capital users. However, should savings remain largely unaffected, the burden would fall on capital owners. He would only say that a tax that seriously decreased net returns could be shifted, especially in the very long run.[66]

Brown saw some merit to the taxation of inherited wealth even where it took the form of non-land property, especially where it did not appreciably diminish the motive for accumulation, fell primarily on direct descendents and was progressive in lightly affecting smaller estates. Yet all these conditions he saw as uncertain and evasion difficult to legally prevent.

The possible incidence of excess profits taxes was analyzed. (In 1919, such a tax had been enacted by Congress.) Brown indicated three ways in which this tax could be shifted. He thought that the tax may retard the redistribution of capital and penalize risky industries. The tax might reduce the accumulation of capital, as may a tax on capital. Brown did admit that a monopoly could be taxed so no shifting of the tax was possible. But he added that the cost and difficulties of evasion could still have economic effects, especially if the tax were viewed as temporary.

Other Taxes

Brown wrote at great length on the subject of taxes on land. His conclusion that a tax on pure land value would fall exclusively on landowners and would be fully capitalized in the price of land was the traditional one where static, general equilibrium analysis was employed. Although some writers in the past had attempted to challenge the view that a tax on land value could be shifted, none did so successfully. Few ideas in economic thought remain sacrosanct. Martin Feldstein in 1977 argued that shifting of a pure land tax could take place due to induced capital accumulation or portfolio balance requirements.[67] However, in response, Calvo, Kotlikoff and Rodriguez maintained that shifting depended on the nature of the life-cycle model used in the dynamic analysis.[68] They went on to demonstrate that a compensated tax on pure land rents would not be shifted in the long run in a life-cycle model with intergenerational transfers. On Brown's part, the only qualification of the principle were instances where a tax on land value actually taxed more than the site value, including elements that were better classified as capital. The impossibility of decreasing the supply of land made shifting likewise impossible. (Because most of Brown's analysis and advocacy of land value taxation are treated in the following chapter, I shall postpone further discussion of his arguments in this area.)

He did, however, treat some tax incidence questions related to land taxation that do not bear directly on land value taxation. He discussed the relationship between taxation and capitalization, the incidence of taxes on land according to quantity and the general question of whether all taxes discourage accumulation. On the last question Brown pointed out that one must hypothesize as to the use to which tax revenues are put.

He noted that even if the source is a non-shiftable base such as land values or net monopoly profits, were the government to waste this wealth the taxes would diminish accumulation. If, however, the assumption is that the state makes reasonable use of its revenues the result may be no diminution of accumulation, or even an increase. Shiftable taxes which adversely affected the motivation to accumulate in addition to taking away wealth, he argued, represented inferior public policy.

As earlier mentioned, Brown found much actual taxation to involve compound taxation. The two most prominent instances were property and income taxes. The general property tax was thus a tax on rent of land and the interest from its associated capital. An income tax would draw in addition on wages broadly defined. Writing in the early years of federal income tax Brown expressed a common concern with evasion, particularly in the cases where incomes were determined by declaration. As has been alluded to above, some of Brown's ideas relative to the incidence of property taxation have become associated with what has been called the "new" or more recently "capital tax" view. As most of this discussion took place subsequent to his death one can only speculate that although Brown may have been flattered by this attention he would have felt uncomfortable even in this "Room with Three Views" wherein the focus is upon the capital portion of the residential property tax.[69]

Brown's treatment of the incidence of inherited wealth or death taxes in *The Economics of Taxation* came up in James K. Hall paper, presented to a 1940 AEA Round Table on the Incidence of Taxation which Brown chaired. Hall summarized Brown's position as that of seeing the burden falling upon the successors with disincentives to save resulting in a smaller capital stock which leads to a long-term sharing of the incidence by the successors with laborers and landowners in general.[70] Brown did, however, stress the speculative nature of the disincentive effects and the likelihood of evasion. He also noted the growing popularity of such taxes and opined that, were the duties sufficiently progressive, such taxation was not "entirely without merit."[71] (This Round Table was made much more memorable by Henry C. Simons' paper which urged tax specialists to pursue differential incidence in general equilibrium framework with definite monetary assumptions.)

Brown chose to include consideration of the incidence of import and export levies or tariffs in his text. In considering a protective tariff as a tax, he concluded that in general the tariff or export duty burdened consumers more than it aided the protected producers. It would require exceptional circumstances for some or all of a tariff to fall on foreign producers.[72]

"The Incidence of a General Output or a General Sales Tax"

BROWN'S LAST ARTICLE ON TAX INCIDENCE, "The Incidence of a General Output or a General Sales Tax," appeared in 1939 in the *Journal of Political Economy*.[73]

This article represented a refinement of his earlier thought as well as a correction of some earlier views. His interest in this subject perhaps was sparked by the rise of state retail taxation during the 1930s and by what he perceived to be a faulty analysis of the incidence of such taxation. The then commonplace conclusion was that taxes on retail sales would be passed on to consumers. Due noted Brown as an exception to this view in his book, which was completed in thesis form but not published until after Brown's article appeared. Brown's conclusion was that, with certain qualifications, such a tax would fall on the owners of the factors of production. Due said:

> It is interesting to note that no discussion of retail tax incidence has considered this aspect at all; the usual brief analysis merely indicates that the tax will pass to consumers, and ignored entirely the reactions on investment, employment and interest rates which are inevitable under the orthodox theory of distribution on which the analyses are based.[74]

In 1953, Richard Musgrave credited Brown with being the first to note the fallacy in the presumption that a general sales tax would raise the prices of consumer goods and not reduce cost payments to factors.[75] Earl Rolph in 1952 commented,

> In 1939 Professor H.G. Brown demonstrated in a rigorous fashion that a general system of excises is not shifted to consumers, does not affect the product mix, but does reduce factor incomes. For reasons not easily discerned, his argument has rarely even been thought worth refuting.[76]

Brown began his argument by assuming that the tax would apply to "all lines of production," including purchases by the government. He implicitly assumed perfect competition in both factor and commodity markets, a given supply of money and perfectly inelastic factor supplies. Brown, as in other analyses, was vague with regard to the uses of what he assumed to be new revenue. Due suggested that Brown assumed the use of the revenue would not alter the aggregate money demand for goods.[77] However, H. P. B. Jenkins thought that Brown intended that the tax would not cause any additional divergencies between marginal rates of substitution of goods in production and those in exchange.[78] In any case, Brown was aware that collective versus individual spending patterns could alter relative demands for goods and have an effect on relative prices.

Brown maintained that a general sales tax would not reduce output and thus that prices need not rise unless for exogenous reasons the money supply were increased. Here he appears to be following J. S. Mill.[79] Brown further argued that the reduction in factor incomes would be proportionate, which in turn implied that labor would contribute more than capitalists and landowners in absolute terms. He described the general output tax as "in practical effect, the same as if it raised prices . . . without either decreasing or increasing money incomes."[80]

Brown then turned to a more practical analysis of state retail taxes wherein rates vary from state to state. Here he found that retail prices would rise by roughly the amount of the tax in the taxing state while slightly lowering retail prices in surrounding states. He saw the tax driving a "wedge" between retail and wholesale prices. In a correction to the article, he stressed that

> average prices (counting producers,' wholesale and retail prices and also individually received wages, interest and rent and the governmentally received tax monies) as actually charged and paid in markets, are not made either higher or lower by output or sales taxes, and the average is, therefore, the same regardless of where the "wedge" is driven.[81]

He added in the correction that the additional transactions created by collection of the taxes may slow the spending of money for goods, which is the equivalent of saying that the velocity of circulation would be reduced. However, he thought this to be of little quantitative significance. The existence of friction in the form of sticky prices and wages was used by Brown to show how the introduction of sales taxes may have contributed to the unemployment problems of the era. This obtains from his argument that in the long run the general sales tax could not raise commodity prices.

Brown sent copies of his article to several economists who were specialists in taxation and received responses from Howard Bowen and Richard Musgrave, among others. Bowen praised the article: "I am glad that you have pointed out so clearly the true nature of general output and sales taxes."[82] Musgrave, although agreeing that the tax was likely to be shifted backward, felt that an increase in money velocity could also result in forward shifting of the tax.[83] Brown responded that he could see no reason to attribute a rise in money velocity to the imposition of a general sales tax, but he did concede that money velocity might fall slightly.[84] Musgrave expressed other objections, which he elaborated in subsequent publications. Subsequent to his exchange of letters with Musgrave, Brown never published again on the questions of tax incidence.

With one exception,[85] Brown's article received no published response for several years, as Rolph noted. Due, in his *Theory of Incidence of Sales Taxation,* appeared to accept Brown's reasoning if what he called the "traditional analysis" is employed and a given level of income is assumed. Due later came to refer to this as the "Brown Case" or the "Rolph-Brown Case."[86] Rolph's paper was a direct challenge to the orthodox view of sales tax incidence. He not only accepted Brown's view of sales tax incidence, but argued it should be extended to the case of partial excise taxes as well. Both Due and Musgrave objected to the views of Brown and Rolph for different reasons. Due in his 1953 article found that Brown's assumptions, explicit and implicit, led to a case of "very limited scope and usefulness."[87]

The assumptions of perfect competition with perfectly inelastic factor supplies do certainly limit the analysis; however, they do provide a convenient and useful starting point for such analysis.

The lack of a clearly stated assumption with regard to the effect of a new tax revenue upon product and factor demand was also emphasized by Due in his criticism. Brown seemed to envision somewhat vaguely a neutral or minor effect. In 1953, Musgrave conceded that factor payments may fall, but found fallacious the view that the tax would fall ultimately on the factors in a manner equivalent to a proportional income tax. "The direction of adjustment does not determine incidence,"[88] he declared. The difference for Musgrave was that adjustments on the income-uses side would not leave the two taxes equivalent, as the market price for unripened capital goods would fall relative to the market price of consumer goods. Brown made no provision for "unripened" capital goods and appeared to have conceived the general sales tax as affecting both capital and consumer goods, whether purchased by the private or public sector. Jenkins, writing in 1955, found that Brown was "not quite able to distinguish between the price effects of his tax and those of his assumed constant quantity of money."[89] However, he found Brown quite close to grasping the significance of the distinction between the direction of adjustment to the tax and the direction of tax shifting.

Brown's statement as to the direction of adjustment was interpreted by Jenkins as a prediction of a partial forward shifting and backward adjustment. He faulted Brown for not attributing this to a decrease in the circular velocity of money in active circulation or the monetary effect of the tax.

James M. Buchanan entered the discussion first in a 1955 article in Italian that was subsequently republished in a modified form in his 1960 collection of essays, *Fiscal Theory and Political Economy*. Although Buchanan focuses on the contributions of Rolph, Due, Musgrave, Jenkins and Parravicini, he presents some points of interest on Brown's contribution to the debate. Buchanan found as "substantially correct" Brown's conclusion as to the backward shifting of a genuinely general excise tax, finding that the traditional "all-too-facile" extension of partial equilibrium tools had lead to "wrong" conclusions.[90] Further, Buchanan stressed a fundamental difference between Brown's and Rolph's analysis: "The difference is that the Brown analysis is admittedly framed in terms of balanced-budget incidence, with particular attention given to the government's securing and spending of newly collected tax revenues."[91] Thus Brown was not unaware that the composition of output could be altered by the tax. Buchanan points specifically to Brown's cautionary statement: "Of course, less individual spending and more collective spending might change the relative demands for and marginal cost of various kinds of goods and so have some effects on their relative prices."[92] Buchanan, somewhat prophetically, ends his article commenting on the importance of the proper monetary framework for tax incidence analysis and the admixture of analytical and methodological questions that were yet to be clarified.

A further contribution of Buchanan in this period was to "reconnect" the largely American or Anglo-Saxon public finance literature to that of an ongoing Italian equivalent. One expression of this, especially relevant to Brown, is Domenico da Empoli's 1966 book, *Critical Analysis of Some Effects of a General Sales Tax.*[93] Da Empoli chose to examine closely Brown's article—not for its originality,[94] which is questioned, but for the acuity of his treatment and its position as the genus of such a long-running controversy whose breadth cannot be fully captured without reference to the Italian commentary, little of which has been translated. In a manner similar to that of Buchanan, da Empoli found Brown's assumptions to be acceptable for approximate, if not definitive, conclusions. Further, he questioned whether the "Brown case" required an explicit assumption of fixed factor supplies to hold. Brown did, in his reply to Musgrave, indicate that a distinction between short- and long-run elasticities of supplies of factors should be taken into account.[95]

Despite Peter Mieszkowski's 1967 charge that in general equilibrium terms the questions of tax shifting forward or backward are rendered "sterile,"[96] in 1978 Edgar Browning chose to readdress the question of sales tax incidence.[97] He included transfers in his model and found that the burden of sales and excise taxes fell on factors earnings rather than on consumers. John F. Due responded to a 1985 clarification of Browning's argument in the next year by criticizing among other things the all-consumption nature of Browning's model.[98] Browning replied, defending the usefulness of this type of model.[99]

Conclusion

IN CONCLUSION, BROWN'S WORK in the area of taxation was an important contribution. Nevertheless, it is only very rarely referred to in contemporary texts.[100] A comment on Brown by Joseph A. Pechman is illustrative, perhaps more than intended, of Brown's position in the field of public finance. In his last book, *Who Paid the Taxes, 1966–1985?* in a chapter on incidence assumptions Pechman made the following statement and footnote: "During the past twenty-five years there has been substantial change in the method used by economists to analyze tax incidence.[2]" "(2.) Essential elements of the basic theory can be found in Harry Gunnison Brown, *The Economics of* Taxation (Holt, 1924), but his views had relatively little influence. . . ."[101] This is a compliment but at the same time suggests a commentary. In this field Brown was somewhat of an outsider. He did not join nor participate in the National Tax Association. Had it not been for his efforts with Henry Holt & Company and the appreciation of the editors of the *Journal of Political Economy,* he would have had no influence whatsoever. Indeed, many economists who came to appreciate his contributions came to know them only in a variety of indirect fashions, such as noticing his slim volume in a library's stacks. From the 1960s on it is rare to come across a major study that does not have some sort of sponsorship by institutes or foundations. Brown was not of this era.

From the post-World War II era on, the level of sophistication in tax incidence studies has risen markedly, yet Brown's work should be counted as one of the bases upon which this advance took place. In particular he was a precursor of a general equilibrium approach to the study of tax incidence or, in Horst Claus Recktenwald's terms, a continuator in the development of "macroeconomic incidence."[102] Arnold Harberger commented in a letter to the author:

> My respect for him is enormous. He belongs in a league with Seligman and Hotelling as the best contributors to the literature of public finance over an entire generation of economists.[103]

Notes

1. Henry C. Simons (1926). "Review of *The Economics of Taxation*." *Journal of Political Economy* 34 (February): 134–136.
Frank Knight (1925). "Review of *The Economics of Taxation*." *National Municipal Review* 14 (April): 377–378.
Fred Rogers Fairchild (1926). "Review of *The Economics of Taxation*." *American Economic Review* 16 (June): 343–344.
2. Simons (1926): 136.
3. Knight (1925): 377.
4. W. Twerdocleboff (1929). "Die Theorie der Steuerüberwälzung in der neustern Literatur." *Zeitschrift für die gesamte Staatwissenschaft* 86 (3): 513–543.
5. I have found a notice of a Spanish translation of the book which was published in Lima, Peru in the early Forties, but I have been unable to locate it.
6. Harry Gunnison Brown (1979[1924]). *The Economics of Taxation*. Chicago, IL: University of Chicago Press. See back cover for A. Harberger's comment.
7. *Ibid.*: vi.
8. Fairchild (1926): 343.
9. Brown felt that the data available was likely to be inadequate and referred to the problem of utilizing the method of "least residues," which would entail a very large task.
10. Knight (1925): 377.
11. Brown (1924): 9.
12. Harry Gunnison Brown (October 13, 1927). Letter to Glenn Hoover. Joint Collection University of Missouri Western Historical Manuscript Collection-Columbia and State Historical Society of Missouri Manuscripts: 2.
13. Brown (1924): 56.
14. Simons (1926): 135.
15. Brown (1924): 19.
16. Ephriam Kleiman (2000). "Early Inflation Tax Theory and Estimates." *History of Political Economy* 32 (2): 233–265.
17. *Ibid.*: 245, n. 21, and 236–237.
18. *Ibid.*: 253.
See also Robert W. Dimand (1997). "Editorial Introduction." *The Works of Irving Fisher*. Vol. 7. Ed. William Barber: 1–5.
19. Kleiman (2000): 252.
20. Brown (1924): 36.
21. Herbert J. Davenport (1919). "The War Tax Paradox." *American Economic Review* 9 (March): 34–36.
22. Harry Gunnison Brown (1951). "The Size of the National Debt." *American Journal of Economics and Sociology* 11 (October): 55–60.

23. John F. Due (1942). *The Theory of Incidence of Sales Taxation.* Morningside Heights, NY: King Crown Press.

24. Simons (1926): 135.

25. Due (1942): 215.

26. *Ibid.*: 212.

27. Brown (1924): 92–93.

28. Knight (1925): 378.

29. Due (1942): 218.

30. Alfred Marshall (1938). *Principles of Economics.* 8th ed. London: Macmillan & Co.: 480–483.

31. E. R. A. Seligman (1921). *The Shifting and Incidence of Taxation.* 4th ed. New York: Columbia University Press: 347.
F. Y. Edgeworth (1899). "Professor Seligman on the Mathematical Method in Political Economy." *Economic Journal* 9 (June): 286–315.

32. Brown used as an example a monopoly based on control of resources.

33. Brown (1924): 117–118.

34. *Ibid.*: 129.

35. E. R. A. Seligman (1892). "The Shifting and Incidence of Taxation." *Publications of the American Economic Association* 7 (March and May): 156–159.
H. C. Adams (1898). *The Science of Finance.* New York: Henry Holt & Co.: 398.
F. Y. Edgeworth (1897). "The Pure Theory of Taxation." *Economic Journal* 70 (June): 226–238.

36. Brown (1924): 131.

37. Richard Musgrave (1959). *The Theory of Public Finance.* New York: McGraw-Hill: 304–305.

38. Otto von Mering (1942). *The Shifting and Incidence of Taxation.* Philadelphia: Blakiston Co.

39. *Ibid.*: 103.

40. Brown (1924): 142.

41. Harry Gunnison Brown (1922). "The Incidence of Compulsory Insurance of Workmen." *Journal of Political Economy* 30 (February): 67–77.

42. Frank W. Taussig (1926). *Principles of Economics.* Vol. 2. 3rd ed. New York: Macmillan Co.: 353–356.

43. *Ibid.*: 354–356.

44. Dale Yoder (1931). "Some Economic Implications of Unemployment Insurance." *Quarterly Journal of Economics* 45 (4): 636.

45. J. A. Brittain (1971). "The Incidence of Social Security Payroll Taxes." *American Economic Review* 61 (March): 113.

46. Earl Rolph and George Break (1961). *Public Finance.* New York: Ronald Press: 61.

47. Paul Peretz (1997). "Social Security and Political Investment." *Polity* 30 (1): 99.

48. Joseph Dorfman (1959). *The Economic Mind in American Civilization*. Vol. 4. New York: Viking Press: 115.

49. Herbert A. Simon (1943). "The Incidence of a Tax on Urban Real Property." *Quarterly Journal of Economics* 57 (May): 416–429.

50. This point will be examined in Chapter 6.

51. Brown (1924): 183–184.

52. *Ibid.*: 183.

53. Jens Peter Jensen (1931). *Property Taxation in the United States.* Chicago: University of Chicago Press: 57–58.

54. Simon (1943): 402.

55. Simon (1943): 405.

56. Peter Mieszkowski (1969). "Tax Incidence Theory: The Effect of Taxes on the Distribution of Income." *Journal of Economic Literature* 7 (4): 1110.

57. Peter Mieszkowski and George Zodrow (1985). "The Incidence of Partial State Corporate Income Tax." *National Tax Journal* 38 (December): 490.

58. Peter Mieszkowski (1972). "The Property Tax: An Excise or Profits Tax?" *Journal of Public Economics* 1 (April): 73.

59. Peter Mieszkowski and George Zodrow (1989). "Taxation and the Tiebout Model: The Differential Effects of Head Taxes, Taxes on Land Rents, Property Taxes." *Journal of Economic Literature* 7 (3): 1116–1117.

60. David F. Bradford (1978). "Factor Prices May Be Constant But Factor Returns Are Not." *Economic Letters* 1: 199.

61. David E. Wildasin (1988). "Indirect Distributional Effects in Benefit-Cost Analysis of Small Projects." *Economic Journal* 98 (September): 802.

62. David E. Wildasin (2000). "Factor Mobility and Fiscal Policy in the EU: Policy Issues and Analytical Approaches." *Fiscal Policy* 31 (October): 343–344.

63. William C. Wheaton (2000). "Decentralized Welfare: Will There Be Underprovision?" *Journal of Urban Economics* 48 (3): 537.

64. Brown (1924): 184.

65. While Wildasin (1988:802) says, "Brown argues, however, that on balance the wages of workers in general will fall by the amount of the tax, that is, the small reduction in net wages for workers as a whole will be equal to the total tax collected," Brown (1924:148) wrote, "A tax on wages in any one line tends, therefore, to be distributed over wages in general, leaving them in about the same relation to each other as before."

66. Alfred G. Buehler (1940). *Public Finance* New York: McGraw-Hill Book Company: 357. Buehler cites Brown (1924:190) as making a "somewhat more positive statement" than the Colwyn Committee. (D. H. Rob-

ertson [1927]. "The Colwyn Committee on the Income Tax, and the Price Level." *Economic Journal* 37: 580.)

67. Martin Feldstein (1977). "The Surprising Incidence of a Tax on Pure Rent: A New Answer to an Old Question." *Journal of Political Economy* 85 (April): 349–360.

68. Guillermo A. Calvo, Laurence J. Kotlikoff and Carlos Alfredo Rodriguez (1979). "The Incidence of a Tax on Pure Rent: A New (?) Reason for an Old Answer." *Journal of Political Economy* 87 (August): 254–262.

69. See George R. Zodrow (2001). " The Property Tax as a Capital Tax: A Room with Three Views." *National Tax Journal* 54 (1): 139–156.

70. James K. Hall (1940). "The Incidence of Death Duties." Round Table Discussion on the Incidence of Taxation. *American Economic Review* 30 (March): 241–242.

71. Brown (1924): 208–210.

72. *Ibid.*: 301–304.

73. Harry Gunnison Brown (1939). "The Incidence of a General Output or a General Sales Tax." *Journal of Political Economy* 47 (April): 254–262.

74. Due (1942): 148.

75. Richard Musgrave (1953). "On Incidence." *Journal of Political Economy* 61 (August): 318.

76. Earl R. Rolph (1952). "A Proposed Revision of Excise-Tax Theory." *Journal of Political Economy* 55 (April): 103.

77. John F. Due (1953). "Toward a General Theory of Sale Tax Incidence." *Quarterly Journal of Economics* 68, May: 258.

78. H. P. B. Jenkins (1955). "Excise Tax Shifting and Incidence: A Money Flows Approach." *Journal of Political Economy* 62 (April): 125–149.

79. John Stuart Mill (1909). *Principles of Political Economy.* London: Longmans, Green & Co. Book 5, Chap. 5.

80. Brown (1939): 257.

81. Harry Gunnison Brown (1939a). "The Incidence of a General Output or General Sales Tax: A Correction." *Journal of Political Economy* 49 (June): 419.

82. Howard Bowen (May 19, 1939). Letter to Harry Gunnison Brown. Joint Collection, University of Missouri Western Historical Manuscript Collection, Columbia, MO.

83. Richard Musgrave (November 21, 1939). Letter to Harry Gunnison Brown. Joint Collection University of Missouri Western Historical Manuscript Collection-Columbia and State Historical Society of Missouri Manuscripts.

84. Harry Gunnison Brown (November 28, 1939). Letter to Richard Musgrave. Joint Collection University of Missouri Western Historical Manuscript Collection-Columbia and State Historical Society of Missouri Manuscripts.

85. As James Buchanan (1960) noted (in his *Fiscal Theory and Political Economy: Selected Essays,* Chapel Hill: The University of North Carolina Press: 126, f. 5) that Henry C. Simons may have been supportive of Brown's view, but only an abstract of a paper he presented in a Round Table on the incidence of taxation in the *Proceedings* published in March, 1940 (*American Economic Review:* 242–244) which made no specific reference to Brown's article. Brown chaired this discussion.

86. Due (1953): 258.

87. *Ibid.:* 260.

88. Musgrave (1953): 318.

89. Jenkins (1955): 125.

90. James M. Buchanan (1960). "The Methodology of Incidence Theory: A Critical Review of Some Recent Contributions." *Fiscal Theory and Political Economy.* Chapel Hill, NC: University of North Carolina Press: 139–140.

91. *Ibid.:* 140.

92. Brown (1939): 260.

93. Domenico da Empoli (1966). *Analisi critica di alcuni effetti dell'imposta generale sulle vendite.* Milan: Giuffrè.

94. Domencio da Empoli following von Mering (1942:176, f. 1) suggests as a example of an earlier "similar view" that of J. A. Schumpeter in a 1928 article, "Wen trifft die Umsatzsteuer?" (*Der Deutche Volkswirt* November 16: 207–209). Mering reports Schumpeter as claiming that "at least a substantial part of the sales tax is borne by the producers."

95. Harry Gunnison Brown (November 28, 1939): 1.

96. Peter Mieszkowski (1967). "On the Theory of Tax Incidence." *Journal of Political Economy* 75: 250–262.

97. Edgar K. Browning (1978). "The Burden of Taxation." *Journal of Political Economy* 86 (April): 649–674.

98. John F. Due (1986). "Tax Incidence, Indirect Taxes and Transfers—A Comment." *National Tax Journal* 39: 539–540.

99. Browning (1986). " Reply to Professor Due." *National Tax Journal* 39: 541–542.

100. Based on a brief informal survey of texts in public finance or public economics, I found that texts of the of the post-World War II period up to the mid-1960s tended to cite Brown, while later ones do not.

101. Joseph A. Pechman (1985). *Who Paid the Taxes, 1966–1985?* Washington DC: The Brookings Institution: 23. (My thanks to Mason Gaffney for pointing out this reference.)

102. Horst Claus Recktenwald (1971). *Tax Incidence and Income Redistribution: An Introduction.* Detroit, MI: Wayne State University Press: 24.

103. Arnold Harberger (October 15, 1984). Letter to author. Personal files, Iowa City, IA.

Appendix 5A

Harry Gunnison Brown and Kinked Demand Curves

THE GERMAN ÉMIGRÉ economist Otto von Mering reported on two early usages of the kinked demand curve idea in his 1942 *The Shifting and Incidence of Taxation*. He stated: "The increase in the elasticity of demand on which both authors [E. R. A. Seligman and Harry Gunnison Brown] base their arguments implies a discontinuous demand curve or at least a kink in the demand curve."[1]

Joseph Spengler thought that H. G. Hayes was the first to utilize kinked demand curves in his *Our Economic System* in 1928.[2] George Stigler dismissed Hayes and other precursors such as Joan Robinson brought forward by Spengler for not displaying "the economic content of asymmetrical oligopolistic behavior."[3] Gavin Reid accepted several forerunners of Sweezy and Hall and Hitch, but noted that Hayes's treatment was unlikely to have been influential and was, moreover, seriously flawed.[4] Reid further posited that a common concern of Sweezy and Hall & Hitch was that of observed price rigidity in certain markets, which had been brought into public focus principally by Gardiner Means in the mid-1930s. Reid also appears to agree with Stigler that the appropriate standard to judge the forerunners was whether they understood that the issue was "whether asymmetric conjectural coefficients in prices are thought to hold for local variations about the equilibrium price."[5] Stigler's interpretation, particularly of Sweezy, has recently been challenged by Craig Freedman as being intentionally too narrow so as to facilitate a defense of traditional price theory.[6] Ironically, Brown's usage of the kinked demand curve concept has as its origin a much earlier disputation as to "correct" price theory.

In Seligman's treatment of the incidence of a tax on monopoly output he argued, in contradistinction to Cournot's well-known proposition, that the monopolist may chose to bear the burden of the tax and alter neither the price or output. He showed this to be the case with arithmetical examples wherein the discrete price/output combinations formed, relative to the original profit maximizing combination, an elastic segment of the monopolist's demand "curve." Seligman offered no explanation for the nature of the supposed demand relationship.[7] Edgeworth had objected to Seligman's analysis, essentially pointing out that were the demand curve continuous, the monopolist would shift forward some portion of the tax. However, he conceded grudgingly that: "it is impossible to say whether the increase in elasticity conduces to the increase or decrease of the efficiency of the tax to raise price; unless we are given not only c' [marginal cost] (which is supposed), but also e' [the rate at which the own price elasticity increases with the increase in price] involving the curvature of the demand curve, which is not, I think, usually given, even as to sign, much less the quantitative precision which would be necessary for the present purpose."[8] Edgeworth was correct, but seemed unable to understand why Seligman (as well as professors Graziani and Jannacone who supported his position) insisted on the relevance or importance of a discontinuous demand relationship. Seligman stated in the later editions of his text that he was assuming "a demand which becomes more or less elastic after the point of maximum revenue is reached."[9] Specific to his examples, this would be "becomes more elastic after the point of maximum profit is reached." Thus in his discontinuous examples he could have been thinking of a kinked demand curve but was unable to make this clear to his critic.[10]

In contrast, Brown's treatment of this proposed exception to Cournot's proposition was much clearer. Although he made no mention of the Seligman-Edgeworth exchanges, he was a careful reader and critic of Seligman's analysis. However, in this case Brown implicitly supports Seligman's claim. To illustrate the "extreme" case wherein a monopolist may not raise its price as a result of an output tax Brown said, "[S]uppose the demand for a certain kind of goods produced by a monopoly to be inelastic up to a given price, and beyond that price to be extremely elastic."[11] He supplemented his reasoning with a numerical example similar to Seligman's which when graphed, results in an obtuse kink roughly at the profit maximizing output.[12] Brown's rationale for the kink may have been based on Marshall's "fear of spoiling the market"[13] as pointed to by Reid. Brown stated that "any appreciable rise above the given price would practically destroy demand."[14] Thus he, unlike most writers in public finance of the time, sided with Seligman in arguing that a rise in the monopolist's price was not the inevitable result of a tax on output for reasons other than perfect inelasticity of supply or perfect elasticity of demand.[15]

Brown also, perhaps again following Seligman's direction, considered a demand that had a reflex kink and could result in an increase in price greater than the amount of the tax. Brown's reasoning for such a kink was that a rise in price would eliminate "a certain class of buyers while buyers of another class would continue to buy."[16]

Reid has commented that by the 1930s, given the rather low order of analytical skill required to formulate a kinked demand curve, "the idea might well have emerged from the mind of any economist with or without the aid of Hayes."[17] This may well apply as well to the Seligman-Brown usages, as neither Sweezy nor Hall and Hitch make reference to them. Neither Brown's nor much less Seligman's examples meet the strict tests of Stigler or Reid for fully anticipating Sweezy and Hall and Hitch. Yet, one might still be tempted to speculate about some subjective or unnoticed influences for the following reason: Seligman's and Brown's texts, unlike Hayes's book, were well-known and highly regarded. These discussions, in addition to the relevant articles in the *Economic Journal*, may well have been germinal. Such rarefied speculation apart, the early usages by Seligman and Brown should be noted.

Notes

1. Otto von Mering (1942). *The Shifting and Incidence of Taxation.* Philadelphia: Blackiston Co.: 33.

2. Joseph J. Spengler (1965). "Kinked Demand Curves: By Whom First Used?" *Southern Economic Journal* 32: 82–83.

3. George J. Stigler (1978). "The Literature of Economics: The Case of the Kinked Oligopoly Demand Curve." *Economic Inquiry* 16: 186.

4. Gavin C. Reid (1981). *The Kinked Demand Curve Analysis of Oligopoly.* Edinburgh: Edinburgh University Press: 3–5.

5. Gavin C. Reid (November 21, 1990). Letter to author. Personal files.

6. Craig Freedman (1995). "The Economist as Mythmaker—Stigler's Kinky Transformation." *Journal of Economic Issues* 24 (March): 175–209.

7. E. R. A. Seligman (1921). *The Shifting and Incidence of Taxation.* 4th ed. New York: Columbia University Press: 342–348.

8. Francis Y. Edgeworth (1899). "Professor Seligman and the Mathematical Method in Political Economy." *Economic Journal* 9: 312.

9. Seligman (1921): 347.

10. For an overview of the Edgeworth-Seligman exchange, see Laurence S. Moss (forthcoming), "The Seligman-Edgeworth Controversy about Tax Incidence: An Interpretation." *History of Political Economy.*

11. Harry Gunnnison Brown (1924). *The Economics of Taxation.* New York: Henry Holt & Company: 97.

12. Brown (1924): 100–102.

His example was not as precise as it could have been in that his marginal cost curve would miss slightly the gap in the marginal revenue as calculated from his demand co-ordinates. However, his discrete figures in terms of profits do reflect what he wishes to demonstrate. The hypothetical example he gave is summarized below (assuming a $1.00 per unit tax):

Price	Sales	Expense Per Sale	Profit Per Sale	Profit Pre-Tax	Profit Post-Tax
$15	0	—	—	$0	$0
14	10	$8	$6	60	50
13	100	8	5	500	400
12	200	8	4	800	600
11	260	8	3	780	520
10	330	8	2	660	330
9	410	8	1	410	0
8	500	8	0	0	−500

13. Alfred Marshall (1920). *Principles of Economics.* 8th ed. London: MacMillan: 337.

14. Brown (1924): 97.

15. The public finance texts I examined were Adams (1898), Plehn (1909), Hunter (1921), Dalton (1923), Jensen (1924) and Lutz (1925).

16. Brown (1924): 98.

17. Reid (1981): 4.

Appendix 5B

Predecessor(s) of the Brown Proposition: Ricardo? Marshall? Walras?

The "earlier contributors" alluded to in the text are found in a footnote Brown's *The Economics of Taxation*. For purposes of exposition I will reproduce the footnote and the sentence footnoted.

> The conclusion would seem to be, then, that the burden of the tax on some capital is finally (assuming that it does not tend to decrease the aggregate volume of capital) distributed upon the owners of all capital in the taxed community.[1]
>
> (1) This point was first suggested to the writer by Professor H. J. Davenport in the spring of 1916. It was set forth in an article by T. S. Adams on "Tax Exemption through Tax Capitalization" in the American Economic Review, June, 1916, p. 278, and in an article in the March, 1917, number of the same magazine by Davenport entitled "Theoretical Issues in the Single Tax."[1]

Douglas Mair and Richard Damania in a 1988 *Cambridge Journal of Economics* article challenged the attribution by Simon and Mieszkowski of what they term "the capital-in-general" argument to Brown.[2] Their paper argues that the correct attribution should be to Ricardo, with Marshall bringing forward in time the Ricardian tax incidence doctrine. The authors further charge Simon and Mieszkowski with failing to record Brown's footnote. In 1989 Mieszkowski (and Zodrow) would make reference to the footnote.[3] However, Simon did not only report on Brown's footnote but improved upon it by expanding the reference to include a comment on T. S. Adams's article by E. R. A. Seligman (1916, *American Economic Review* December: 790–807).[4] This error is inconsequential except that it lends an air of discovery that does not fit, as Simon and Miezskowski were well aware of Brown's Georgist views.

The authors quote Davenport in affirming the Ricardian rent doctrine and state, "The capital-in-general argument, which is seen as distinguishing and improving the neoclassical property tax doctrine over the classical has, through its attribution to Brown, its origins in the single tax movement. The single tax movement in turn drew its inspiration from Ricardo, the Physiocrats and the Millses."[5] In order to best evaluate this Brown-Single Tax Movement-Ricardo connection it would seem best to examine what was actually said by Adams, Davenport and Seligman to see how Brown drew on this earlier exchange, keeping in mind that Simon obviously read all and found Brown's statements to be worthy of attribution.

Such an examination requires the consideration of another writer—Charles Bowdoin Fillebrown. Adams's article had one major purpose, which was to expose a single tax fallacy proclaimed most notably by Fillebrown in his *The A B C of Taxation*. In the preface to this book Fillebrown stated: "Twelve years of zealous study and discussion of the subject of taxation have brought me at last to what should be the starting point of every student, to wit: the recognition that investments in land are exempt from taxation."[6] Fillebrown's 1928 *Who's Who in America* entry includes: distinguished Civil War service, two years attendance at the Massachusetts Technological Institute, president and general manager of a knitting company, long-time service as president of the Massachusetts Single Tax League and present occupation as a single tax propagandist. Fillebrown singled out for criticism Richard Ely's *Outlines of Economics* (1908), of which T. S. Adams was one of the co-authors. Thomas Sewell Adams was a 1899 Johns Hopkins Ph.D. who had just arrived at Yale in 1916 after many years at Wisconsin, making him, in effect, Brown's replacement.

Adams's argument and dissent from Seligman can be seen in the following sentences:

> If [property] taxes are not paid directly they are paid silently and indirectly through the competition of capital for the extra profit represented by the absent tax.... Stated in terms of pure theory, the rate of capitalization is the resultant of all known opportunities of investment and all known taxes. It registers automatically the average tax burden. When a man buys durable property he capitalizes its net yield or in-

come at a rate which is lower when the general tax burden is high, and higher when the general tax burden is low.[7]

Seligman replied to Adams in the December issue of the journal.

Summing up this entire argument, we see that it is, indeed, true that the imposition of a tax on capital may, in some cases, have a depressing effect upon the rate of interest. This point has, indeed, not been adequately emphasized before, and Professor Adams deserves credit for calling attention to it. But we must be careful not to overemphasize the point. As we have just shown, the tendency of taxation to depress interest rates is, in the first place, exceptional; it is, in the second place, often counteracted or actually outweighed by the opposite tendency; and, in the third place, even in the rare cases where it exists, it is so slight as to be negligible.[8]

Davenport as well as Brown had to have been amused and delighted with Adams's article. Amused, because Adams managed to entangle Seligman with Fillebrown. Seligman was a longtime and adamant opponent of the single tax. Delighted, especially because, when Seligman's reply to Adams's article was made known to him, Davenport was not only able to divest from single tax advocacy the "C" from Fillebrown's A B Cs or the erroneous idea of "burdenless taxes," but also to contest both Adams's and Seligman's views and present his own. (Davenport and Brown were both teaching at the University of Missouri during 1916 and undoubtedly had extensive conversations on their mutual interest.) Davenport noted, "the ultimate issue appears to turn upon the relation between property taxes and interest rates."[9] In this long footnote Davenport accepts in part Adams' analysis:

[Adams] holds that the very fact of taxation upon property must be ranked as one of the influences restricting the net returns from property and thereby restricting interest rates. These burdens upon the investors manifest themselves precisely in the fact that they make net income dearer, in terms of present purchasing price. The investor gets less income from his money.[10]

Thus in review Brown was correct to cite Adams and Davenport for pointing out that interest rates may fall as a result of the tax. However, neither presentation can be considered an adequate analysis of the incidence of a tax on some capital, as Seligman complained in the case of Adams. They both fail to explain how Seligman's "negligible" effects could be significant. Furthermore, Brown's analysis drew very little from the opinions of Adams or Davenport, neither of whom invoked any Ricardian principle other than the familiar rent doctrine, which, of course, has no application to a tax on capital.

Ricardo

YET, EVEN WITHOUT A "SINGLE TAX" CONNECTION, the question of Ricardo's precedence in the capital-in-general argument remains to be examined. Mair and Damania argue that Ricardo's treatment of taxes on houses should be incorporated with that of poor rates. They accomplish this by quoting Ricardo in the following manner:

> If, at any time, all manufacturing capital contributed to the poor rates in the same proportion as the capital expended by the farmer or the landlord [or the builder], then it would no longer be a partial tax on the profits of the farmer's or the landlord's [or the builder's] capital, but a tax on the capital of all producers, and therefore, it could no longer be shifted either on the consumer of raw produce or on the landlord. (Principles: 259)[11] (parentheses and emphasis added by the authors)

This should be compared to Ricardo's original statement:

> If, at any time, all manufacturing capital contributed to the poor rates in the same proportion as the capital expended by the farmer or the landlord in improving the land, then it would no longer be a partial tax on the profits of the farmer's or the landlord's capital, but a tax on the capital of all producers; and, therefore, it could no longer be shifted either on the consumer of the raw produce or on the landlord.[12] [emphasis added]

Since this is a case of a general tax on capital, not that of a tax on some capital, the authors go on to establish that Ricardo did not believe the poor rates to be a uniform tax in practice, as the valuation of the farmers' and manufacturers' capital was inconsistent. Thus either (usually) farmers or manufacturers would be relatively burdened. Ricardo carefully notes in this case that the farmers' (or landlords') capital expended "in improving the land" is not as comparably mobile as that of other manufacturers. For them, as the authors note, "There can be no reason why their profits should be reduced below the general rate when their capitals might be easily removed to agriculture"[13] (emphasis mine). Notable also are Ricardo's suggestions for interim adjustments to the assumed changed rates in the form of higher prices for raw produce (unsuccessful in the farmers' case) and higher prices for goods of the manufacturer (successful). This is precisely the interpretation that Brown found superficial.[14]

Mair and Damania conclude that they find in Ricardo a "statement" of the capital-in-general argument attributed by Simon and Mieszkowski and Zodrow to Brown. Ricardo does appear to suggest it, but it is not surprising that Shoup[15] failed to note it and no other writer (save possibly Marshall) brought the concept forth. Also the important corollary concept of slight-changes-affecting-significant-results recognized by Simon is clearly absent.

Marshall

ALFRED MARSHALL WROTE RELATIVELY LITTLE on taxation. Mair and Damania found, however, in his *Official Papers by Alfred Marshall* (J. M. Keynes 1926) evidence that he supported the Ricardian capital-in-general conclusion. They find this in his reply to the 1897 Royal Commission on Local Taxation specifically inquiring as to his view on the real incidence of "taxes on trade profits." As they note, he expresses his opinion that profits do not constitute an economic entity, but do include "some interest on capital, some earnings of ability and work, and, often, some insurance against risk." Then he concludes: "Generally speaking, the incidence of taxes on profits is widely and evenly diffused; they run from one trade to other trades. And this is one reason why there are very few incomes from movable or personal property in England that have not helped to bear the burden of rates."[16]

Marshall's careful statement is clearly within a Smithian-Ricardian view that returns to capital should tend toward equalization, but seems to bear only vaguely with the question of a tax on some capital in a local setting, even if he does make reference to a tendency to check the growth of capital and lead to the emigration of capital to less taxed locations and of people to less taxed vocations. (Of course, Brown was not remotely likely to have been aware of Marshall's earlier views.)

Walras

OTTO VON MERING, IN HIS EXAMINATION OF a partial tax on capital, suggested that Leon Walras has expressed a "similar opinion" as had Brown on his page 183.[17] Mering stated: "it has been rightly pointed out that the transfer of capital from taxed to untaxed fields will increase the supply of capital in industries not subjected to the levy. This would—if the taxed industries constitute a sufficiently large part of total investment so that much capital would be transferred—lower the reward for the supply of capital in non-taxed industries and consequently the average rate of interest."[18] The "similarity" Mering found in Walras's treatment was in his concluding portions of his "Lesson 42" on taxation, wherein he stated:

> Hence a tax on house rent would work out like a tax on consumption—at least in part, for, if we look at the matter closely, we observe that a portion of the burden is borne by the capitalist. Since some of the capital goods previously employed in the construction of houses will be transferred to all sorts of other employments, a general decline in the rate of income (from capital goods) will result, and this decline will be to the detriment of all capitalists including house-owners, and to the advantage of all consumers including tenants. [parentheses Jaffe][19]

In his brief discussion of Walras' treatment, Richard Musgrave noted that Walras recognized what Musgrave referred to as the "spillover" effect of a tax on the earnings of capital in a particular industry.[20] In a footnote, Musgrave further states, "It may be noted that prior to the third edition Walras, like Ricardo, made no allowance whatsoever for the spillover effect, but concluded that the entire tax was to be borne by the consumer of the product supplied by the industry in which capital is taxed."[21] With regard to Walras, Musgrave seems correct, as Jaffe noted that Walras omitted in his third edition "the remainder of the section" wherein he clearly concludes that such a tax was an indirect consumption tax.[22] One may wonder if Walras changed his mind in this regard between the first and third editions and why? With regard to Musgrave's reading of Ricardo we find simply more evidence that Mair and Damania's interpretation of Ricardo was not readily apparent.[23] Brown never mentioned Walras but, as Irving Fisher's student, may have indirectly been influenced by Fisher's careful attention to Walras' work.

Conclusion

To conclude, I can find no clear predecessor(s) for the "Brown proposition" in earlier literature, classical or otherwise. This is not to conclude, however, that Ricardo or other writers played no role in the development of these ideas, only that we cannot readily show how they did. Rather than end in such a negative or inconclusive fashion, I would like to suggest a compromise of sorts. Brown's general affinity with Ricardo's emphasis on the importance of tax incidence on societal welfare is a notable link. (Not that Marshall and Walras did not share this concern, but their tax treatments were in Musgrave's term "rather sketchy."[24]) The Brown-Ricardo connection is not due to the single tax movement, but rather a shared attempt, a hundred years apart, to analyze the long-term economic consequences of choosing to tax capital, both in part or as a whole.

Notes

1. Harry Gunnison Brown (1979[1924]). *The Economics of Taxation.* Chicago: University of Chicago Press, Midway Reprints: 183.
2. Douglas Mair and Richard Damania (1988). "The Ricardian Tradition and Local Property Taxation." *Cambridge Journal of Economics* 12: 435–449.
3. Peter Mieszkowski and George Zodrow (1989). "Taxation and the Tiebout Model: The Differential Effects of Head Taxes, Taxes on Land Rent, and Property Taxes." *Journal of Economic Literature* 27: 1098–1146.
4. Herbert A. Simon (1943). "The Incidence of a Tax on Urban Real Property." *Quarterly Journal of Economics* 57: 402.
5. Douglas Mair and Richard Damania (1988): 437.
6. Charles Bowdoin Fillebrown (1909). *The A B C of Taxation.* 2nd ed. New York: Doubleday, Page & Company: v.
7. T. S. Adams (1916). "Tax Exemption through Capitalization: A Fiscal Fallacy." *American Economic Review* 6 (June): 278.

8. E. R. A. Seligman (1916). "Tax Exemption through Capitalization: A Reply." *American Economic Review* 6 (December): 801.

9. Herbert J. Davenport (1917). "Theoretical Issues in the Single Tax." *American Economic Review* 7 (March): 26–27.

10. *Ibid.*

11. Douglas Mair and Richard Damania (1988): 439.

12. David Ricardo (1951–1971). *Principles. Works of David Ricardo, Vol. 1, Principles of Political Economy.* Ed. P. Scraffa. Cambridge: Cambridge University Press: 259

13. *Ibid.*: 261.

14. Harry Gunnison Brown (1979[1924]): 181.

15. Carl Shoup (1960). *Ricardo on Taxation.* New York: Columbia University Press.

16. John Maynard Keynes (1926). *Official Papers of Alfred Marshall.* London: Macmillan: 356–357.

17. Otto von Mering (1942). *The Shifting and Incidence of Taxation.* Philadelphia: The Blakiston Company: 204, f. 2.

18. *Ibid.*

19. Léon Walras (1954). *Elements of Pure Economics.* Tr. William Jaffe. London: George Allen & Unwin: 455–456.

20. Richard Musgrave (1959). *The Theory of Public Finance.* New York: McGraw-Hill Company: 400.

21. *Ibid.*: 401

22. Walras, *op.cit.*: 609.

23. Richard Musgrave (1959): 385–392.

24. *Ibid.*: 401.

Chapter 6

Land Value Taxation[1]

Introduction

IN 1916, THE YEAR BROWN JOINED THE FACULTY of the University of Missouri, the first major study of the single tax movement in the United States was published. Its author, Arthur Nichols Young, in a concluding survey, indicated that:

> The American single tax movement has not had large accomplishments either in the way of legislation secured or number of adherents gained for its essential principles.[2]

In his study, Young did not identify any academic economist who defended these "essential principles." In the succeeding years, Harry Gunnison Brown would move purposefully to fill this void.

That the economics profession was opposed to George's proposed reform is not an unfair exaggeration. A simple listing of prominent American political economists who adamantly opposed the single tax idea is indicative of the position of the profession. Beginning with William Graham Sumner and Francis A. Walker, a brief list would include John Bates Clark, Richard Ely, Simon Patten, Frank Fetter, E. R. A. Seligman and Frank Knight.[3] Outside of this country a few of the notable opponents were Edwin Cannan, F. Y. Edgeworth and Gustav Cassel.[4] This is not to imply that these diverse and prestigious scholars were uniformly hostile to Henry George and his ideas. According to Joseph Dorfman, Frank Fetter was influenced to pursue the study of political economy by George's *Progress and Poverty.*[5] Seligman found support in George's writing for his own denunciation of the existing property tax system.[6] Ely was careful to praise George for "bringing forth the land problem as one of paramount importance."[7]

The view of Brown as a solitary crusader is somewhat misleading. Many economists of his time favored modified versions of the
single tax, in particular where it would be applied only to future
increments in the value of land. In 1904, Charles Fillebrown circu-
lated a questionnaire to members of the American Economics Association, which stated: "It would be sound public policy to make
the future increase in ground rent a subject of special taxation."
Seventy-seven of the eighty-seven who replied agreed with the
statement.[8] Thomas Nixon Carver, Frank Taussig, John Commons
and Herbert J. Davenport[9] were some of the economists of the
time with whom Brown could find varying degrees of affinity.[10]
Irving Fisher (according to Brown)[11] maintained a long silence on
this question.[12] Somewhat later, Brown quoted favorable expressions made by Fisher, Commons, Carver and Davenport along
with Frank Graham, Raymond Bye, Glenn Hoover, William H.
Dinkins and T. J. Anderson, Jr. and noted other economists who
had expressed favorable opinions as well.[13] Outside of this country P. H. Wicksteed, Leon Walras and Knut Wicksell can be considered proponents of land value taxation.[14]

Brown's advocacy of land value[15] taxation does stand in marked
distinction to that of his colleagues of note, with the possible exception of John Commons. Brown's position was between that of
the orthodox "single-taxers" and the "single-taxers of a looser ob-
servance" as Davenport declared himself to be. Brown's advocacy,
introduced in 1917 by "The Ethics of Land Value Taxation" in the
JPE, would entail multiple considerations. First, theoretical questions in economics, such as the place of land in economic theory
as well as the meaning given to the concept of rent, were treated
in part in Chapters 2 and 3 of this study. He also was concerned
with examining the economic effects of increased land value taxation in order to defend what he perceived as beneficial outcomes
and to refute erroneous criticisms. As ethical or philosophical concerns were endemic to the proposed tax reform, he addressed
them as well. Also, strategies on how to best promote land value
taxation to enhance not only its intellectual but also its political
acceptance could not be ignored.[16] Finally, Brown was forced to
react to changing social and economic conditions as well as to
varying intellectual currents of thought.

Brown incorporated the aforementioned article into a book published in 1918, *The Theory of Earned and Unearned Incomes.*[17] In 1921 he produced a smaller work, *The Taxation of Unearned Incomes*, which was revised and expanded in a 1925 edition. This book in turn was expanded into *The Economic Basis of Tax Reform*[18] in 1932. He published many articles on land value taxation in a wide variety of journals, and when the *American Journal of Economics and Sociology* was founded in 1941, he became one of its major contributors as well as a member of its editorial board.

Brown's Position

BROWN'S INTERPRETATION OF THE SINGLE TAX IDEA was that income derived from the site value of land (which he considered to be unearned) should constitute the first source for governmental taxation. A program for tax reform would entail the eventual substitution—to the extent possible—of land value taxation for all other types of taxation, which he considered to be economically harmful and philosophically unsound. He never maintained that the revenues from the taxation of land values would suffice. His son, Phillips H. Brown, related to me that his father privately referred to himself as a "triple-taxer"[19] and was willing to accept inheritance taxation, income taxation and perhaps, use taxation (such as a gasoline tax) to obtain the needed revenues that the taxation of land value could not generate. In addition, Brown was willing to entertain considerations that would allow landowners to claim some portion of their rent corresponding to site value. In contrast to Davenport, Carver and others, Brown rejected the view that only future increments in land value be taxed.

In this regard, and in implicitly arguing for a very large percentage tax on land value, Brown could claim little or no active support within the profession.[20] He rejected the natural rights and labor theory of value elements in George's thought as unnecessary to the support of land value taxation. Also, in contrast to some Georgists, he did not feel that the tax program, in and of itself, was an economic and social panacea. Although he favored nationwide taxation of land values, from the outset he was willing to support (as he did later, quite actively) local experimentation with such taxation. However, he did fear that a too-moderate or too-gradual implementation of the tax program could blur the benefits and in some case have perverse results. He noted in a 1936 article that

> I am sometimes spoken of as a single-taxer by persons who are opposed to the single tax, while some of the thorough-going single-taxers profess themselves not wholly satisfied with my orthodoxy. The truth is that I recognize the fundamental justice and common sense of the single tax idea.[21]

As could be observed in Chapter 2 and 3, Brown's arguments for the place of land in economic theory and the interpretation of economic rent had strong overtones of the classical writers, in particular Ricardo and J. S. Mill. Brown frequently referred to himself as an economist "unemancipated" from the classical tradition, implying ironically that his opponents had gone too far in the break with classical teachings. He thus attempted to fuse the doctrines of the classical writers, who emphasized the unique role of land in the determination of value, and the marginal utility analysis of the more "modern" economists. His key device in this attempt was an interpretation of the opportunity cost concept which he attributed to Davenport. Brown viewed long-run demand as affected in part by the cost of production.

> Normal or long-run demand may therefore be said to depend on the utility or desirability of the goods demanded, on the utility or desirability of other goods which have to be sacrificed if these are to be enjoyed, on the disutility or sacrifice of producing the goods necessary to pay for the goods, and by way of comparison, on the disutility or sacrifice necessary to produce, instead of buying the goods desired.[22]

This last comparison, he maintained, was equivalent to the opportunity cost principle of Davenport. John Commons noted that Brown, somewhat inadvertently, had shown the equivalency of Henry Carey's "disopportunity value" and Davenport's opportunity-cost principle to the "cost of reproduction."[23] In simpler terms, Brown declared,

> There is a very real sense, then, in which the demand for an article, and the amount which consumers will pay for it, depends upon its cost

of production. They will not, in the long run, pay more for it than the amount of other goods which the same sacrifice will produce.[24]

He defined "land" as land space excluding fertility and improvements, such as drainage and other items that he considered capital. The key property of land space was its nonreproducibility. Thus, land space could have no cost of production and constituted the most important element in what he called the second class of commodities. The demand for goods of this type depends only on their utility. The demand for commodities of the first class or ordinary goods depends upon their cost of production as well as their utility. In this manner, Brown justified a separate treatment of land in economic theory. He added that the return to land was unearned.

In his 1925 review of Brown's *Economic Science and the Common Welfare*, John Commons indicated his acceptance of Brown's view on land value taxation. He stated:

> His analysis at this point is quite superior to that of David Ricardo and Henry George, since its makes scarcity the central feature and not the reduction of efficiency at the agricultural margin of cultivation. I believe it places the argument for special taxation of bare-land values on stronger and better grounds than those that have hitherto been offered by the followers of the Ricardian analysis.[25]

Earned and Unearned Incomes

THAT THE ECONOMIC RETURN TO LAND was not wholly earned by its owners was a tenet of classical political economy. Adam Smith, David Ricardo and John Stuart Mill all tended to take this view. However, this proposition was vigorously and diversely attacked from the onset. In a somewhat latter-day example in 1893, J. Shield Nicholson wrote:

> Mill himself was partly to blame for the excursions which he made into the application of social philosophy to practice. It is these excursions we are indebted to for the fantastical notion of the unearned increment.[26]

In contrast, L. L. Price in an *Economic Journal* article in 1891 commented, "The unearned character of a payment for the 'original and indestructible powers of the soil' can hardly be denied."[27] The two statements are illustrative of a division within the discipline with regard to the manner and extent to which ethical or moral considerations should be entertained in economic studies. The practice of distinguishing earned from unearned incomes carried over into the twentieth century in the language of economics, but it faced increasing dissent. Thomas Nixon Carver, for example, suggested as an alternative a tripartite division of forms of income into earnings, findings and stealings, under which increments to site values were considered findings.[28] Herbert J. Davenport, who labored to rid economic theory of such value judgments, nevertheless was very reluctant to relinquish this distinction because this would excuse incomes that he considered to be socially unproductive. He divided these incomes into the capitalized bounty of nature, capitalized privilege and capitalized predation.[29] For many, the inclination was to reject such a division or to use the term "unearned" only in parentheses. However, usage of the terms was common even among those who opposed the single tax notion or socialistic views.

In *The Theory of Earned and Unearned Incomes*, Brown presented his rationale for declaring payments to landowners to be unearned. The marginal product of land, or the "economic rent," was unearned in that the landowner proportioned no equivalent service to the community. A renter received only a privilege to utilize the land while a receiver of an interest payment had proportioned a service in the form of saving. Brown went on to argue that the site value of land was originally zero and that the present value is attributable not to its present owner, but to society. Brown made clear that unearned incomes were not unique to land. A monopolist's profit or wage was also unearned, as were positive returns to disservices and negative services. Brown argued that the transfer of land did not legitimize the incomes earned, even if "earned" incomes were used to purchase it. The new owner, as had the old owner, would proceed to collect, explicitly or implicitly, for the value of the services of the land that neither the first nor second owner produced. Brown asked, "Is such doctrine good utilitarianism? Is its application good social policy?"[30] Brown similarly viewed (with minor qualifications) the returns to owners of natural resources such as mines, oil deposits, virgin timber-lands, and so on.

Of course, Brown's position on these questions followed that of Henry George, as did Brown's proposed remedy. He rejected public ownership of land and other natural resources through purchase because it would represent a validation of unjust claims. Therefore, in a competitive business system, only the appropriation of economic rent through taxation for the general benefit would remedy the situation.

Among the rebuttals to Brown's argumentation was a challenge of the terms "earned" and "unearned" with respect to incomes. Willford I. King directly attacked such usage in 1921.[31] He noted that it was becoming increasingly common and that despite the lack of sanction for it in "standard" texts on economics, many economists used it or admitted its validity. He maintained that for practical considerations, the distinction was not useful, nor could it be made so in a logical manner. He argued that all incomes were not necessarily earned but should be treated as such in economics.

> The attempt to divide incomes into categories designated as "earned" and "unearned" seems to serve no purpose and this classification appears to have been devised, not with an intent to aid science or statescraft, but in an effort to stigmatize the institution of private property.[32]

Although King's article was very critical of Brown's views, Brown made no immediate reply. John Commons did comment on the article in his *Institutional Economics*. He agreed that from the viewpoint of private business enterprise, King's denial of the distinction of incomes was sound. However, from the viewpoint of society, this was not so, given the effects of speculation in land on industry and agriculture.[33] Commons agreed in part with Brown that income from speculation in land could be distinguished from other incomes because individuals do not create site value; thus, speculation in site values represents no contribution to the commonwealth.

In a review for *The Nation* of Brown's 1925 *The Taxation of Unearned Incomes,* Henry Raymond Mussey (a Wellesley economics professor) stated:

It is full time for some competently equipped economist to take up the cudgels in behalf of the economically tenable parts of Henry George's doctrine. Mr. Brown has done it with zeal, and on the whole with skill. Of course this puts him outside the fold of the safe and sane economists, and the vigor of his onslaught has already occasioned some little fluttering in the academic dovecotes.[34]

To Tax Current Rent or Future Increments Only?

IF LAND WERE TAXED, should the current rent be taxed or should the tax only be on the future increments to the rent? Several economists who were inclined to support taxation along "single-tax" lines, such as Taussig, Carver and Davenport, adamantly insisted that only future increments be taxed. The taxation of these increments to land value derived from John Stuart Mill, whose father, James, also advocated it, as had the Scotsman William Ogilvie.[35] Germany had experimented most extensively with such a tax, and it was a controversial element in the Lloyd George budget of 1909.[36] Arthur Young pointed out that the province of Alberta was the first government in North America to employ a tax of this type. Knut Wicksell expressed an opinion on this subject, with which John Commons would have agreed.

> Incidentally, once the right of expropriation of private land for public purposes is recognized, the proposed participation of the community in future increase in land values can hardly be opposed.[37]

Brown from the outset, debated this issue, taking the side of the Georgists. He referred to the question as one of "vested rights" in property. He attempted to meet the objection voiced in one instance by Fred Fairchild, that to take a part or a whole of the value of land through discriminatory taxation without compensation would be like "changing the rules of a game, while the game is in progress to the disadvantage of one contestant."[38] Brown began with an analogy that an increased tax upon income (although personal income may not normally be capitalized and sold) was fundamentally no different from a like percentage increase in land value taxes. He noted that with an increased tax on personal incomes, "confiscation" or a violation of an implied pledge by society would seldom be mentioned in a discussion of a higher tax. He further noted that monopoly profits had been permitted in the past and that owners of the monopoly had certainly formed expectations of continued profits. In a similar manner, protective tariffs had been implemented in the past, discriminatorily affecting incomes received.

As the regulation of a monopoly or the removal of a tariff was normally undertaken without consideration of compensation for those adversely affected, Brown questioned why land value taxation could not be similarly treated. In his view, the return to landowners corresponding to the situation value of the holdings was better seen as a tribute that corresponded to no service, past or present, in the benefit of those who must pay it. Landholding was only a negotiable privilege or franchise that society could, should it so choose, remove most expediently through a program of gradually increased land value taxation. He felt that a gradual program, which would probably be implemented through local action, would not cause great losses to the majority of landowners, especially small holders who live on their own land.

Brown pointed out that the advocacy of taxing only the future increments was inconsistent if it were done to avoid the question of "vested rights." In a growing country, the capitalized value of land is likely to reflect in part the expectation of rising land prices, and to tax away these future increases in yield would be confiscation in the same sense as would a tax on the current yield. Admitting that the degree of confiscation may be less, he maintained that any defense of the more moderate approach relied upon arguments that would support a more far-reaching reform.[39]

Brown's arguments on vested rights, which appeared frequently in his writing, received little reaction. Frank Knight, noting his own "altogether negative" view of the single tax, agreed with Brown that objections to the single tax were equally operative in opposing a tax only on future increments.[40] Ward L. Bishop, in reviewing *The Economic Basis of Tax Reform*, said that Brown had made "probably as strong an argument as can be made against the sanctity of 'vested rights.'"[41] An anonymous reviewer of *The Theory of Earned and Unearned Incomes* in a 1920 issue of the *Political Science Quarterly* said that Brown's discussion of vested rights deserved attention. This reviewer also commented: "The book should disprove once and for all the shallow myth that no economist has favored the single tax."[42] Lastly, Harold Hotelling in a 1938 article noted: "The proposition that there is no ethical objection to the confiscation of site value of land by taxation . . . has been ably defended by H. G. Brown."[43]

Some Early Arguments on the Economic Effects of Land Value Taxation

THE SINGLE TAX IDEA, especially where moderately interpreted as a program to increase the taxation of site values and relieve the tax burden on "improvements," elicited arguments that tended to be more economic than ethical in nature. In Great Britain an exchange of articles in the *Economic Journal* on the question of the economic effects of the taxation of site values preceded and followed the Lloyd George budget of 1909. The principal concern was the effect that increased site value taxation relative to taxes on buildings and improvements would have on urban population density. Edwin Cannan argued that the effect would be to increase urban congestion. "What is taken away in site values is simply slopped away in increased costs."[44] By "increased costs" Cannan appeared to be referring to negative externalities arising from greater population density.

Edgar Harper and C. F. Bickerdike contested Cannan's conclusions. Bickerdike maintained that there could well be positive production externalities, and in addition, were the additional site value taxes earmarked for community improvements, the net result should be positive.[45] The negative externalities would serve ultimately as a check on undue growth of center cities. Of an altogether different disposition were Charles Trevelyn and Joseph Wedgewood, MP, who favored a nationwide program of increased site value taxation. Trevelyn argued that in the existing system both urban and rural landlords "force" small manufacturing concerns to the cities, thus contributing to the over-population there.[46] Wedgewood, an avowed land-taxer, objected that the discussants had based their arguments on "purely utilitarian grounds" and had ignored considerations of freedom and justice.[47]

In the United States, urban congestion was not so great a concern at the time, and these debates were ignored until the early 1960s. However, single tax proposals and propaganda in this country and in Canada appeared to have provoked renewed opposition from many economists. The rebuttals to these charges were provided largely by Brown, Davenport and Commons.

Alvin Saunders Johnson, a former student of J. B. Clark, published an article in *The Atlantic Monthly* in 1914 titled "The Case Against the Single Tax." Johnson reintroduced an argument of J. B. Clark's, that the unearned increment played a vital role in this country's economic development. "It was the unearned increment which opened the West and laid the basis for our present colossal industrialism."[48] He reasoned that the extension of the economically productive border of the country was hastened as the prospect of the increment induced pioneers to endure hardships and substandard present returns. A by-product of the western migration was the positive effect upon the return to the workers remaining in the eastern areas. In 1916, T. S. Adams, a colleague of Ely's at Wisconsin, used this same argument as one case of a more general diffusion of the unearned increment. He concluded that "farmers and farms are more numerous, farm products more plentiful, and farm prices lower, because of the unearned increment."[49] In addition, he argued that the increment resulted in lower railroad rates.

Both Brown and Davenport separately replied to these points in 1917. Brown first questioned whether the real inducement for the pioneers was not the prospect of a higher return on their labor rather than a problematic rise in land values. Second, even if the prospect of rising land values were an essential part of the incentives, he questioned whether a more gradual spreading of the population westward might not have been preferable. He also pointed out that the contentions ignored the role of government subsidization in the form, for example, of the protection provided by the army. Davenport stressed in his article that the claim for the unearned increment was grossly exaggerated.

> But I submit that the net social result of sending men out where "farmers work for less than a day's wages, if we measure his reward in an-

nual income alone," is, so far, to waste the labor of each man. . . . In the form of a mortgage on the future we have been paying the pioneers for wasting their time.[50]

In fact, some later-day studies of the role of the federal land grant subsidies tend to show that they were of dubious value.[51]

Richard Ely formulated another argument that sought to establish that the increments to land value actually were earned. In 1920, he suggested that the classical theory of rent had not adequately considered the costs a landowner, urban or rural, incurred in the period of transition from one use to another, higher one. The "ripening" costs were socially necessary for the land to reach the higher plateau of use, and thus the income from the utilization or sale of the land was earned. A land tax would tend to force the land into production before the ripening period was completed, which would result in a lower productivity than could otherwise be achieved. Ely reasoned that the classical economists had been concerned primarily with agricultural land and had not seen (as was clear with urban property) that bringing land into production required time and should not be considered costless.[52] Harold Groves suggested in his *Tax Philosophers* that Ely's "ripening costs" seem at least in part to refer to interest and risk on investments. Brown would classify this as the capital component of land value apart from its site value.

Although Ely did not explicitly associate his theory of "ripening costs" with speculation in land, he did utilize expectations with respect to the future value of land. J. B. Clark, Alvin Johnson and T. S. Adams saw land speculation as accelerating the utilization of land. Brown noted a seeming contradiction between this view and that of Ely, who saw "speculation" as delaying the use of land. He also contrasted Ely's view to that of economists who maintained that land speculation resulted in very little land being held out of use. On several occasions Brown sought to defend George's thesis that speculation in land tended to, as Brown interpreted, "hold good land out of use, so forcing resort to poorer land, decreasing the productivity of industry, lowering wages and raising land rent."[53] In reply to Ely, Brown conceded that some service may be rendered by land speculation, and he cited Fisher's *The Nature of*

Capital and Income in support of this opinion. However, Brown argued that disservices are likely to be rendered as well in the form of the economic waste produced by the unnecessary extension of the infrastructure of services and transportation costs. But he did concede to Ely that land speculation did not necessarily result in unusual gains on the average. Brown noted that George had not made this argument either. However, Brown felt that the economic effects of this seemingly irrational "gambling" on the part of only a minority should not be ignored.

Frank Knight, in a brief review of Brown's 1925 book, objected to the "familiar single-tax heresy that taxes on land value would have any appreciable effect in the way of bringing additional land into use."[54] From another perspective, Davenport opined that unless 100 percent of the rent of land were taxed away, land speculation actually would increase with higher rates of taxation.[55] He declared as a "fundamental" principle of taxation that any taxation should be proportionate to present income.

Brown's differences with these two writers appear to lie in the nature of land speculation in the case of Knight and in the method of taxation in that of Davenport. Brown maintained that when *both* used and unused land were taxed alike, the tendency would be for the speculative return to land holdings to fall, thus increasing land usage. He assumed in his argument that the speculator was not capable of or was uninterested in making improvements and, in addition, tended to overestimate the prospective rise in land value. Thus, the prospective return for such a landholder must fall relative to that of those who intend to make improvements on the land, regardless of the percentage of rent taken by the tax. Moreover, if taxes on capital were relieved as a result of the increased land tax, the differential would be even greater. However, Brown noted that in quantitative terms this advantage of land value taxation was relatively minor.[56] Brown's reluctance to emphasize this advantage was not characteristic of later expressions on the subject. He may have felt uncertain as to the magnitude of the economic effects, which seem to rely on the size of the purely speculative forces induced to leave the land market as a result of the tax.

Problems of Assessment and Revenue Adequacy

ANOTHER ARGUMENT COMMONLY ADVANCED against the implementation of high land value taxation was whether the site value of land could be accurately assessed in practice. Early opinions in this regard varied widely. Seligman said in one instance,

> it is quite impossible in practice to distinguish improvements on the land from improvements in the land. No attempt is ever made, in assessing land values, to differentiate the two.[57]

Brown pointed out that Seligman's use of words in this instance was confusing, as the proposition was to separate site values from the value of all improvements. Alfred Marshall considered the difficulty "undoubtedly very great" but

> of a kind to be diminished rapidly by experience: the first thousand such assessments might probably give more trouble, and yet be less accurately made than the next twenty thousand.[58]

Commons felt that the greatest difficulty was in valuing the fertility value relative to the value of bare land and that urban site valuation should be easier and more accurate.[59]

Brown did not comment extensively on the problem. He conceded that there was a possibility of some unfairness due to inaccurate assessments. However, he viewed these as temporary problems and argued that errors or inadequate data would create minor penalties on thrift and improvement compared to a system of taxation that deliberately penalized thrift and improvement. In a 1970 study, Ursula Hicks commented that a number of countries presently use land value taxation, so it cannot be said that it is not practicable.[60] In the same study, Kenneth Back said: "I am satisfied that highly accurate and consistent land valuations can be established."[61] He added that although administratively feasible, it would not necessarily be administratively simple or less costly.

Yet another source of opposition to the single tax idea was that land was an inadequate tax base. This was an early criticism that questioned whether a 100 percent tax on land would provide sufficient revenue. In that era the question was largely conjectural. Brown, as previously noted, never held that such a tax would suffice. He argued that economic rent being economically significant whether it should be adequate for local or other governmental needs was an irrelevant objection to its application as a first source of public revenue.

The adequacy of land as a base for local governmental revenue continues to be a matter of debate. Many economists still feel that land value taxation would not be a significant source of revenue. Mason Gaffney has argued that land values have been underestimated for a number of reasons, and other effects of land value taxation have been ignored frequently in attempts to assess the adequacy of land as a tax base. He concluded in one study that land values equal or exceed building values in the United States.[62] Dick Netzer once commented on the local adequacy of land value taxation in a letter to Brown: "Once school costs are removed from consideration, the land value tax does come very close to satisfying the revenue adequacy criterion, I believe."[63] In 1986, Steven Cord has found that "land rent (both collected and imputed) is at least 28 percent of the U. S. national income in 1981."[64]

Brown's Special Considerations

BROWN WAS WILLING TO ENTERTAIN CONSIDERATIONS that would allow landowners the right to retain some portion of the rental return. He agreed that in cases where land value had been increased due to street construction and the owner had contributed by way of special assessment, the owner was entitled to a return on this investment if one were forthcoming. Brown was more circumspect regarding the return on what we would call "land development." He preferred to place this in the category of a limited service analogous to that of an invention. Thereby, he argued that some special return be allowed but, as with a patent, only during a limited period of time. His reluctance to accept a return was founded on his belief that investors in such development projects should not utilize expected increments in land value in their calculations. He maintained that foresight with regard to the shifting or increasing of population rendered no real service and was not deserving of a special return.

In discussing the "ability to pay" theory of taxation, Brown conceded that there might be some adverse distributional effects in a heavy reliance on land value taxation. He rejected the ability-to-pay principle as the sole basis for a reform of the tax system. In a manner similar to Commons,[65] Brown maintained that if such a principle were to be applied, it must in the case of "earned" income be prevented from interfering greatly with the principle of "proportioning incomes received to services rendered."[66]

The possibly adverse effects of land value taxation were that among those receiving a large proportion of their income in land rent may be found the "ubiquitous widows and orphans" and that among those receiving only a small portion of their income in land rent may be the very wealthy. Brown responded that in the first case that special provisions may be made and in the second that special taxes could be devised. His point was that these circumstances should not impede a tax reform leading to greater land value taxation and resulting benefits, both economic and ethical.

Robert V. Andelson has noted that Brown on one occasion described himself as a Malthusian.[67] To the extent this is true, it forms a marked contrast with the views of George on population. Brown did express concern with overpopulation in general and rather openly advocated family planning in his texts.[68] This concern led him to make a minor theoretical qualification to his argument on the effects of greater land value taxation. He felt that such taxation might work, however slightly, to the disadvantage of families who purposefully restricted their size so as to better endow their progeny. Brown clearly was thinking about the situation of a small, family farm with all rent taxed away for general benefit in times of increasing population. This family in restricting its size may find its standard of living relatively reduced. Here Brown would consider leaving the owner some portion of the rent so as to avoid this injustice.

"The Single-Tax Complex of Some Contemporary Economists"

IN 1924 BROWN PUBLISHED "The Single-Tax Complex of Some Contemporary Economists."[69] He was undoubtedly aware of the long-standing mutual antipathy between professional economists and the followers of Henry George. One extreme example of the attitude of these economists can be found in Francis A. Walker's reference to George's proposal: "I will not insult my readers by discussing a project so steeped in infamy."[70] Single-taxers, meanwhile, tended to question the credentials of the profession, both scientific and moral. Brown's approach was more restrained; he implied that contemporary writers of texts in economics and in public finance were in varying degrees the victims of a legacy of bias. The bias was expressed in an excessively negative and frequently erroneous conception of the single tax idea. He reviewed the treatment accorded the single tax on land values in several texts and was criticized by one commentator for the causticity of his criticism of them. The basis of the bias was, he felt, a type of "defense complex" wherein "a reasonable consideration of the merits of the case will not be tolerated."[71] He further argued that the objectors had made rights in land property a sacred cow and were unwilling or unable to consider the single tax proposal objectively. Among those criticized were E. R. A. Seligman, C. C. Plehn, Winthrop Daniels, Fred Fairchild, Merlin Hunter and C. J. Bullock. Seligman, the most prominent of those listed, was thought privately by Brown to have attained a stature in the field of taxation that was not wholly deserved.[72] Jacob Viner had written a review article in 1922 on textbooks on government finance that was highly critical of recent publications in this area.[73] Brown cited two of his criticisms which were made in his article. In one, Viner charged Merlin Hunter with misreading Seligman and mistakenly stating that the *impôt unique* of the Physiocrats actually had been adopted and abandoned as a failure.

Willford I. King responded to Brown's article with a rebuttal, "The Single-Tax Complex Analyzed,"[74] about which Seligman commented that it "effectively ridiculed" Brown's contentions.[75] Whereas Brown's arguments were wry, King's response was not only clever in its mockery but even sardonic.[76] King admitted that two of Brown's objections were valid and then proceeded to attack the single tax by reiterating old and answered arguments. King insisted, as had Seligman, that the term "single tax" be considered only in the precise context of George's proposal. Brown preferred to advocate greater land value taxation, which he viewed as complementary to the goals of single taxation. He had asked that the particular argument of his article not be considered a defense of single tax principles, and perhaps for this reason did not respond to King's article for several years. In 1943, he pointed out that King's views were typical of the authors of textbooks in public finance.[77] Brown continued to be unrepentant in his criticism of authors whom he felt slighted land value taxation. (See Appendix 6.)

Economic Arguments on the Effects of Land Value Taxation: Rothbard and Knight

BROWN DESCRIBED WHAT HE SAW TO BE THE "probable effects of making land rent the chief source of public revenue."[78] He assumed that this would remove most of the existing taxation of capital. There would be a rise in the rate of interest and a fall in the price of land; interest rates would rise as the net return to capital rose until more saving was forthcoming; land prices would fall with the capitalization of the higher tax on land rent, and also with the temporarily higher interest rate.[79] He then applied these effects to the case of a small farmer, noting that such farmers would have the taxes on improvements of all types reduced. Thus, all or most of the farmer's taxes would be based on the unimproved or "run down" value of his landholdings. The farmer could accumulate wealth at a greater rate, and if indebted, could pay off the debt more easily. Were the farmer marginal, in the sense that average earnings only were commensurate with a fair return on labor and capital invested despite good management, he would pay only a nominal tax. Assuming that the necessary governmental expenses would be paid by better-situated farmers and urban landholders, the small farmer, so described, would benefit from public services to which he was temporarily unable to contribute.

Next, Brown examined the case of the prospective farm owner or tenant that would be nearly identical to that of a prospective homeowner. Land value taxation would facilitate the purchase of land through the savings on the purchase price as the higher taxes on land value could be paid with the interest on savings. To argue this, Brown appears to assume that the prospective owner has the funds equal to the original price and invests the savings. If so, Brown did not prove his point. He clarified this later by saying that: "even if the lower price of land does no more than balance the higher tax on it, the reduction or removal of the other taxes is all clear gain."[80]

Thus, he argued that tenancy should be reduced and prospective farmers aided. He envisioned the tax reform as a partial removal of occupational barriers wherein those with little means could begin anew in farming. He saw the land tax in 1932 as representing a lighter burden on farmers during sustained periods of low farm prices because rental value of farmland would fall in these periods. He admitted that some farmers would be worse off—at least temporarily—as a result of the tax but that these farmers in general would be in a better position to bear this burden and should consider the interests of their progeny.

Many critics of the single tax had pointed out that a 100 percent tax on land's economic rent was tantamount to a confiscation or nationalization of these lands. They frequently referred to this as a step toward socialism while others, such as Frank Knight, believed it to be the equivalent of anarchy.[81] The confiscation of land values by the government was considered economically disastrous because it would imply government ownership and management of land, which would not attain the standard of efficiency achievable through competitive private ownership. Murray Rothbard commented in a similar manner on the scenario created by a 100 percent tax on land rent.[82] He argued that upon the application of the tax, land would become valueless or free and that owners would have no incentive to charge any rent. Thus, no revenue would be forthcoming from the tax, and furthermore no market allocation of the land sites would be available and "everyone will rush to grab the best locations."[83]

The full implications of a 100 percent tax were rarely discussed in detail by either its proponents or its opponents, as the question tended to strain one's imagination. Some critics did stress the ensuing economic chaos of such as dramatic change in the tax as well as the property system. Brown, like other advocates, did not accept that the reform would in a sense "confiscate" all site value.

Property would retain "value" in terms of the improvements made upon it.

Brown responded to Rothbard in a 1958 article arguing that his deductions were erroneous and contradictory.[84] The owners' incentive to collect their rent, even if the owners own no improvements on the land, would be provided by the taxing body on penalty of sacrificing the title. In the more likely case where owners have invested in improvements, they retain an incentive to collect the rent in order to pay the tax and retain the title. Those who have not or do not intend to make improvements on the land held could immediately give up their title, but the tax could then be collected from the renter, were there one, or within due time from the new owner. Brown argued that if land were to be in a "state of non-ownership" as Rothbard proposed, why then the chaotic rush to grab up the best locations? He did not go on to answer Rothbard's implied question and Knight's as well: How would an efficient allocation of sites be accomplished given that the sites would remain economically scarce? Were Brown to have answered, one can suppose that in large part the allocation would be according to market principles with certain aid from governmental agencies. Ignoring the added difficulties of expectations with respect to the tax reform, the agency in charge would try to maximize the yield on the tax. C. Lowell Harris pointed this out in his commentary on Rothbard in *Critics of Henry George*.[85] Even with the 100 percent tax there would remain incentives to bid for the use of land on the part of those presently using it and those who wish to in the future. The agency controlling the title would grant to the highest bidder the right to use the land as long as the taxes were paid and to "sell" this right at their discretion. The bids presumably would be taken as revenue as well by the agency. Transfer or sale from one user to another may present a problem even if accurate assessments were made on the potential yield of the site value. The problem would be one discussed previously: To what extent would "speculation" in land values perform a service in directing land to its most efficient use? Assuming it to be minimal, the land "market" would function on the basis of the expected returns to the application of labor and capital to the site, although the site itself nominally can have no return. There are, of course, other possible complications, but Brown would have stressed in this case the tax relief gained for labor and capital. Rothbard, Knight and others were correct in pointing out, in this extreme case, the greater reliance on the auspices of governmental agencies in terms of the requirement of assessment accuracy and performance of the state's broker role. Yet, some urban and land-use planners might welcome these opportunities. Such a radical change would be highly disruptive, but as Brown and others maintained, no such change was contemplated or thought practical. For Brown, the 100 percent land value tax was, I believe, an ethical ideal somewhat analogous to Marx's pure communism that did not demand immediate and detailed analysis.

In 1936, George R. Geiger,[86] a student of John Dewey, published *The Theory of the Land Question*. Brown was cited as having read the manuscript, and he strongly influenced portions of the book.[87] Geiger's earlier book on the philosophy of Henry George[88] was subject to a caustic review by Frank Knight. Knight maintained that

> there is no evidence, a priori or empirical, either (a) that speculative activity yields a higher return, in any representative sample of cases, than does activity where the results are actually in accord with expectations, or (b) that land acquisition or holding presents anything peculiar in comparison with other activities.[89]

In a letter to John Ise, Brown described Knight's review as "a bit rabid."[90] In 1943 Brown responded that George did not base his proposition on the belief that landowners receive an exceptional rate of return. To Knight's second point Brown responded that George's view of land was analogous to slaveholding in that, regardless of the rate of return, the incomes derived were exploitative in nature. Brown constructed another analogy wherein at some nominal cost the ownership of a lake (Michigan) is acquired and charges for its use would then represent something "peculiar in comparison with other economic activities."[91] Knight would reiterate his view in a 1953 article: "There is no socially-created unearned increment in the possession of landowners."[92]

Brown's Abridgements of George's
Progress and Poverty

BROWN WISHED THAT THE READERSHIP of *Progress and Poverty* not only by students but also by the general public would not abate as the book "aged." In 1928 he produced a radical abridgement, from 600 to 80 pages, under the title *Significant Paragraphs from Henry George's Progress and Poverty,*[93] which was authorized by Anna George de Mille and underwritten by the Robert Schalkenbach Foundation. Brown removed all of Book I on wages and capital and all but a small portion of Books II and III on population and laws of distribution, respectively. Book IV, George's thesis on the effect of economic growth on the distribution of wealth, was cut from 28 to 4 pages. He pared at the remaining Books but managed to offer the essence of George's remedy and its effects as well as a good sampling of George's rhetorical ability. He also added a few comments and interpretations. John Dewey, who provided an introductory essay to the book, praised Brown's work, but indicated that this summary should not serve as a substitute for the original because it did not capture George's social theory. Dewey declared: "No man, no graduate of a higher educational institution, has a right to regard himself as an educated man in social thought unless he has some firsthand acquaintance with the theoretical contribution of this great American thinker."[94] Brown's 1940 abridgement was considerably less radical, as it resulted in a book of 232 pages.[95] He made no comments in the text, but continued to achieve much of the reduction in length by excising George's treatment of Malthus, the wages-fund, and laws of distribution. The success or failure of Brown's quite considerable efforts might be judged by knowing the precise years for which the abridgements were available and their sales in those years. I have not been able to find such information, but, judging by the infrequency with which these books appear in university and college catalogues, one might speculate that they attained only a limited circulation, despite being very inexpensive.

Brown's Later Articles and Advocacy of Land Value Taxation

BROWN HAD OCCASION in a 1941 "communication" to the *American Economic Review* to chide Kenneth Boulding for an inconsistency in his *Economic Analysis*. Brown found fault with Boulding's definition of economic rent. In one instance, Boulding defined it as the return to any factor in excess of the minimum amount necessary to keep that factor "in its present occupation," and in another he substituted the phrase "in continuous service." For Brown this minor slip was of importance, as he wished to retain the use of the term *economic rent* to signify the rent of land exclusive of the return to improvements. He asked, "Is the expression 'economic rent' now to do duty for every sense in which we may say there is a 'surplus'?"[96] Ben Fine found Brown's question to be illustrative of the position of those who "reacted against the euthanasia for rent theory as a specific source of revenue tied to the land."[97]

In his later articles, Brown increasingly referred to the urban problems of slums, blighted areas and suburban sprawl. Land value taxation, he thought, would assist in preventing or alleviating these problems by creating incentives for improvements and by lessening speculation in building sites. In addition, he felt that lower-cost housing would result which would reduce the need for subsidization of housing and home ownership.

Studies of Australian land taxation by A. R. Hutchinson convinced Brown in 1949 that there was empirical support for the claims made for greater land taxation.[98] Hutchinson compared the Australian states based on the proportion of local real estate taxes levied on land value. He ignored the state and national land taxes, as they produced relatively little revenue. (The national tax in effect in Australia between 1910 and 1952 has been discussed by many writers including, in 1960, Richard M. Bird, who noted that analysis of the effects of the tax was complicated by the continual alterations in the rates and exemption levels.[99] Bird found that when the tax was abolished in 1952, it provided only 1 percent of federal revenue.) Hutchinson found that, in general, in those states taxing land value highly relative to improvements, housing construction, areas under cultivation and population inflow increased substantially in comparison to those states that did not base the property tax largely on land values. Brown recognized that the study was not conclusive as there might not have been sufficient similarity among the states, yet he felt it was a good prima facie case and worthy of further investigation. Mary Edwards in 1984 carried out a statistical study that supported Hutchinson's conclusions; she found that not taxing improvements tended to lead to an increase in the value of housing and the value of the total housing stock.[100] Brown served on the board of editors for a 1955 publication, *Land Value Taxation Around the World*, which was a unique resource for study in this area of taxation.[101] A greatly expanded second and third edition of this book, now edited by Robert V. Andelson, have recently been published.[102] In this revised study Geoffrey A. Foster concluded in his study of the case of Australia: "the various studies (mainly in Victoria) in local government areas give empirical vindication of the economic and ethical soundness of the site-value approach."[103]

While living in Pennsylvania, Brown became active in promoting local land value taxation. In 1951, the Pennsylvania legislature passed a bill allowing "third-class" cities to voluntarily adopt a graded tax plan wherein the cities could assess land and improvements separately and gradually increase the tax on land value relative to that on improvements.[104] In 1913, Pittsburgh and Scranton had adopted a similar plan. The new plan did not set fixed limits on the ratio between land and building taxes. Brown and his wife, Elizabeth, aided in the attempt to convince city authorities to adopt the plan. However, the results were disappointing, and the Browns attributed this to a lack of understanding of the benefits and to the opposition of those with special interests.[105] Later, the fortunes of land value taxation in the state, improved with new cities adopting the plan and cities such as Pittsburgh increasing the ratio of land to improvements taxation. Steven Cord, an active supporter of this movement and editor of *Incentive Taxation*, was quoted as saying that the land-tax idea "has moved out of the hands of the aficionados and into the mainstream of local politics" in western Pennsylvania.[106] Cord's 1983 statement was prophetic for all of the state of Pennsylvania. A portion of the abstract of a 1997 study by Wallace Oates and Robert

Schwab of the rejuvenation of the city of Pittsburgh reads: "The analysis suggests that, while the shortage of commercial space was a primary driving force behind the expansion, the reliance on increased land taxation played a supportive role by enabling the city to avoid rate increases in other taxes that could have impeded development."[107] One can speculate that Brown would have applauded the authors for their objectivity and recognition of the importance of the study despite its inherent difficulty. He may as well have quibbled with the authors' above statement, and asked if the previous tax regime was a contributor to the shortage of commercial space. If this were so, then the role of land value taxation may have been something more than merely supportive.

Throughout his life Brown was active in organizations supporting the single tax idea and was a contributor to *Land and Freedom, The Freeman* and the *Henry George News*, among others, and, from its inception, the *American Journal of Economics and Sociology*. As mentioned earlier, he served on the editorial board of this journal along with, for a number of years, two other economists, Harold Hotelling and John Ise. Hotelling was sympathetic to land value taxation as was Ise originally, although the latter was shown to have altered his view by E. R. Brown.[108] Brown was also a founding member of the *The Freeman*'s editorial council along with William C. de Mille, John Dewey, George Raymond Geiger, Henry George III, Joseph Dana Miller, Albert Jay Nock and Kathleen Norris. His contributions to this journal (1938–1943) were highly polemical with titles such as: "The Clarions of the Battle Call," "The Void in College Curricula" and "Why States Go Totalitarian." *The Freeman* became the *Henry George News* in early 1943. Brown contributed many articles to this newsletter.

Some Notable Developments Subsequent to Brown's Death

In 1994 the National Tax Association conducted a tax policy opinion survey of its individual membership which repeated verbatim a 1934 survey of American public finance professors carried out by Mabel Walker of the Tax Policy League. Question 13 of this survey reads: "Should there be a special tax on [the] unearned increment of land values?"[109] The response to this poorly worded question was 62% positive in 1934 and only 22% in 1994! The 1994 survey was broken into five age groups from 20–30 years old, etc., to over 60 in age. The youngest and the oldest groups with 38% and 34%, respectively, were much more favorable to this form of land value taxation than the middle groups with 16%, 19% and 23%. On a related question (#11), "Should improvements be taxed at a lower rate than land?" the 1934 positive response was 54%, which dropped to 38% in 1994, indicating some inconsistency in the responses. Re: question 13, the poor wording might explain the huge drop-off in support as "special tax" is not explained and the term "unearned increment" is somewhat pedantic. The professors in 1934 were much more likely to have decoded the question as calling for some degree of support for Henry George's single taxation. Joel Slemrod, who commented on the results of the survey, interpreted "unearned increment in land values" to be "presumably" the "capital gains not due to improvements." Slemrod then attempted to explain the significant drop-off as "one example of the greater tendency in 1934 to favor higher taxes on capital income compared to labor income."[110] A much more likely explanation is that contemporary tax specialists tend to find any question nonsensical if it treats land differently than capital. The survey question in 1934 when land was still considered a factor of production distinct from capital by most economists was a meaningful one. If the Fillebrown 1908 questionnaire is comparable to these surveys, then we can observe a decline in support by the profession as characterizing the whole of the last century. This would, of course, be discouraging for Brown, with the only possible bright spot being the 38% support evinced by the youngest age cohort.

Brown would have been more pleased in general with the, at times, more lively and open discussion of land value taxation in public sector journals and the continued dedication to Georgist themes in the *American Journal of Economics and Sociology* with the continued sponsorship of the Francis Nielson Fund and the Robert Schalkenbach Foundation. Will Lissner, its founding editor, lived to see the chief editorship pass successfully to first Frank C.

Genovese and then to Laurence S. Moss in the journal's almost complete 60 years of publication.

Two Ph.D. theses in economics have notably focused on land value taxation. Terence Michael Dwyer's 1980 Harvard thesis, *A History of the Theory of Land Value Taxation*,[111] is the most comprehensive study of its kind. The title is somewhat deceptive in that the study is more than a history; it treats and contributes to ongoing arguments with respect to the efficiency and equity of land value taxation. Dwyer draws extensively on Brown's writings on taxation and land value taxation. Kris A. Feder's 1993 Temple thesis titled *Issues in the Theory of Land Value Taxation*[112] profits from Dwyer's study and in particular the numerous contributions on the subject by Mason Gaffney while not ignoring Brown's key articles. Kenneth Boulding's "neo-Georgist" position is examined and over one-half of the study is dedicated to examining the relation of land speculation to land value taxation. Feder concludes her thesis pointing to "Unsettled Questions Regarding Land and Its Taxation." This theme is much that of Dick Netzer's recently published article, "What We Need to Know About Land Value Taxation."[113] For Netzer the key questions are land value taxation's contemporary relevancy and feasibility.

Application of Georgist ideas to problems in economic development and the "new" environmentalism were areas that came into focus quite late in Brown's life; thus he made no direct contribution to these questions. This void has been more than adequately filled by a number of scholars. Besides the above-mentioned Gaffney and Feder, I would add the names of James L. Busey, Jerome F. Heavey, Jürgen Backhaus, Jacob Jan Krabbe, David Richards, Roger Sandilands and Fred Foldvary.

Conclusion

INTELLECTUAL AND POLITICAL CURRENTS during Brown's 60-odd years of advocacy of land value taxation were generally not favorable to his cause. Progressive and populist movements existing in his early years were not drawn toward the single tax idea per se. Labor movements of a more radical bent were inclined to adopt socialistic programs. Moderate labor unions, despite Samuel Gompers' support of George in his mayoral contest, in general found no place for land value taxation in their agendas. Prominent intellectual periodicals, such as the *New Republic, The Dial* and the *Atlantic Monthly*, despite their vacillations, were never taken with this proposed reform.[114] Despite the affinity between Georgist and Austrian thought, two of the latter's prominent expositors were adamant opponents of the single tax (Rothbard and Ludwig von Mises). Nor is there any traceable influence in the traditional political parties.[115]

The earlier work of the Joseph Fels Fund and that of the Henry George Schools and Clubs, the Robert Schalkenbach Foundation, the Henry George Foundation and the Lincoln Institute of Land Policy[116] in the promotion of land value taxation has not commanded widespread attention. However, the ongoing efforts of these entities are indicative of the continuing attraction and relevancy of the ideas expressed by George well over 100 years ago. In academia, the Committee on Taxation, Resource and Economic Development has published several studies. Among its contributing members, several are sympathetic to land value taxation with Mason Gaffney emerging as this cause's leading advocate. More recently the Centre for Incentive Taxation in London has been the source of several studies. In addition, the University of Rochester Press in 1997 published a series, *The Henry George Centennial Trilogy*, edited by Kenneth C. Wenzer. He also edited a 1999 study, *Land Value Taxation: The Equitable and Efficient Source of Public Finance*, which includes a reprint of Brown's 1927 *Journal of Political Economy* article, "Land Speculation and Land-Value Taxation."[117]

The *Critics of Henry George*, edited by Robert V. Andelson, and Steven Cord's *Henry George: Dreamer or Realist?*[118] are outstanding examples of works which have served to renew interest in and respect for the work of Henry George. Mason Gaffney and Fred Harrison's *The Corruption of Economics* appears to have caught the attention of a good portion of the profession. A very distinguished group of scholars including now four Nobel prize for economics recipients signed an open letter (November 7, 1990) to Mikhail Gorbachev urging him to adopt an essentially Georgist approach to the privatization of markets in that land would remain in public ownership and the rents paid to the government would provide a large portion of needed public revenue. Although it cannot be known for certain, it would seem likely that William Vickrey would have spoken out favorably of land value taxation had fate allowed him to make his Nobel Prize acceptance address. One can only catagorize as "surprising" the recent avowal of support for Georgist reform by one of the long time, leading expositors of the history of economic thought: Mark Blaug.[119] Outside of academia I will draw upon a further example of land value taxation's persevering influence from a 1997 *Des Moines Register* op-ed. Bill Reichardt, a well-known former businessman, state legislator and star football player for the University of Iowa, offered an opinion piece titled "Tax the land, not improvements, and renew our cities."[120] He ended the editorial by referencing the paper's readers to not only George's *Progress and Poverty*, but also to Robert V. Andelson's *From Wasteland to Promised Land* and Nicholas Tideman's *Land and Taxation*.[121] The relationship or affinity of an Andelson, a Cord, a Gaffney, a Harris, an Oates, a Netzer, a Tideman, a Vickrey or any other of the above-mentioned writers to Harry Gunnison Brown varies from slight to significant. What clearly links them, however, is that they represent a generation that succeeded that of Brown's, and Brown was just as clearly an important link, perhaps the most important, back to the teachings of Henry George and his predecessors.

In conclusion, questions as to the most advantageous land tax policies remain with us, and their importance has not diminished. Brown's lifelong work in demonstrating the relevancy of land value taxation to these questions forms a important legacy for students, whether they come to share his conclusions or not. Pinkney Walker, a student and colleague of Brown's in his later years at Missouri, commented that Brown chose to actively support land value taxation because so few economists were supporting any reform in this direction.[122]

Notes

1. Several commentators have observed that a more accurate term would be *land rent taxation*. Although I think they have a valid point, I will follow the more readily recognizable terminology.

2. Arthur Nichols Young (1916). *The Single Tax Movement in the United States*. Princeton, NJ: Princeton University Press: 312.

3. [William Graham Sumner] (1881). "Review of *Progress and Poverty*." *Scribner's Monthly* 28 (June): 312–313.

Francis Amasa Walker (1883). *Land and Its Rent*. Boston: Little, Brown.

John Bates Clark (1890). "The Ethics of Land Tenure." *International Journal of Ethics* 1 (October): 62–79.

Richard T. Ely, Thomas S. Adams, Max O. Lorenz and Allyn Young (1930). *Outlines of Economics*. 5th ed. New York: Macmillan Co.: 462.

Simon Nelson Patten (1891). "Another View of the Ethics of Land Tenure." *International Journal of Ethics* 1 (April): 357–360.

Frank A. Fetter (1904). *The Principles of Economics*. New York: Century Co.: 374–375.

Edwin R. A. Seligman (1925). *Essays in Taxation*. 10th ed. New York: Macmillan & Co.: 66–69.

Frank Knight (1953). "The Fallacies in the Single Tax." *The Freeman* 3 (August) : 809–811.

4. Edwin Cannon (1930). *A Review of Economic Theory*. London: P. S. King & Son: 400–403.

F. Y. Edgeworth (1925). *Papers Relating to Political Economy*. Vol. 2. London: Macmillan & Co.: 187, 192, 225 and 232.

Gustav Cassel (1932). *The Theory of Social Economy*.   New York: Harcourt , Brace & Co.: 260–279.

5. Joseph Dorfman (1959). *The Economic Mind in American Civilization*. Vol. 3. New York: Viking Press: 360.

6. Edwin R. A. Seligman (1912). "Recent Tax Reforms Abroad." *Political Science Quarterly* 27 (March): 469.

7. Richard T. Ely (1917). "Land Property as an Economic Concept and Field of Research." *American Economic Review* 7 (March): 33.

8. Charles Fillebrown (1908). Chairman of a Round Table Discussion. "Agreements in Political Economy." *Publications of the American Economics Association*, Ser. 3, no. 5: 117–123.

9. J. Patrick Gunning (1997) has pointed out the quite equivocal "support" Davenport lent single taxation which neither George Geiger (1936) or for that matter Brown had failed to take note of. I will not pursue the questions raised here, but only attest to the difficulty of interpreting *in toto* Davenport's oblique writing mannerisms. Also it may be noted that after leaving Missouri for Cornell, he wrote nothing more on the subject.

10. Thomas Nixon Carver (1915). *Essays in Social Justice*. Cambridge, MA: Harvard University Press: 281–303.

Frank Taussig (1926). *Principles of Economics*. Vol. 2. 3rd ed. New York: Macmillan & Co.: 80–82.

John Commons (1922). "A Progressive Tax on Land Values." *Political Science Quarterly* 38 (March): 41–68.

Herbert J. Davenport (1917). "Theoretical Issues in the Single Tax." *American Economic Review* 7 (March): 1–30.

11. The history of Irving Fisher's position on the single tax as best I can reconstruct is the following. Brown wrote Fisher in 1925 reminding him of conversations they had had concerning Fisher's intention of writing a chain of books which would include one addressing the question: What is Wrong with Us? Brown argued that the present system of taxation an important part of the answer to this question and it had not been competently studied to date. He went on to urge Fisher to write on this subject. (Letter, March 14, 1925, Irving Fisher Papers, Yale University Library) In the correspondence there is no reply from Fisher on this entreaty. Louis Post reported in his 1926 book, *What is the Single Tax?* (New York: Vanguard Press), that Fisher made the following statement in a speech at a formal dinner in New York City: "Premising that so important a change should not be made abruptly, I favor a gradual reduction, as far as possible, of the burden on industry and labor, and taking instead the economic rent of bare land. I am, however, opposed to the 'single tax' in the sense that land value should be the sole source of public revenue." (106) This was the basis for Brown's 1928 appendix citation of Fisher as one whose expressed opinion tended to be supportive of single taxation.

George R. Geiger next reported to have heard Fisher say that he was "90 per cent a single taxer." He further stated: ". . . his chief objection to George was the metaphysics of the single tax system, i.e. its absolutism." (*The Philosophy of Henry George*. New York: The Macmillan Company, 1933: 468.)

In 1932 Fisher published a short article that stressed his objections to the confiscation element in the single tax and its "singleness." The article, titled "The Single Tax," appeared in *The International Musician* in the September issue of this obscure (for economists at least) publication. I came to know of the article only through a lambasting critique of it in the Georgist journal, *Land and Freedom*. ("The Professor and The Single Tax" 32[6]: 206–207) Fisher's very brief article essentially elaborates on his objection to the confiscatory element in the single tax program, but recognizes that there are no special "vested rights" in land value such that increased taxation of land value as well as increases in land value in the future (within reasonable limits) was acceptable and to be desired due to the non-shiftability of the tax. Fisher's other objection was to the "orthodox" single-taxer position that only land value be the subject of taxation. Arguing somewhat whimsically, he declared that this may lead to excessive government revenue such that the proceeds would be wasted, or in the other extreme that such a tax would yield no revenue at all. Fisher was probably harking back to an earlier criticism made by Charles Spahr ("The Single Tax." *Political Science Quarterly* 6, 1891: 628–631) which Gaffney

(1994:71) has pointed out seems applicable only to local as opposed to nationwide land value taxation.

In 1942 Fisher's *Constructive Income Taxation: A Proposal forReform* was published which brought together his long-time concerns about the double taxation of savings and capital gains taxation as well as his general preference for expenditure taxation. (See William Barber, ed. [1997] *The Works of Irving Fisher.* Volume 12: *Contributions to the Theory and Practice of Public Finance.* London: Pickering & Chatto.) Brown made no written comment on Fisher's proposal.

12. Harry Gunnison Brown (1925). *The Taxation of Unearned Incomes.* Columbia, MO: Lucas Brothers: 126.

13. They did so in response to an inquiry by the American Association for Scientific Taxation as noted in *Significant Paragraphs from Henry George's Progress and Poverty* (Ed. Harry Gunnison Brown. New York: Doubleday, Doran & Co., 1928. Appendix: 77–80. Those who had made "similar expressions" were: Arthur T. Hadley, Tipton R. Snavely, Paul Douglas, Thaddeus P. Thomas and the Rev. John A. Ryan.

14. Lionel Robbins (1967[1932]). Introduction. *The Common Sense of Political Economy.* By Philip H. Wicksteed. Vol. 1. New York: Augustus M. Kelly: vi–vii.

Renato Cirillo (1984). "Leon Walras and Social Justice." *American Journal of Economics and Sociology* 43 (January): 53–60.

Knut Wicksell (1958). "A New Principle of Just Taxation." *Classics in the Theory of Public Finance.* Eds. Richard Musgrave and Alan Peacock. London: Macmillan & Co.: 72–118.

15. I have chosen to use primarily the term "land value" without hyphenation to express the economic value of land apart from improvements made on or in it. Other terms I believe to be synonymous are used at times, such as "bare land value" and "site value" where the context makes the meaning clear.

16. Warren Samuels had noted that: ". . . inasmuch as land has been so economically, socially and politically important, land ownership has a transcendental if not sacral status in the minds of both landowning and non-landowning people, one frequent consequence of which is common attitudes adverse to land taxation." (Foreword. "Land Value Taxation Around the World." Ed. Robert V. Andelson. *American Journal of Economics and Sociology* 59 (Supplement): ix.)

17. Harry Gunnison Brown (1918). *The Theory of Earned and Unearned Incomes.* Columbia, MO: Missouri Book Co.

18. Harry Gunnison Brown (1932). *The Economic Basis of Tax Reform.* Columbia, MO: Lucas Brothers.

19. Phillips Hamlin Brown (December 15, 1981). Letter to author. Personal files, Iowa City, IA.

20. This is not to imply that there were no economists other than those mentioned previously who supported the single tax idea. It does imply that I have found no economist of Brown's stature who openly supported Brown's view. For example, William N. Loucks of the University of Pennsylvania wrote an article in the *Annals of the American Academy of Political and Social Sciences* in 1930 in which he indicated strong support, yet I have not found any other writing by him on this theme.

21. Harry Gunnison Brown (1936). "A Defense of the Single-Tax Principle." *Annals of the American Academy of Political and Social Sciences* 183 (January): 63.

22. Harry Gunnison Brown (1931). *Economic Science and the Common Welfare.* 5th ed. Columbia, MO: Lucas Brothers: 244–245.

23. John R. Commons (1934). *Institutional Economics.* New York: Macmillan & Co.: 813–814.

24. Brown (1931): 24.

25. John C. Commons (1925). "Review of *Economic Science and the Common Welfare.*" *American Economic Review* 15 (September): 484.

26. J. Shield Nicholson (1893). "Address to the Economic Science and Statistics Section of the British Association." *Journal of Political Economy* 1 (December): 124.

27. L. L. Price (1891). "Review of the Duke of Argyll's *The Unseen Foundations of Society.*" *Economic Journal* 3: 264–271.

28. Carver (1915): 282–303.

29. Herbert J. Davenport (1911). "The Extent and Significance of the Unearned Increment." *Publications of the American Economic Association* 11: 322–331.

30. Brown (1918): 208.

31. Willford I. King (1921). "Earned and Unearned Income." *Annals of the American Academy of Political and Social Sciences* 95 (May): 251–259.

32. *Ibid.*: 259.

33. Commons (1934): 840–841.

34. Henry Raymond Mussey (1925). "Talking Taxes." *The Nation.* October 7: 389.

35. Nichols (1916): 259.

36. This budget was rejected by the House of Lords.

37. Wicksell (1958): 113.

38. Fred Rogers Fairchild (1923). *Essentials of Economics.* New York: American Book Co.: 507.

39. Brown (1932): 191–195.

40. Frank Knight (1925). "Review of Brown's *The Taxation of Unearned Incomes.*" *National Municipal Review* 14 (June): 378.

41. Ward Bishop (1933). "Review of *The Economic Basis of Tax Reform.*" *American Economic Review* 23 (December): 761–763.

42. Anonymous (1920). "Review of *The Theory of Earned and Unearned Incomes.*" *Political Science Quarterly* 35: 693–694.

43. Harold Hotelling (1938). "The General Welfare in Relation to the Problems of Taxation and Railway and Utility Rates." *Econometrica* 6 (July): 256.

44. Edwin Cannan (1907). "The Proposed Relief of Buildings from Local Rates." *Economic Journal* 17: 36–46.

45. C. F. Bickerdike (1912). "The Principle of Land Value Taxation." *Economic Journal* 22: 1–15.

46. Charles Trevelyn (1907). "Land Value Taxation and the Use of Land." *Economic Journal* 17: 30–35.

47. Joseph Wedgewood (1912). "The Principle of Land Value Taxation." *Economic Journal* 22: 388–397.

48. Alvin S. Johnson (1914). "The Case Against the Single Tax." *The Atlantic Monthly* 113 (January): 33.

49. Thomas S. Adams (1916). "Tax Exemption through Tax Capitalization: A Fiscal Fallacy." *American Economic Review* 5 (June): 279.

50. Davenport (1917): 25.

51. One example is Susan Previant Lee and Peter Passel (1979) *A New Economic View of American History.* New York: W.W. Norton & Co.: 307–325.

52. Richard Ely et. al. (1933). *Outline of Economics.* New York: Macmillan & Co.: 447–449.

53. Brown (1925) *The Taxation of Unearned Incomes*: 128.

54. Knight (1925) "Review of *The Taxation of Unearned Incomes*": 378.

55. Davenport (1917): 16.

56. Harry Gunnison Brown (1927). "Land Speculation and Land Value Taxation." *Journal of Political Economy* 35 (June): 402.

57. Seligman (1925) *Essays in Taxation*: 91.

58. Alfred Marshall (1938). *Principles of Economics.* London: Macmillan & Co.: 804.

59. Commons (1922) "A Progressive Tax on Land Values": 53–59.

60. Ursula Hicks (1970). "Can Land be Assessed for Purposes of Site Value Taxation." *The Assessment of Land Value.* Ed. Daniel Holland. Madison, WI: University of Wisconsin Press: 9–24.

61. Kenneth Back (1970). "Land Value Taxation in Light of Current Assessment Theory and Practice": 54.

62. Mason Gaffney (1970). "Adequacy of Land as a Tax Base": 157–212.

63. Dick Netzer (February 11, 1969). Letter to Harry Gunnison Brown. Author's personal files, Iowa City, IA.

64. Steven Cord (1986). "How Much Revenue Would a Full Land Value Tax Yield?" *American Journal of Economics and Sociology* 44 (July): 291.

65. Commons (1922): 46–48.

66. Brown (1932): 123.

67. Robert V. Andelson, ed. (1979). *The Critics of Henry George*. Rutherford, NJ: Fairleigh Dickinson University Press: 385.

68. Harry Gunnison Brown (1942). *Basic Principles of Economics*. Columbia, MO: Lucas Brothers: 445–449.

69. Harry Gunnison Brown (1924). "The Single-Tax Complex of Some Contemporary Economists."
Journal of Political Economy 32 (April): 164–190.

70. Francis A. Walker (1887). *Political Economy*. New York: Henry Holt & Co.: 419.

71. James Harvey Robinson (1921). *The Mind in the Making*. New York: Harpers: 92.

72. Harry Gunnison Brown (October 4, 1930). Letter to James Harvey Rogers. Rogers Papers, Yale University Library, New Haven, CT.

73. Jacob Viner (1922). "Textbooks in Government Finance." *Journal of Political Economy* 30: 242–256.

74. Willford I. King (1924). "The Single-Tax Complex Analyzed." *Journal of Political Economy* 32 (October): 604–612.

75. Seligman (1925) *Essays in Taxation*: 97.

76. King (1924:604) began his rebuttal with the following witticism: "As Mrs. O'Flanagan was on her way home from a review of the regiment of which her son was a member, she overtook a neighbor. 'Faith,' said Mrs. O'Flanagan, 'Oi'm proud of me Terence. Whin the byes came marchin' by in a long straight line, ivery man in the regiment was out of step except Terence."

77. Harry Gunnison Brown (1943). "Anticipation of an Increment and the 'Unearned Decrement' in Land Values." *American Journal of Economics and Sociology* 2 (April): 347.

78. Brown (1932): 215.

79. Compare with Jan K. Brueckner (1986). "A Modern Analysis of the Effects of Site Value Taxation." *National Tax Journal* 39 (March): 49–58.

80. Brown (1932): 231.

81. Knight (1953): 810.

82. Murray Rothbard (1970). *Power and Markets*. Menlo Park, CA: Institute for Humane Studies: 95.

83. *Ibid.*

84. Harry Gunnison Brown (1958). "Foundations, Professors and 'Economic Education.'" *American Journal of Economics and Sociology* 17 (January_: 149–152.

85. C. Lowell Harris (1979). "Rothbard's Anarcho-Capitalist Critique." in *Critics of Henry George* : 354–370.

86. Geiger was the son of Oscar Geiger, who founded in New York the Henry George School of Social Science. For more on George R. Geiger see Christopher K. Ryan and Helen B. Ryan (1999) "Remembrance and

Appreciation Feature: George Raymond Geiger (1903–1998)." *American Journal of Economic and Sociology* 58 (1): 7–15.

87. George R. Geiger (1936). *The Theory of the Land Question.* New York: The Macmillan Company.

88. George R. Geiger (1933). *The Philosophy of Henry George.* New York: The Macmillan Company.

89. Frank Knight (1933). "Review of George R. Geiger's *The Philosophy of Henry George.*" *Journal of Political Economy* 41 (October): 688.

90. Harry Gunnison Brown (January 9, 1939). Letter to John Ise. Joint Collection of Missouri Western Historical Manuscripts Collection-Columbia and State Historical Society of Missouri.

91. Brown (1943): 351.

92. Knight (1953): 810.

93. The use of number of pages is, of course, a crude measure. Word count using scanning devices would be a much better measure; but, it is not, I feel, required for this comparison.

94. John Dewey (1928). Preface. *Significant Paragraphs from Henry George's Progress and Poverty.* By Harry Gunnison Brown. New York: Doubleday, Doran & Company: 2.

95. Henry George (1940). *Progress and Poverty.* Rearranged and abridged by Harry Gunnison Brown. New York: Henry George School of Social Science.

96. Harry Gunnison Brown (1941). "Economic Rent: In What Sense a Surplus?" *American Economic Review* 31 (December): 833–835.

97. Ben Fine (1983). "The Historical Approach to Rent and Price Theory Reconsidered." *Australian Economic Papers* 22 (June): 141.

98. Harry Gunnison Brown (1949). "The Challenge of Australian Tax Policy." *American Journal of Economics and Sociology* 8 (July): 377–400.

99. Richard M. Bird (1960). "A National Tax on the Unimproved Value of Land: The Australian Experience." *National Tax Journal* 13 December: 386–392.

100. Mary Edwards (1984). "Site Value Taxation in Australia: Where Land is Taxed More and Improvements Less, Average Housing Value and Stock Are Higher." *American Journal of Economics and Sociology* 43 (October): 481–495.

101. Robert V. Andelson et al., ed. (1955). *Land Value Taxation Around the World.* New York: Robert Schalkenbach Foundation.

102. Robert V. Andelson, ed. (2000). "Land-Value Taxation Around the World." *American Journal of Economics and Sociology* 59 (Suppplement). (Also, *Land-value Taxation Around the World.* Ed. Robert V Andelson. Boston: Blackwell Publishers, 2000.)

103. Geoffrey A. Foster (2000). "Australia." *Land Value Taxation Around the World*: 415.

104. Will Lissner (1951). "Pennsylvania's New Optional Graded Tax Law." *American Journal of Economics and Sociology* 10 (October): 41–43.

105. Harry Gunnison Brown and Elizabeth Read Brown (1968). "Obstacles to the Adoption of Land Value Taxation." *American Journal of Economics and Sociology* 27 (October): 387–392.

106. Gurney Breckenfeld (1983). "Higher Taxes that Promote Development." *Fortune* 18 (August): 69.

107. Wallace E. Oates and Robert M. Schwab (1997). "The Impact of Urban Land Taxation: The Pittsburgh Experience." *National Tax Journal* 50 (March): 1.

108. Elizabeth Read Brown (1961). "How College Textbooks Treat Land Value Taxation." *American Journal of Economics and Sociology* 20 (January): 162–163.

109. Joel Slemrod (1994). "Professional Opinions about Tax Policy: 1994 and 1934." *National Tax Journal* 48: 125.

110. *Ibid.*: 133.

111. Terence Michael Dwyer (1980). *A History of the Theory of Land Value Taxation.* Diss. Harvard University. Ann Arbor, MI: UMI. (Due to the university library's lending policies I was unable to make use of this study in the first edition of this book.)

112. Kris A. Feder (1993). *Issues in the Theory of Land Value Taxation.* Diss. Temple University.

113. Dick Netzer (2001). "What Do We Need to Know about Land Value Taxation?" *American Journal of Economics and Sociology* 60 (Supplement). (Although it was not made clear in this publication, Netzer's article seems to have been written earlier, circa 1994, based upon the references made in the text.)

114. Brown was not unmindful of this tendency. In an address to the 1936 Henry George Congress published in *Land and Freedom* with the title "Radical Literary Intelligentsia and Hard-headed Propertied Conservatives: A Study in Similarities," he lashed out against the intellectual trend of the inter-war years. As the title suggests he found the generally "left-leaning" intellectual journals, by ignoring or treating as passé George's remedy, were playing into the hands of the "industrial magnates" who on their part championed freedom and individualism as a "smoke screen" to hide and maintain their "special privileges." (v. 36: 171–175)

115. Mason Gaffney has pointed out that, in large, American historians have neglected the political importance of the single tax movement in the years 1901–1924. Modified Georgist ideas melded with the progressive movement that dominated national politics for much of the period via both major parties but most evidently in the Wilson administration. Although Harding's election marked the end of a progressive presidency, the movement continued in Congress and in Georgist-inspired legislative initiatives in several states. See Gaffney (1994) "The Stratagem against

Henry George." *The Corruption of Economics.* By Mason Gaffney and Fred Harrison. London: Shepheard-Walwyn Publishers: 34–39.

116. The role of the Lincoln Foundation has been controversial.

117. Kenneth C. Wenzer, ed. (1997). *The Henry George Centennial Trilogy.* Vol. I–III. Rochester, NY: University of Rochester Press.

Kenneth C. Wenzer, ed. (1999). *Land-Value Taxation: The Equitable and Efficient Source of Public Finance.* Armonk, NY: M. E. Sharpe and London: Shephard Walwyn.

118. Steven Cord (1965). *Henry George: Dreamer or Realist?* New York: Robert Schalkenbach Foundation.

119. Mark Blaug (2000). "Henry George: Rebel with a Cause." *European Journal of the History of Economic Thought* 7 (2): 270–288.

120. William Reichardt (1997). *Des Moines Sunday Register*, August 24. Section C: 1 and 2.

121. Robert V. Andelson and James W. Dawsey (1992). *From Wasteland to Promised Land: Liberation Theology for a Post-Marxist World.* New York: Maryknoll NY: Orbis Books and London: Shephard-Walwyn.

Nicholaus Tideman, ed. (1994). *Land and Taxation.* London: Shephard-Walwyn in association with the Centre for Incentive Taxation.

122. Pinkney Walker, "In Memoriam," as quoted by Paul Junk in his Preface to *Selected Articles by Harry Gunnison Brown.* New York: Robert Schalkenbach Foundation, 1980.

Appendix 6A

Brown's Stratagem in Light of Gaffney's "Neo-Classical Economics as a Stratagem Against Henry George"

Brown's advocacy of land value taxation entailed certain strategic decisions, several of which have been alluded to in the preceding chapters. Evidence of his ideas on how to best champion his chosen cause can be found in his writing in and outside of the discipline and especially in some of his correspondence. Mason Gaffney in his lengthy contribution to *The Corruption of Economics* (1994) declares: "Brown was a neo-classically trained economist who used neo-classical tools to plead the Georgist case before other NCEists. He projected his own conscientious sincerity onto others. He thought he could reach them through reason, using their own tools and concepts. He was a very capable theorist; he pretty well failed."[1] Gaffney was clearly referring to Brown's failure with respect to his "chosen reference group,"[2] which I interpret to be academic economists and in particular public finance economists. Gaffney is correct. Yet Brown's "failure" remains of interest in that his was the most notable attempt by an economist to translate and carry forward the message of George's "remedy" for 50-some years.

Most strikingly Gaffney's narrative but also Steven Cord's (1965) *Henry George: Dreamer or Realist* and *The Critics of Henry George* edited by Robert V. Andelson (1979) provide an historical background to appraise Brown's strategies. Neither Charles Albro Barker's (1955) venerable biography of Henry George nor other standard references are of much help, as they lose the slim trail that Georgism left in academic economics.[3] Because Brown's writings had only one reaction outside of this country, I will confine my comments to American economists—the span being from J. B. Clark to George Stigler. My further focus in time will be roughly on the period 1917–1933 which Cord characterized as featuring "The Cold Winds of Conservatism."

Antagonists

BROWN IS SAID TO HAVE SOLIDIFIED his convictions about land value taxation in the early 1910s while serving as an instructor at Yale. He knew who the principal single tax antagonists were: E. R. A. Seligman and J. B. Clark of Columbia, Simon Patten of Princeton, Frank A. Fetter of Cornell and Princeton, Alvin S. Johnson of Cornell, Richard T. Ely of Wisconsin and Frank Knight of Iowa and Chicago who was Johnson's student at Cornell. There were, of course, many other prominent opponents such as William Graham Sumner, Francis Walker, H. C. Adams, Charles Spahr or Henry Seager, but their influence had waned by this period. This first group was still active, influential and well-situated. Their interconnectedness and influence can be demonstrated with a few examples.

(1) Alvin S. Johnson, as Gaffney notes, was J. B. Clark's personal secretary and his student at Cornell. Johnson published "The Case against the Single Tax" in the prestigious *Atlantic Monthly* in 1914. Johnson reiterated his argument in the 1927 publication that was sponsored by the American Economic Association whose publication committee consisted of Seligman, Ely, J. Hollander, B. M. Anderson, Jr. and J. M. Clark.[4] In an earlier issue the case for the single tax had been made by F. W. Garrison (grandson of the famous abolitionist) who was a lawyer by trade.[5] It was thoroughly Georgist in tone and optimistic about recent trends. Johnson's theme, derided by Gaffney, was that the single tax was "a device for the spoliation of the middle class."[6]

(2) Frank A. Fetter closely supervised Arthur Nichols Young's published thesis at Princeton, *The Single Tax Movement in the United States*. Cord comments: "Young was opposed to the single tax idea although he displayed a certain sympathetic fascination with it."[7] I agree with Cord that it was an extensively researched, scholarly work. Yet its "Concluding Sur-

vey" reads like a premature obituary for the Georgist movement. In 1921 Fetter inspired and wrote the introduction to John Roscoe Turner's published dissertation, *The Ricardian Rent Theory in Early American Economics*. This too is a worthy study. Although justifiable, Turner's ending his survey with Arthur L. Perry is also convenient in that no consideration of Henry George nor even Francis Walker is allowed to muddle his central story of early American opposition to Ricardo's rent theory.

(3) Willford I. King, one of the long listing of Richard T. Ely's collaborators, published with Macmillan in 1915 his National Bureau of Economic Research study, *The Wealth and Income of the People of the United States*. Its publication was under the rubric of The Citizen's Library of Economics, Politics and Sociology series edited by Ely. King is identified as an Instructor in Statistics at the University of Wisconsin. Allyn Young, another one-time collaborator with Ely, reviewed this pioneering work in economic statistics for the *Quarterly Journal of Economics*. Young reviewed the effort with an admixture of praise and skepticism. Given that Young's reputation for fairness is comparable to that of W. C. Mitchell's, I will simply replicate the paragraph of greatest interest to followers of Henry George:

> Even more daring is the attempt to apportion the national income in each of these census years among the different factors of production. There are a host of difficulties in such an undertaking, and Dr. King does not tell enough about his methods to enable one to say just how far his ingenuity has enable him to surmount them. He has confidence in his figures for wages and salaries, and does not believe that those for rent are in error by more than 20 per cent. He does not attach much importance, however, to the line which he draws between interest and profits. Of particular interest is the stability and relatively small size of the share of the national income imputed to rent (never over 9 per cent).[8]

Uncritical acceptance of King's findings (which were quite different from the less "scientific" estimations of Davenport

[1910] and others) may have had the effect, as Cord noted, of diverting attention away from the "land question."[9]

(4) Cord reports that when in 1915 New York City was considering adopting the "Pittsburg-Scranton" type plan for graded taxation, E. R. A. Seligman endeavored to get his former student, Robert M. Haig, to supervise two studies of the proposal. Haig's reports were negative.[10] Seligman would later select Frank A. Fetter to provide the entries on Rent and on Capital for *The Encyclopedia of the Social Sciences*. Fetter's views even by the early 1930s were controversial.

(5) C. R. McCann, Jr. and Mark Perlman make quite clear that George Stigler should not in general be considered a disciple of Frank Knight.[11] However, in regard to Stigler's celebrated 1941 dissertation written under Knight, one may reasonably expect a high degree of like-mindedness between them at that time. In his *Production and Distribution Theories*, Stigler is selective in a not very subtle manner when he examines the positions of the theorists on the question of the factors of production and in particular the importance of a distinction between land and capital. I am not implying any outright misinterpretation on his part, but even in the application of his famed sarcasm Stigler betrays his theoretical preferences. (e.g., "These distinctions need not be considered here; they are cited only to show how classical and naïve Böhm-Bawerk's position is."[12]) His preferences are clear and at least on these questions no different from Knight's. Forty years later he picked a seemingly gratuitous example to make a point: "If anyone in this audience wishes to become an apostle of the single tax after the scripture of Henry George, for example, I recommend that he or she acquire and cherish a wealthy, indulgent spouse."[13] In his essay, "Does Economics Have a Useful Past?," Stigler states: "An incomparably less important but otherwise similar group [to the Marxists] is the single taxers who arose under Henry George."[14] Although Mason Gaffney's introduction of the term "bafflegabbers" may be consid-

ered excessive, its application to Stigler, at least in this instance, may be appropriate.

These examples are not meant to suggest a conspiracy as such, but to display an implacable enmity among economists of the time, who were well-trained and placed and in some cases well-funded. These economists were unintentionally aided by other economists who, to some degree, favored land value taxation or older land nationalization programs. As pointed out in Chapter 2, the theoretic formulations of Leon Walras, P. H. Wicksteed, Irving Fisher and Paul Douglas (with Charles Cobb) presented difficulties for proponents of this tax reform. Their contributions undoubtedly advanced economic thought, but at the cost of leading most economists to ignore or underestimate the potential of land value taxation.

Brown's Stratagem

AS POINTED OUT IN THE FIRST PART OF CHAPTER 6, Brown could identify several economists of note who were sympathetic with land value taxation. Herbert J. Davenport was generally seen as a "limited" supporter, but John Commons was, perhaps, the more consistent advocate. Yet studies of Commons frequently fail to mention this component of his views. Brown could not have been unaware that he was virtually alone in the task he described to Dick Netzer as his "main contribution," that of putting the theory of land value taxation into "the language of contemporary economics."[15]

Yale to Missouri

Brown spent six years at Yale as an economics instructor. As a graduate student and instructor there he wrote nine journal articles and had three books published by Macmillan. Although Brown made only positive comments about his life in New Haven and his subsequent move to Columbia upon the invitation of Herbert J. Davenport, it is difficult to explain why Brown was not promoted at Yale. Although the department (of business and economics) at Missouri enjoyed the temporary fame of hosting Veblen as well as

Davenport, both would leave within a year. In the Fisher-Brown correspondence there is no evidence of a "falling out" despite their published differences of opinion on capital and interest theories. None of Brown's publications dealt directly with land value taxation, but he was presumably candid about his views with his colleagues. Brown's motive for going to Missouri may have simply been pecuniary, a higher salary and greater ease in obtaining promotions. However from a strategic standpoint the venue of a Yale (despite the relative weakness of its economics department) would seem to have been preferable to that of Missouri in the promotion of his cause. One suspicious development was that Yale hired T. S. Adams away from Wisconsin in 1917 and Adams, a tax and labor specialist, was an adamant anti single-taxer.

J. B. Clark[16]

It was from Missouri that Brown "announced" his advocacy in a 1917 JPE article, "The Ethics of Land-Value Taxation." In terms of his stratagem Brown had accomplished a prerequisite for any effective advocacy: he was a trained and recognized (published) economist. He did not write his books on international trade and transportation rates for this purpose. He would demonstrate continuing interest in these areas of economics, but the books and articles did serve to bolster his credibility as an economist when he began to publish on land value taxation. The article sets the tone and style of Brown's advocacy that would continue for more than 50 years. Moreover, it was the nucleus upon which further refinement would be attempted in three subsequent books that would cumulate in his 1932 *The Economic Basis of Tax Reform.* The JPE article's title is somewhat misleading as Brown's discussion is multifaceted, but in addressing the ethical objections to single taxation he was acknowledging the long-time source of much antipathy to George's proposal and confronting it directly. Yet Brown began the article by referring back to his earlier exchanges with Fisher and Fetter (and by extension with Clark) on the importance of the distinction between land and capital. The article both elaborates on the single tax idea without a single reference to Henry George and refutes several of the most common objections to land value taxation. Two opponents are named: J. B. Clark for his "lure of the increment's role in the settlement of the American West" argument (ignoring A. S. Johnson's more recent restatement of the argument) and F. A. Walker for his (and many others') contention of "unfair confiscation" in the single tax idea. Brown made clear his differences with John Stuart Mill, Frank Taussig and Davenport on the question of whether only the unearned increment should be taxed away.[17] What he failed to do in the article was to make the positive case for the results of land value taxation that he subsequently turned to, especially in his 1923 text, *Economic Science and the Common Welfare*.

E. R. A. Seligman

Neither Brown's nor Davenport's 1917 articles provoked a response from the profession. This could have been interpreted in two ways: they held the high theoretical ground in the matters they brought up, or they were being ignored. Brown began to publish articles in the JPE on tax incidence and in a note in the QJE, "An Oversight in the Theory of Incidence," he criticized a segment of Seligman's analysis in the third edition of his *The Shifting and Incidence of Taxation*. Seligman did not respond. Brown's choice of the QJE was perhaps somewhat calculated, as Taussig and Seligman were tacit rivals. In 1924 Brown published his *Economics of Taxation* (with seven explicit criticisms of Seligman's analytical prowess) as well as his combative "The Single-Tax Complex of Some Contemporary Economists." His text did succeed in establishing himself as an "authority" or "specialist" in the field of public finance. Further articles, in particular his 1939 JPE article on the incidence of a general sales tax, added to this recognition.[18] Yet Brown knew that he was unlikely to succeed in greatly influencing the "reference group" to which Gaffney referred. In a letter to a sympathetic Glenn Hoover in 1927 Brown explained: "The Seligmans, Hunters, Adams, Elys, Plehns, Lutzs [Harley Leist], et. al. aided and abetted by the National Tax Association and the National Association of Real Estate Boards constitute an effective group, largely because they have directly or indirectly access to nearly all students and the rest of us to just a few.

Those trained under them use their texts and repeat their views."[19] Seligman's only response or mention of Brown came in a note to his 30-page chapter on the single tax of the 10th edition of his *Essays in Taxation* of 1925.[20] This chapter, which was never substantively altered over the long course of text's run, has been challenged by Andelson and Gaffney[21] and by Gaffney.[22] In his note Seligman said: "A more recent defender of the single tax is H. G. Brown, Two Essays on the Taxation of Unearned Income, Columbia, Mo., 1921, whose contentions are effectively ridiculed in an amusing article by W. I. King, "The Single-Tax Complex Analyzed. . . ."[23] The cosmopolitan, erudite and generally quite liberal Seligman did a disservice to his discipline and his own reputation by never recognizing Brown's *Economics of Taxation* as the most constructive book on tax incidence (in English) in the interim between Edgeworth's 1897 "The Pure Theory of Taxation" and the early 1940s books of Due and Von Mering.

Richard T. Ely

In a 1927 letter to Emil O. Jorgensen, Brown revealed not only his opinion of Richard T. Ely and his Institute, but also his somewhat vacillating thought on how to best deal with antagonists such as Ely. Jorgensen's *False Education in our Colleges and Universities* is more accurately described by its subtitle, *An Expose of Prof. Richard T. Ely and His "Institute for Research in Land Economics and Public Utilities."* (By 1925 the Institute was located at Northwestern University but had no official affiliation with the university.) Jorgensen's tactic, mildly put, was one of denunciation. Brown, who seems to have known him, wrote with the purpose of explaining why he had not "endorsed" Jorgensen's expose by adding his name to what he called "your Education Protective Association." Brown began relating an encounter at an AEA meeting with a University of Wisconsin professor who was also a member of the Institute, M. G. Glaeser. Glaeser announced to the roundtable group discussing public utility regulation that he wished the subject were taxation so that he could demonstrate that at least he did not have a "single tax complex." Brown, after meeting the man, indicated that he was impressed with his sincerity and commented: "I am of the impression that there is distinctly less prejudice than there used to be but that the majority of economists do not thoroughly understand the problem." Further he suggested that the Institute might not be as bad as Jorgensen had implied. With a hint of sarcasm Brown wrote: "I rather suspect that its main purpose is less to influence legislation that it is to give prestige to real estate men through making it appear that the work of a realtor is 'professional,' analogous to that of the lawyer, doctor or engineer and requiring university training for its most successful pursuit."[24]

Brown seemed to want to give Ely, personally, the benefit of the doubt. "It is quite possible that he is unconsciously prejudiced—I very much doubt that he is consciously dishonest—by his own economic gains from land speculation. At any rate, his thinking on the subject is terribly confused, but no more so, perhaps, than the thinking and writing on various phases of taxation of the redoubtable Edwin R. A. Seligman of Columbia University."[25] But Brown was not finished with Ely.

> I quite agree that Ely is entirely wrong as regards the particular points in dispute, but my guess would be that his being wrong is the result of muddle-headedness or a very great prejudice, or both, rather than of conscious intellectual crookedness. In short, while you assert that Ely is competent and that therefore he must be intellectually dishonest, I am not so sure that he is competent in this field. My guess is that he is hopelessly incompetent, that he has no clear conception of the problem and that, as it is usually impossible to "teach an old dog new tricks," he never will be.[26]

In his letter Brown went on to chide Jorgensen for possibly alienating public utilities by depicting them as completely supporting Ely's taxation views. He personally thought that some utilities had relatively little of their property in the form of land ownership and thus had no strong reason to oppose land value taxation. This of course presupposed that they were properly regulated so as to indemnify the public for the franchises which the utilities had been granted. He added that he knew parties in the Southwestern Bell Telephone Company whose views were closer to his and Jorgensen's.

He closed the letter by praising Jorgensen's chapter "The Fallacies of Professor Ely" for its arguments and for employing what Brown termed the "laughter" method as opposed to Jorgensen's general tone of denunciation.[27]

Brown apparently immediately decided to test the water and submitted an article to *The Journal of Land & Public Utility Economics*. "Should Bare-Land Value Be Taxed More Heavily" appeared in Volume 4 of the journal. The article is notable for the tone and style adopted by Brown to reach what he perceived the readers of such a journal to be. That a cat and mouse game was afoot was probably clear to all. A rejection would have been "proof" of prejudice while acceptance was "proof" that there was no prejudice.

Brown continued his "experiment" by publishing in the *Public Utility Fortnightly* in 1929 and in *Tax Facts* in 1930.

Frank H. Knight

Gaffney's implication that Brown was somewhat naïve in his assessments of his opponents such as Ely can be better assessed after taking into consideration what Gaffney termed "The Chicago School Poison." A better term would be simply the "Knight-Stigler Poison," as Gaffney's treatment bears witness to. Brown published frequently in the JPE from 1917 to 1928. There were nine articles, six of which dealt with aspects of land value taxation. Jacob Viner and H. C. Simons demonstrated over the years an appreciation for Brown's work on tax incidence. Although neither was known to favor the single tax idea, they shared with Brown a strong discontent with Seligman and his students' domination of the field. Frank Knight was at the University of Iowa from 1919 to 1927. Thus I would disagree with Gaffney that the editors of the JPE "baited" Brown into submitting his "Single Tax Complex" article.[28] I do agree with his assessment of Willford I. King's response. Despite the nature of King's attack, Brown seemed not to be upset by it, perhaps because he knew himself to be in part responsible for creating this opening.

Knight had announced his thorough opposition to single taxation early on but did not "show his hand" explicitly until his 1953

Freeman article, "Fallacies in the Single Tax," with one exception. The Brown-Knight correspondence indicates a collegial friendship. In one letter Knight was inquiring about a position at Missouri for Aaron Director who Knight indicated was having difficulty finding an appropriate position and enclosed an open letter of recommendation from Lionel Robbins.[29] Brown responded that his department would welcome such a highly qualified candidate, but that the opening Knight had heard of was only for one year.[30] Knight and Brown shared, for diametrically opposed reasons, an aversion for time preference explanations of interest. Finally, C. Lowell Harris recalls that Knight spoke highly of Brown despite their differences.[31]

The exception mentioned above was a 1933 review by Knight of George R. Geiger's *The Philosophy of Henry George*. In a letter to John Ise discussing who would be a good choice to lead the attack on the single tax at a forthcoming session at the Mid-West Economics Society meeting, Brown cited the following section of Knight's review as a demonstration that Knight was "a bit rabid in his opposition."[32]

> All this reasoning is on a mental level not above that involved in the simpler operations of arithmetic. The economic and social ideas of Henry George are as a whole at the same pre-arithmetical level, the level of those held before and since his time by all who have held any at all, apart from an insignificant handful of competent economists and other negligible exceptions. Henry George's claim to be an economist (or social philosopher either) rests on the possession of linguistic powers not uncommon among frontier preachers, politicians, and journalists, and on the fact that his particular nostrum for the salvation of society appeals to a number of people, no doubt for much the same reasons that made it appeal to him, and which give many other nostrums their appeal. Such economic ideas are important because they are, apparently, prerequisite to the achievement of any prominence at all in the promotion of economic reform.
>
> It seems a fact, reasonable a priori and conformable to history and experience, that popular thinking about the criteria of thinking runs into instrumentalism; and that in the field of social relations the formula "truth is what works" means that it is what sells goods, wins votes, and in general brings distinction and power, the things men desire in social relations . . .

Under such conditions, truth must very shortly come to mean what serves the purposes of those "in power." An instrumentalist theory of social truth has meaning only with reference to a dictatorship, i.e., as a form of power, or with reference to an end of social action universally and unquestionably accepted—which is contrary to fact and is indeed the essence of the social problem. It should not be thought accidental or unnatural that a large fraction of the peoples of European civilization have already accepted political systems in which the pretense that public policy can be determined by free popular discussion—or safely permitted to be the subject of such discussion—is dropped. Every indication points to an early extension of such a system over the nations where it does not already obtain. The newspaper and radio have made of every national group a crowd, and the idea that a crowd could possess political intelligence and virtue can no longer be taken seriously. If society is to get the management required for the effective application of modern technology and the maintenance of social against special interests, it will apparently have to get it in the historically venerable way of Dei gratia! The notion that management might be left to the intelligence and impartiality of the citizenry was a dream of a century which did not foresee modern technology or means of communication—but more particularly did not foresee modern psychology, especially in its practical sense, the twin arts of salesmanship and propaganda.[33]

Given this, Brown didn't think Knight would be a good choice. He commented: "But Knight's approach is so peculiar, so likely to have a recondite, psychological, and even a metaphysical tinge that I fear attention will be turned away from the arguments usually appealed to by the opposition, allow no chance to answer these usual arguments, and, therefore, no chance to weaken the hold of the arguments most needing to be weakened."[34]

Brown, for his part, had favorably reviewed Geiger's book for *The Philosophical Review*. In the review he commented: "It must be admitted with regard to economists, whatever may be true of philosophers, that very many, probably the majority, are antagonistic. Such forthright views about the rent of land as those of Henry George are not favored in what are currently reckoned, academically, as 'the best circles' and are not conducive to the acquisition of academic prestige."[35]

Conclusion

WAS BROWN NAÏVE? YES AND NO. No, because he pretty much knew what was going on, as is indicated above. He knew he was not succeeding in convincing very many of his fellow economists and especially those specializing in public finance. Yes, in the sense that he believed a bit too much in the good will of his fellow economists and probably tended to exaggerate what little support he had in academia. Yes again, if naiveté is defined as dogged optimism. In 1927 he responded to a letter from John H. Sherman of Lake Forest College, Illinois:

> Thanks for the implied compliment—if it be such!—that I enjoy the fervor of a "crusader" and the satisfaction of a "martyr." So far as I can see, I have at least no martyrdom either to glory in or to lament. Thus far my job appears to be secure and, as jobs go, it does very well. That I should have any better job in different circumstances, is much to be doubted. As regards a "crusader's" fervor, I confess to mixed motives. It is an economist's business to point out, when he can, how our quasi-voluntary co-operative system of getting a living can be improved and, of course, I have some interest in that task. But along with any enthusiasm which I have on that account, there is also a very strong emotion of mixed despair, disgust and contempt—does it seem to you sometimes that it is rage?—for the exceedingly sloppy thinking of which supposedly distinguished economists allow themselves to be guilty in this matter. . . . Inertia and tradition are immensely powerful even among those who pass as the intelligentsia.[36]

Brown published extensively in Georgist journals in the 1930s and early 1940s.

From its founding in 1941 he wrote almost exclusively for the *American Journal of Economics and Sociology* for almost 30 years. In one of the 40-plus articles he wrote Brown drew an analogy that was meant to be instructive, but was at the same time personal. In the 1956 article titled "Academic Freedom and the Defense of Capitalism,"[37] he wove into this theme the medical history of puerperal (or childbed) fever. In essence the cause of the death of one of twenty women in childbirth was recognized in 1847 by a young Hungarian obstetrician, Ignaz Phillip Semmelweiss. It was a physician-carried infection easily avoided, Semmelwiess found, by antiseptic cleansing of the hands. The medical establishment of the time had catalogued a list of 30 possible causes of wildly different origins and drove Semmelwiess from his post. Using now de Kruif's Microbe Hunters,[38] Brown finishes the history with Louis Pasteur's dramatic interruption of a lecture on the subject of the fever by a learned physician in the late 1870s. Pasteur, a chemist, declared the cause was microbes carried to their patients by doctors. When the lecturer allowed that Pasteur may be right but opined that finding such a thing as a microbe was impossible, an enraged Pasteur went forward, grabbed a piece of chalk, declared he had found it and drew a chain of circles on the blackboard. Brown then related that his own mother, despite the general acceptance of Semmelwiess's prescription, had died, to the best of his knowledge, of puerperal fever in 1891. He then drew the rather dramatic comparison of a smug profession ignoring truth or reason for 50 years and in doing so violating the oath of "do no harm" to that of his own. Brown's story omitted some details. He was eleven when his mother died. Pasteur was almost 60 at the time of the incident and shared with Brown a crippling leg affliction.

In summary, Brown's stratagem was a simple one. He was said to be first and foremost a teacher. Any dedicated teacher's strategy involves informing, reasoning, provoking, interacting, iteration, patience and hoping for the best.

Notes

1. Mason Gaffney (1994). "Neo-classical Economics as a Stratagem against Henry George." *The Corruption of Economics.* Eds. Mason Gaffney and Fred Harrison. London: Shepheard-Walwyn: 123.

2. Mason Gaffney (November 26, 1997). Letter to author: 1. Personal Files. Iowa City, IA.

3. I do not wish to slight especially Joseph Dorfman's *The Economic Mind in American Civilization* or the *New Palgraves* and other period studies which I regularly consult. Although the three studies I cite might be termed "biased," such bias provides a needed focus which is lacking in other studies.

4. Mason Gaffney (1994): 77.

5. F. W. Garrison (1913). "The Case of the Single Tax." *The Atlantic Monthly* December: 737–746.

6. Mason Gaffney (1994): 76–77.

7. Steven B. Cord (1984[1965]). *Henry George: Dreamer or Realist?* 2nd ed. New York: Robert Schalkenbach Foundation: 115

8. Allyn A. Young (1916). "Nearing's Income; King's Wealth and Income." *Quarterly Journal of Economics* 30 (3): 586.

9. Steven B. Cord (1984): 121–123.

10. *Ibid.*: 104.

11. C. R. McCann, Jr. and Mark Perlman (1993). "On Thinking About George Stigler." *The Economic Journal* 103 (July): 996–997.

12. George J. Stigler (1941). *Production and Distribution Theories*. New York: Agathon Press Inc.: 193.

13. George J. Stigler (1982). *The Economist as Preacher and Other Essays*. Chicago: University of Chicago Press: 33.

14. *Ibid.*: 116–17. The complete paragraph is the following:

> A school may be based upon policy views rather than upon economic analysis or scientific methodology, and its life will normally become longer. Marxism is perhaps as much a political party as a school, but its longevity as a school is due to the fact that it is not a scientific body of knowledge (although its works have scientific content). Given its non-scientific role as an instrument of economic reform, it can ignore and has ignored almost every advance in economic theory and research which it has been unable to reconcile with its scripture. An incomparably less important but otherwise similar group is the single taxers who arose under Henry George.

15. Dick Netzer (2001). "What Do We Need to Know about Land Value Taxation." *American Journal of Economic and Sociology* 60 (Supplement): 99.

16. Brown discussed Clark more directly in later articles. See, for example, Harry Gunnison Brown (1958) "Foundations, Professors and 'Economic Education.'" *American Journal of Economics* 17 (January): 152–155.

17. An extensive examination of Brown's article can be found in William A. Fischel's contribution, "The Ethics of Land Value Taxation Revisted: Has the Millennium Arrived Without Anyone Noticing?" in *Land Value Taxation: Can It and Will It Work Today?* (Ed. Dick Netzer. Cambridge, MA: Lincoln Institute of Land Policy, 1998). Fischel's treatment is not unsympathetic, but rather overemphasizes Brown's willingness to entertain special considerations for landowners and his acceptance of a gradualist implementation of land value taxation. In later writings Brown would emphasize that his special considerations constituted "a slight theoretical qualification." (*Economic Science and the Common Welfare*, 6th ed., 1936: 404) Brown elsewhere interpreted a gradual approach as a definite step by step process of substantial periodic lowering of the taxation of improvements in tandem with a raising of the tax on land rent.

18. Harry Gunnison Brown (1939). "The Incidence of a General Output or a General Sales Tax." *Journal of Political Economy* 47 (April): 254–262, and "A Correction." *Journal of Political Economy* 47 (June): 418–420.

19. Harry Gunnison Brown (October 13, 1927). Letter to Glenn L. Hoover. Joint Collection University of Missouri Western Historical Manuscript Collection-Columbia and State Historical Society of Missouri Manuscripts: 1–2.

20. E. R. A. Seligman (1925). *Essays in Taxation.* 10th ed. New York : The Macmillan Company.

21. Robert V. Andelson and Mason Gaffney (1979). "Seligman and His Critique from Social Utility." *Critics of Henry George: A Centenary Appraisal of Their Strictures on* Progress and Poverty. Ed. Robert V. Andelson. Rutherford, NJ: Fairleigh Dickinson University Press: 279–290.

22. Mason Gaffney (1994): 59–63.

23. E. R. A. Seligman (1925): 97.

24. Harry Gunnison Brown (January 14, 1927). Letter to Emil O. Jorgensen. Joint Collection University of Missouri Western Historical Manuscript Collection-Columbia and State Historical Society of Missouri Manuscripts:1.

25. *Ibid.*: 2

26. *Ibid.*

27. Emil O. Jorgensen (1925). "The Fallacies of Professor Ely." *False Education In Our Colleges and Universities.* Chicago: Manufacturers and Merchants Federal Tax League: 34–183. Steven Cord and Robert V. Andelson discuss some of Jorgensen's points in "Ely: A Liberal Economist Defends Landlordism" in *Critics of Henry George* (1979): 313–325. See also Gaffney (1994): 82–103.

28. Gaffney (1994): 123.

29. Frank H. Knight (April 24, 1939). Letter to Harry Gunnison Brown. Joint Collection University of Missouri Western Historical Manuscript Collection-Columbia and State Historical Society of Missouri Manuscripts.

30. Harry Gunnison Brown (April 27, 1939). Letter to Frank H. Knight. Joint Collection University of Missouri Western Historical Manuscript Collection-Columbia and State Historical Society of Missouri Manuscripts.

31. [C. Lowell Harris] (1986). Letter to Spencer Carr. Personal Files, Iowa City, IA.

32. Harry Gunnison Brown (January 9, 1939). Letter to John Ise. Joint Collection University of Missouri Western Historical Manuscript Collection-Columbia and State Historical Society of Missouri Manuscripts:1.

33. Frank H. Knight (1933). "Review of *The Philosophy of Henry George* by George R. Geiger." *Journal of Political Economy* 41 (October): 689–690.

34. Harry Gunnison Brown (January 9, 1939): 2.

35. Harry Gunnison Brown (1934). "Review of *The Philosophy of Henry George* by George R. Geiger." *The Philosophical Review* 43: 217.

36. Harry Gunnison Brown (October 13, 1927). Letter to Dean John H. Sherman. Joint Collection University of Missouri Western Historical Manu-

script Collection-Columbia and State Historical Society of Missouri Manuscripts: 1.

37. Harry Gunnison Brown (1956). "Academic Freedom and the Defense of Capitalism." *American Journal of Economics and Sociology* 15 (July): 177–179.

38. Paul de Kruif (1926). *Microbe Hunters.* New York: Harcourt, Brace & Company: 145–146.

Chapter 7

Regulation and Rate-Making

Introduction

AN EARLY AREA OF SPECIALIZATION IN ECONOMICS dealt with theoretical and practical questions on the regulation of transportation and public utility concerns. The *Munn vs. Illinois* decision of the Supreme Court and the Interstate Commerce Act of 1887 moved the railroad industry toward a regulated status, and the 1906 amendment to the act gave the Interstate Commerce Commission the authority to set maximum rates. Along with legislative and judicial bodies and state and federal commissions, economists took an active interest in the attempt to regulate railroads in the public interest. That the "public interest" could be furthered by regulation was an assumption shared by all of these parties as well as, perhaps, the managers of the railroads.[1]

Harry Gunnison Brown's first published article[2] and his doctoral dissertation[3] were concerned with questions related to railroads and rate-making. His interest may have been sparked by the economic implications of recent judicial decisions and legislative acts. Also, Arthur T. Hadley, then president of Yale University and friend of Irving Fisher, was an authority on railroad economics and maintained an interest in this field.[4]

Brown's 1916 *Transportation Rates and Their Regulation*, published by Macmillan, endeavored to present a complete theory on the subject.[5] In the preface, Brown cited John Bauer for a thorough reading and criticism of the text. Brown's 1925 article, "Railroad Valuation and Rate Regulation," featured a defense of reproduction cost as a basis for the valuation to be used in rate-making.[6] This article sparked a long-running debate with John Bauer and James C. Bonbright, among others. Alfred E. Kahn in 1970 said this article contained the classic argument against the original cost valuation method in rate-making.[7] Brown's subsequent articles and exchanges centered on this and related questions.

Early Articles

IN HIS 1907 PAPER, Brown attempted to reconcile two views on how railroad rates should be made. One view was that railroad traffic should be charged "what the traffic will bear," which would admit discriminatory charges. The other view was that charges should correspond strictly to costs. He assumed that the railroads, whether competing or noncompeting, were subject to "increasing returns,"[8] due primarily to the relatively high overhead costs with largely constant operating costs. He noted that in these conditions additional freight should be desired as long as it pays at least the "special additional cost" incurred. Brown regarded the question of whether the extra freight also should pay its portion of the fixed expenses as an open one. He appeared to take "marginal cost" pricing as a first principle and regarded the distribution of the fixed costs as dependent on the competitive conditions.

He then considered the relative rates charged by competing railroads and noncompeting railroads in terms of discrimination among places, commodities and corporations. He found in general that competing railroads, relative to noncompeting ones, would tend to discriminate in favor of some cities, larger corporations and certain commodities. The competing railroads would alter prices to attract business from competitors while the monopoly railroad would reduce rates only to attract new customers. Competition would force a reliance on cost of service as opposed to value of service and would tend to distribute the fixed costs in production to direct costs incurred. He concluded that discriminatory reductions in rates were socially desirable as long as they resulted in increased traffic and not simply the diversion of traffic.

In this article and another published in the next year on the similarities of monopolistic and competitive price-making,[9] Brown clearly was not thinking of the competing railroads as competitive in the usual sense of "perfect competition." Not only was his assumption of declining average costs over the relevant range incompatible with competition over time, but in the case of railroads, only a limited number of competitors was conceivable. He seemed to ignore the possibility of ruinous competition resulting in a monopoly for the advantaged firm. He did indicate that should both rivals follow a price-cutting strategy, both would lose, but he then retreated from this issue.[10]

It is possible that Brown, like Hadley,[11] did not believe railroads to be natural monopolies, and thus, he assumed that declining costs would not prevail in the long run. Nevertheless, Brown's approach seemed to be that of comparing a monopolistic situation with that of imperfect competition, especially emphasizing in the latter case the ability to profitably expand business only at the expense of rival railroads. Thus, the imperfectly competing firms faced a more elastic demand for their services than would a monopoly railroad. Brown called this the "relative responsiveness" as opposed to the "absolute responsiveness" of demand.

The similarity that Brown wrote of in competitive and monopolistic price-making was, in essence, that of the shared condition wherein marginal revenue equals marginal cost. Of course, he did not express it in this manner. He assumed that in both types of market structure, firms or the firm would search for a greater profit by altering their prices. Following Cournot in a (for Brown) rare exercise in mathematics, he demonstrated how a firm would consider a price reduction. He identified the variables in the following fashion: P = original price; ΔP = change in price; $P - \Delta P$ = new price; S = original sales; ΔS = contemplated increase in sales; $S + \Delta S$ = total new sales; E = original total expenses; ΔE = change in expenses; $E + \Delta E$ = total new expenses. He expressed the condition under which the price reduction would be made as (1) $(P - \Delta P)(S + \Delta S) - (E + \Delta E) > (P)(S) - E$. The expression rearranged becomes $[(P)(\Delta S) - (\Delta P)(S) - (\Delta P)(\Delta S)] > \Delta E$, which in discrete form illustrates that price reductions should be carried out to the point where the increment to revenue equals the increment to cost. He elaborated his condition (1) by adding a return to new capital employed, $[(-i)(C)]$, and a return to risk-taking, $(-R)$, to the necessary increase in revenue. Finally he added a term to allow the firm to accept current losses, expecting as a result to gain higher profits in future years from the larger market share acquired in so doing.

The discounted value of these additional estimated profits he added to the left-hand side of the inequality as

$$\frac{G_2}{1-i} + \frac{G_3}{(1-i)^2} + \ldots$$

As noted, he felt that the condition as stated was applicable to both monopolistic and competitive firms.

Transportation Rates and Their Regulation

WHILE STILL AT YALE, Brown reviewed several books for the *American Economic Review* on railroad economics, most notably a translation of C. Colson's *Railway Rates and Traffic*.[12] He also published a long article, "The Competition of Transportation Companies,"[13] which he incorporated into his 1916 text, *Transportation Rates and Their Regulation*. Despite his intention to write a complete treatment of this subject, reviews of the book pointed out areas that were omitted or treated in insufficient detail. The reviews, however, were for the most part laudatory. J. M. Clark and Maxwell Ferguson recommended the book as a supplement to William Z. Ripley's longer text, *Railroads, Rates and Regulation*. J. M. Clark noted several new contributions to the field of study and had special praise for Brown's extensive treatment of freight discrimination.[14] Ferguson and an anonymous reviewer for the *Political Science Quarterly* found controversial Brown's free trade philosophy, which, they claimed, permeated the work. Ferguson also noted Brown's adherence to the "cost-of-service" principle and concluded:

> In the opinion of the reviewer . . . the broadminded analysis of the rate discrimination, in the refreshing clearness with which the salient principles of rate making and rate regulation are set forth, and in the more even distribution of emphasis as between the "inner philosophy of rate regulation" and the "mere record of past legislation and description of existing law," the author has produced a work which has much to commend it.[15]

In the *Economic Journal,* C. F. Bickerdike noted that Brown had produced a "handy volume" with "convenient" summaries of the ICC decisions.[16] Although Brown's book was 347 pages in length, this was about one-half that of similar studies of the time. Bickerdike was not wholly uncritical of the study and was concerned about the differences between present positions of railroads in Europe as compared to those of the United States. He ended his review with the following comment:

> It may be said that that is a point on which practical railwaymen may be left to form their own opinion, and that, in so far as the suggestion is true, self-interest will prevent companies from making anomalous cutting rates. It is questionable, however, whether they are not driven by mere competition into adopting a short-sighted, hand-to-mouth policy which is both damaging to themselves and fruitful in injustice and economic waste for the community in general. It is these fundamental questions at the basis of the whole system of "charging what the traffic will bear" which seem to merit more attention than they receive in this book, and it may be hoped that Professor Brown, whose powers of economic analysis are undoubtedly high, will pursue these matters somewhat further.[17]

In the following year, Brown included a condensed version of this book in his *Principles of Commerce.*[18]

Brown's general approach to the subject of rate-making was to attempt weighing the effects on the general economic welfare. Unjustifiably discriminatory rates, in his view, were analogous to protective tariffs in that they discouraged commerce and created economic incentives and disincentives that tended to reduce society's welfare.

In a 1933 review article, D. Philip Locklin distinguished three approaches in the literature from the 1840s on.[19] The earliest view of Dupuit and others was that overhead costs best explained the differential pricing by railroads. In 1891, Frank Taussig challenged this view by arguing that railroad rates were primarily a case of joint cost and should be analyzed as such.[20] E. R. A. Seligman criticized Taussig's conclusion on the grounds that the existence of monopolistic conditions was the essential explanation of discriminatory pricing.[21] A. C. Pigou's *Wealth and Welfare* of 1912 rekindled the unresolved controversy, and he and Taussig carried on a debate in several issues of the *Quarterly Journal of Economics.*[22] One of the points of contention was whether the costs of providing railway service to different customers should be considered to be joint or simply common costs. Taussig preferred to extend joint cost analysis to much of railroad rates, while Pigou saw common costs as prevailing in general. Pigou also opined that the element of monopoly needed to be present in order to explain discriminatory rates.

Brown commented early in *Transportation Rates and Their Regulation* on this exchange in a footnote.[23] His view was that railroad rates were not perfectly analogous to the normal case of joint costs, such as that of the production of beef and hides. A much closer analogy obtained when the case of back hauls was considered, and Brown saw this as a truer case of joint costs. He noted that as a railroad plant neared full utilization of its capacity, the complementary provision of services would become competitive. In his explanations of discrimination in rate-making, he utilized the overhead cost approach and found monopoly to be essential in explaining such discrimination, especially in the long run. In his general discussion of transportation costs, he utilized the term "sunk costs," which he was likely to have borrowed from Fisher's *Elementary Principles of Economics.*[24] J. M. Clark objected that Brown uncritically included the entire transportation investment in sunk costs and ignored the dynamic aspects of such investment.[25] However, Clark agreed that unregulated railroads would charge "what the traffic will bear"—that is, the competing railroad would charge what the traffic will bear "without being diverted" and what the traffic will bear "without being destroyed" in the case of a monopoly. Brown did not in this text express a firm opinion on the best test of the reasonableness of rates and on what these rates should be based.

Brown was concerned in this text with the nature of competition in railroad and water transportation as well as with its limitation, which was due to monopolistic tendencies throughout the industry. Some earlier writers on the subject had noted that competition in the railroad industry tended to be selective, and they opted to consider particular types of competition.[26] Brown expanded on the usual classification by distinguishing: (1) competition of different shippers over the same route; (2) competition of routes; (3) competition of directions; (4) competition of locations; and (5) competition directed against potential local self-sufficiency. (Earlier treatments had combined competition of directions and locations into the competition of and for markets.) Brown's first category applied only to water and motor vehicle transportation. In terms of the competition of routes, he diagrammed cases where more roundabout routes may be economically defensible. He proposed that the long- and short-haul rule be arranged so that some level of economic waste be accepted in order to gain the stimulus of active competition. This might entail allowing slightly higher rates on intermediate traffic on the roundabout line to allow this line to remain in competition with the more advantageously situated line.[27]

The conditions where competition of directions could take place were shown by Brown to be complex. He argued that where two or more lines led from a producing center in different directions to other markets, their rates could be competitive if, for example, there were other transportation lines capable of serving these markets from other areas. The additional lines could influence prices so as to make the original lines competitive in their rate-making. Competition of locations existed where transportation lines compete in the sense that they attempt by offering low rates on traffic to encourage the development of industries that utilize their services rather than the services of rivals in other locations. Closely related to this idea was Brown's "competition against potential, local self-sufficiency." The transportation line in this case would set rates so as to elicit traffic that would not otherwise be economical and in doing so mitigate against local self-sufficiency.

Brown saw railroads, with few exceptions, as partial monopolies in the sense that the various types of competition would not alter a railroad's dominance over intermediary traffic over its lines. In addition, the tendency toward collusive behavior among railroads contributed to their ability to set rates as they desired. He argued, however, that competition among railroads was not inevitably of the ruinous type unless the railroads were operating substantially below their capacities. He believed that the era of speculative railroad building was past, and he thus maintained that legally enforceable rate agreements and legally recognized pooling would alleviate the discrimination in rates resulting from "cutthroat" competition. He argued that the Interstate Commerce Commission should sanction such open agreements in addition to setting maximum rates. Brown's views were somewhat unusual at the time, but they did reflect in part the earlier views of Arthur T. Hadley.

All of the forms of competition that Brown had considered could result in discrimination in pricing among places. He proceeded to delineate the cases where the resulting discrimination was economically undesirable and where it was economically defensible. From the viewpoint of the general community welfare, he found economic waste when railroads discriminated in favor of competitive and against intermediate traffic. He reasoned that where rates were discriminatory, the average utilization of railroad plant capacity was not furthered. The discrimination in time arbitrarily would deprive certain areas of the benefits of their natural advantages with regard to economic development, while encouraging development of areas that possessed less economic potential. In a similar vein, he argued that should the equally promising intermediate locations be disadvantaged by discriminatory rates, then transportation patterns would be distorted in an uneconomic fashion. He maintained that discrimination of this type resembled a protective tariff in its economic consequences. He also objected to discrimination for or against imported goods in the setting of railroad rates. In addition, the state commission's practice of setting unduly low rates on intrastate traffic to encourage local production he found objectionable.

Brown next examined cases in which rate discrimination among places could be deemed economically defensible. He found discrimination to a limited degree against intermediate points on roundabout routes to be acceptable. The limitations would be that no rate be set below the additional cost involved for competitive or through traffic, and no greater for noncompetitive traffic than what would ensure a reasonable return on the capital required to carry the traffic. He recognized that in practice such rate settings would be a complex matter and could only be approximated so as to leave the two lines in the same competitive conditions as had prevailed before regulation. Were the traffic on the direct line relatively light, then the company may be allowed to discriminate against intermediate traffic to maintain its competitive position. He also found justifiable low rates that favored points in competition with water routes as opposed to points connected only by rail lines. Discrimination in favor of traffic that is competitive with potential local self-sufficiency was also found to be desirable as long as goods could be delivered at less than the local cost of production and pay at least their marginal cost of transport. Brown argued that under certain circumstances discrimination in favor of goods transported for export could be advantageous. This was where net earnings to transportation industries rose as a result, and the gain to domestic producers offset the loss to consumers.

Finally, the case of discrimination between opposite directions in the rates charged different goods was considered. This referred largely to the question of the pricing of back hauls, and he found discrimination here to be acceptable, as it would lead to a greater utilization of transportation facilities. Brown's analysis of discrimination predated the emergence of air and truck transport as viable alternatives to rail and water transport. Although this would complicate questions of discrimination, his general principles still would have application. Alfred E. Kahn noted that he drew heavily on Brown's examples and discussion in the section of *The Economics of Regulation* on rate-making in the presence of competition.[28] Kahn also had praise for "his painstaking elaboration of the consistent economic principles for the guidance of regulatory policy."[29]

Brown then summarized the development of rate regulation and examined the rulings of the Interstate Commerce Commission on what constituted "reasonable" rates. He emphasized the difficulties involved in determining rates due to the variety of railroad services and the extent to which joint costs prevail. The ICC rulings took into account comparisons of rates, cost of service, earnings, and the efficiency of management. Brown concluded that the Commission tended to follow, where possible, the cost-of-service principle. He also noted that reasonable rates should be a reasonable return on the fair value of railroad property. As to whether a fair value was better represented by the original investment or the present physical value, he opined that the Commission was somewhat equivocal in its rulings but tended to favor the latter. Brown next examined representative cases where the Commission ruled on instances of discrimination among places, goods and shippers. He found occasion to criticize some rulings as inconsistent with the principles he had elaborated upon.

In his final chapter, Brown roundly criticized governmental interference and subsidization of transportation. He argued that navigational laws designed to develop a national merchant marine and exclude foreign vessels from coastal trade was economically unsound. With the possible exception of certain defense considerations, he objected to subsidization of shipping in the form of harbor or river improvements at public expense. Even where it was deemed necessary for the government to spend in order to improve waterways, he argued that the clearly benefited localities should pay and, if possible, through user charges. He also objected to the "pork barrel" or "log-rolling" influences in governmental decisions that tended to prevail in the above actions as well as in the setting of protective tariffs. The subsidies for railroad building and in particular the land grants to railroads were questioned similarly. He argued that these policies were of dubious benefit in terms of economic development and represented to some degree an unsanctioned redistribution of wealth. He indicated that there was no way to determine whether these policies had led to an enlargement or shrinkage of national wealth as no means of comparison existed, but he maintained that in terms of general principles the policies did not appear to have been advisedly adopted. It may be noted here that Brown rarely discussed antitrust policies. When he did, he appeared to accept the existing legislation and encouraged its rigorous enforcement. In the 1930s he adamantly opposed relaxation of the laws.

AER Article: "Railroad Valuation and Rate Regulation"

THE 1898 SUPREME COURT DECISION in *Smyth vs. Ames* provided a criterion by which to judge the reasonableness of rates set by the state commissions.[30] The criterion proved not only to be very vague but also to be the subject of controversy until the Hope case of 1944 reversed it.[31] The Court had mentioned in its criteria that consideration be made for the "original cost of production" and for the "present as compared with the original cost of production," along with several other factors. A rising general price level (especially during World War I and the postwar era) sharpened the controversy as to whether "original costs" or "reproduction costs" should be the prime consideration in rate determination. The railroads then favored the use of reproduction costs while the regulatory commissions tended to favor the use of original costs. Justice Louis D. Brandeis in his dissent in the Southwestern Bell Telephone case of 1923 attacked the *Smyth* vs. *Ames* decision as "legally and economically unsound."[32] He favored a prudent investment basis of earning control and found the reproduction cost method of valuation to be the cause of great and continuing difficulties in rate determination.

His view echoed that of several economists specializing in railroad and public utility economics. One of their number, I. Leo Sharfman, was criticized by Brown in 1922. Sharfman, in his *American Railroad Problem: A Study in War and Reconstruction*, had advocated that an original cost basis be employed with the qualification that the original investment had to have been made prudently. Brown declared the issue "to be clearly joined" in his review of the book.[33] The reproduction cost approach he favored was qualified as "the cost of bringing into existence a plant capable of performing the required service."[34] He also indicated that he favored policies that would make the returns to a quasi-monopoly conform to those that arise under competitive conditions. Most of his criticism of Sharfman's views was made more extensively in a later article.

This article, "Railroad Valuation and Rate Regulation," appeared after Frederic G. Dorety (then vice president and general counsel of the Great Northern Railway) had contested Judge Brandeis's views in a *Harvard Law Review* article.[35] Dorety's article contained both legal and economic arguments for the continued consideration of reproduction costs. Brown gave no indication of having read this article, and subsequent critics tended to group it with Brown's article and respond primarily to Brown. In his article, Brown noted that just as the courts were beginning to emphasize the cost of duplicating a service, a number of economists had begun to insist that only the original cost or original investment be considered. He first criticized on grounds of fairness the original-cost doctrine, interpreted without qualification to be the original money cost. He argued that should the price level fall significantly and if valuation were based on original costs, the returns to investors in effect were guaranteed relative to other investors at the expense of the consumers of the service. In the event of rising prices, he maintained that with the reproduction cost standard, neither the public nor the investors taken as a whole would lose or gain in real terms. He did note that bondholders would lose, to the benefit of shareholders. Brown was unhappy with the high percentage of bond investments in railroads and utilities and suggested that measures to redress the balance would be beneficial. (He appeared to assume that railroad and/or utility costs would move coincidentally with the general price level and that lags in the adjustment did not occur.)

Brown's greater concern was with the economic consequences of allocations that would result from original-cost methods. Once again, with changes in the price level, traffic would tend to be unduly discouraged or encouraged. He maintained that when prices fell, rates based on original cost would remain relatively high and would create a distortion because they would not conform to the "rule" of charging only enough to cover the extra or additional cost incurred and thereby discourage traffic. On the other hand, with a significant inflation the original-cost method would result in rates lower than would yield a reasonable rate of return on the present cost of construction while unduly encouraging railroad traffic.[36] This would lead to traffic exceeding the capacity of the plant and force a rationing of service with further undesirable results. The construction of new facilities at higher costs and the charging of higher rates would force an arbitrary discrimination among shippers or other customers and ultimately result in the misallocation of industry and population.[37] He applied the same reasoning to the case where price changes affected only the costs of construction and maintained that, in general, economic loss would result were actual, past cost the basis of rate-making.

Brown turned next to an element in the valuation of railroad property—the value of land. Despite his own views on land value taxation, he indicated that the original cost method of valuation was an inappropriate way of denying the increments in land value to the owners of railroads and public utilities. He argued that such denial would tend to discourage the building of railroads, as the potential buyers of land for other than railroad use could receive increments to the value of other land. Brown's remedy, of course, was to tax all land values equally. He explained that where compensation of some form was to be provided for the loss of the unearned increment in land values, further economic distortion would result.

On more practical grounds, Brown conceded that for "short periods" regulatory commissions should rely on actual book costs. However, if actual costs have widely diverged from the current costs of production, the latter must be given priority.

An important remaining question was how to treat depreciation and obsolescence in rate-making. Brown's view was that, all other things being the same, these factors should not be allowed to influence rates during the life of a plant. Thus, rates should be set so as to meet the repair and replacement costs plus a fair rate of return for the life of the plant. A properly graduated depreciation fund would allow the rates to be invariant with respect to these costs. He noted as well that in the early period of low plant utilization it may be appropriate, as patronage grows, to add these early losses to the cost of construction or duplication.[38]

Finally, he considered the special case of the "weak" versus "strong" railroads wherein both roads connect the same terminals. He reasoned that if the "weak" road could not support itself by charging enough on intermediate traffic to maintain rates competitive with the "strong" road, then abandonment of the line should be considered. Rates set in a manner to allow the "weak" road to survive would create a misallocation of resources. Even the consolidation of the two lines would not necessarily resolve the difficulty, as pricing schemes would either uneconomically favor the terminal or intermediary points or discriminate unfairly among shippers. If the "strong" railroad's advantage was due entirely to its control of the best location and if it was not capable of carrying all traffic, then he conceded that the costs and valuation of the "weak" road should determine the rates, leaving the "strong" road with a return in excess of what it could otherwise earn. He felt that only taxation (not regulation) was the proper means for the community to secure this economic rent.[39]

Response of the Profession and Brown's Replies

JAMES BONBRIGHT WROTE A REVIEW ARTICLE on contemporary books dealing with valuation in a 1926 issue of the *Quarterly Journal of Economics*.[40] He mentioned Brown's article in two different contexts. Bonbright suggested that the current literature in favor of a simple actual cost base of rate control had ignored the problem of economic rent.[41] He noted that the low, actual cost rates on utilities or transportation services amid greater land values and construction costs would not necessarily be of benefit to the community at large. Landowners may be able to increase the rent on properties served by the utilities or railroads and in doing so benefit disproportionately from the low rates. Although Brown did not use this approach, it accords with his view that regulation would only redistribute land value increments among certain groups and not benefit the public as a whole. Bonbright further noted that all the books reviewed, including one by John Bauer[42] (the only one for which he had praise), failed to answer effectively the criticisms Brown made of the original cost basis of rate-making.[43]

John Bauer responded to Bonbright's challenge within the year.[44] Bauer was at the time and continued for many years to be a distinguished specialist in this area, as was Bonbright.[45] Bauer, a 1908 Yale Ph.D. and friend of Brown's, unlike Brown, had practical experience in working with regulatory commissions. Although he believed that the use of reproduction cost in regulation decisions would "destroy" regulation, he did not immediately assault Brown's economic rationale.

> I shall frankly state that except for the requirements of effective regulation and financial stability, I should agree with Brown that the reproduction cost basis would be more in harmony with general economic forces.[46]

He therefore focused on practical considerations and tried to demonstrate that Brown's objections, although in the main economically sound, were of little consequence in actuality.

Taking practical considerations into account, Bauer argued that reproduction cost was far too indefinite a base and the concept had led to endless controversy in the past. Not only was such a base difficult to measure as well as to reach an agreement on how to measure, but it continually was changing as well. He pointed out that approximately 75 percent of railroad expenses were in the form of operating costs and taxes that were calculated on an actual cost basis. The remainder, the return on investment, should have a definite basis for calculation and actual or original cost was the most expedient choice. In addition, to obtain a desirable level of financial stability for railroads and public utilities, the original cost basis would be best suited. He noted in this regard that bond issuance was the major form of financing these institutions and that inflation would tend to incite speculation in railroad and utility stocks; deflation would exert exceptional pressure on the vulnerable financial structures.

In his reply to Bauer, Brown noted that in emphasizing reproduction costs, the courts did so in part because of the perceived unreliability of actual cost figures and the accounting associated with them. Despite the inherent inexactness of reproduction cost estimates, he insisted that their economic importance was such that they could not be ignored when they markedly differed from actual cost figures. He further countered that the financial structure of railroads and utilities was not unique or deserving of special guarantees. Should companies be forced into receivership, he believed that reorganization could be accomplished without undue harm to the interests of the public.[47]

In addressing Brown's economic arguments, Bauer maintained that Brown had exaggerated the potential divergence between calculations of reproduction cost and original cost in several respects. Bauer questioned whether an actual cost basis would discourage investment in a period of rising prices.

> The actual cost basis would provide all the capital economically needed to take care of developing business but would not exercise any artificial influence in stimulating or retarding the flow of capital.[48]

His interpretation of the "artificial influences" was that the reproduction cost basis in an inflation would stimulate investment, assuming adjustment in rates was made promptly.

In reply, Brown argued that such investment would be economically irrational and that the substitution effects of the return to regulated industries falling relative to that of other industries was his real concern.

Bauer questioned the importance accorded to the expectations of buyers of railroad and utility stock regarding a rising price level and increments in the value of land. In reply, Brown noted, in some cases, they indeed may be of little importance, but they remain as reasons for the present cost of the necessary plant to provide the service diverging from the original cost of the plant. Bauer also asked whether the public should deny to railroads and utilities the "unearned" increments to their land values, given the conceded element of public interest in these businesses.

Bauer stressed that even the 25 percent of railroad expenses corresponding to the return on investment would be the subject of a gradual adjustment over time, and thus the small percentage of costs that are not reflected would be counterbalanced by the gains resulting from the ease of application and stability permitted by the original cost formula. He also questioned whether it was a reasonable possibility that the construction of new facilities, as in the case of railroads and utilities, would create a conflict in rate structures between old and new plants. He emphasized in the case of utilities their local nature.

Brown replied that construction of new trackage to accommodate increasing demand was not altogether unlikely and so his point stood. However, he recognized that increased competition of other types, such as trucks and airplanes, may reduce the need for new construction in the future. He also defended his use of large price changes. Bauer found such use too unrealistic; even accepting substantial price variations, the effects of the price changes would be reduced due to the structure of railroad costs. Brown maintained that the extreme conditions that would result in large price movements were recurrent in history and at the present in evidence in Europe and to a lesser extent in the United States. For there to be dramatic changes in the costs to the industry, he pointed to technological breakthroughs or inventions as sources for such changes. He concluded his reply to Bauer by insisting that valuation based on reproduction costs should continue to play a role in regulation despite the difficulties it presents in application. Where the book valuation is thought to have diverged significantly from present costs, then the book costs should be modified with index numbers of general and specific price changes and compared with the engineering estimates. The courts and the commissions could then utilize all this information to make their decisions. For Brown, the added difficulty should result in a worthwhile economic dividend.[49]

In 1927, John Bauer was the chairman of the AEA Round Table Conference on the problem of effective utility regulation.[50] Of the participants in the discussion, only Brown spoke in defense of the use of reproduction cost. As reported by Bauer, Brown reiterated his position that original cost pricing did not accord with the principle of seeking to make rates of public utilities correspond to rates that would prevail under competitive conditions. He also disagreed with a proposal that would tend to assure the financial stability of public utilities. All of the participants challenged Brown's points of view. Robert Hale accused Brown of tacitly assuming a greater mobility of capital than was practicable in the cases of utilities and railroads.[51] He was joined by Professor Ruggles in insisting that the public interest in utilities was sufficient to justify spreading the risk-taking in utility investments beyond the investors to the community or to the general public.[52] Clarence E. McNeill questioned the elasticity of demand for utility services. According to his studies, the demand was "particularly" inelastic; thus, the effects suggested by Brown would be of negligible importance. Finally James Bonbright, noting that Brown's actual proposal was to ascertain the present cost of the most economical plant that might be constructed, concluded that the financing of utilities would become "utterly unmanageable."[53] It was agreed that in the next meeting of the association the subject would be discussed once more.

At this meeting Bonbright and Arthur Hadley presented the major papers, and comments by I. L. Sharfman and Brown were recorded as well.[54] Hadley's paper dealt with the economic meaning of valuation; Bonbright's compared the merits of reproduction cost versus prudent investment on four different grounds. Bonbright stated that with respect to the criterion of efficiency, reproduction cost, interpreted as the cost of providing the service with a new plant, did have advantages over original cost. However, he viewed the application of such a standard to be impossible. He also noted the adverse cyclical effects of original cost pricing as opposed to reproduction cost pricing, but he felt this was of dubious importance. In his discussion of using reproduction cost as a means of attaining rates at competitive levels, he directly attacked Brown's and Dorety's argument that this was necessarily the correct approach to the problem of rate-setting. He pointed out what he saw as the "fatal flaw" in Brown's reasoning, accepting for the sake of argument that the cost of reproducing the service was a practical rate base. Bonbright contended that reproduction cost pricing of services would not conform to the ideal of marginal cost pricing any more than would prudent investment pricing. He further stated:

> Even Professor Brown, who is the leader in this type of defense, recognizes in a measure the dilemma in which he is placed. For while conceding that a price based simply on variable costs would come closest to meeting his ideal as a regulator of socially desirable traffic, he recognizes that the application of such a principle would be quite impossible on grounds of financial expediency.[55]

Bonbright's solution was to allow railroads and utilities to charge rates that in many cases would be in excess of a fair profit on investment and would invoke the recapture clause of the Transportation Act of 1920 to normalize profit-taking.

In response, Brown admitted that reproduction cost prices would be likely to vary from the ideal of long-run marginal cost pricing. However, he maintained that on practical grounds, the better regulatory policy was to allow returns only as high as is necessary to earn a reasonable return on the current cost of plant construction. Where the plant capacity was utilized only partially, he argued that low (marginal cost) rates ultimately would retard economic development as a fuller utilization of capacity was achieved. He asked,

> How test, in the long run, the desirability of such (new) construction other than by charging rates high enough to yield a return thereon, and so judging whether there would be enough business at those rates to justify the construction?[56]

He also added to his earlier arguments against strict reliance on original cost by pointing out that when the obsolescence of a plant was accelerated, to insist that the public continue to pay on the basis of original cost was to impose on the public the rule of "dead hand."

Brown continued to support his position in an address to the American Bar Association,[57] and in an article in the *Public Utilities Fortnightly*.[58] On these occasions, for the most part, he reiterated his earlier arguments. However, he did emphasize that he thought that no formula could be devised to directly determine regulatory rates. He also noted that rates are changed only at intervals in the regulatory process and that the efficiency of management becomes a larger factor in the firm's profitability. After 1930, he made no further comments on the issues other than in the various editions of his textbooks. Bonbright in particular would continue to pursue the arguments especially in his *The Valuation of Property*.[59]

Comments and Conclusions

THE QUESTION (AS BROWN LEFT IT AT THAT JUNCTURE) probably was carried by the proponents of the use of original cost as the rate base (or some variation of it). However, as Bonbright pointed out in a 1940 paper, it was largely on the grounds of administrative feasibility and better financial adaptation that writers favored this approach.[60] A final verdict on the purely economic merits of the two approaches remained unresolved, at least in part. M. G. de Chazeau strongly challenged the application of either method to the determination of service charges as distinct from the determination of appropriate earnings.[61] Hotelling's advocacy of pure marginal cost pricing questioned the relevancy of the use of the average cost pricing implicit in both the original and present cost approaches.[62] Brown's arguments as to the distortional effects of original-cost based pricing encountered the problem of the "second best." His premise that the attempt to set prices of public utility services at competitive levels would further economic efficiency also was questioned, as was the case for marginal cost pricing.

Brown's advocacy of the use of reproduction cost considerations in pricing decisions was not as successful as his attack on original cost usage. However, he was able to raise significant economic questions in this area and emphasize the relevancy of current and future costs for long-run pricing policies. In the difficult search for "general principles" to guide efficient regulatory practice, his was a positive contribution. This view of Brown's contributions is supported in the comments made in 1961 by James C. Bonbright.

> Thirty years or more ago, the case for the replacement-cost principle ... was developed with great skill, and with particular reference to railroad rates, by Professor Harry Gunnison Brown of the University of Missouri. Similar views have been expressed by later writers, but they have lacked both the incisiveness and the firmness of conviction that make Brown's earlier analysis a classic in the history of rate regulation.[63]

Elizabeth Read Brown related to the author that it was the custom of John Bauer while on vacation with his wife to pay a visit to Brown's home, both in Mississippi and Missouri. She said the two Yale classmates would avoid "shop talk" until dinner was over whereupon they would retire to another room and recommence with great relish their debate begun some 30 years in the past.

Notes

1. See Gabriel Kolko (1965). *Railroads and Regulation 1877–1916*. Princeton, NJ: Princeton University Press.

2. Harry Gunnison Brown (1907). "The Basis of Rate-Making as Affected by Competition Versus Combination of Railroads." *Yale Review* May: 79–86.

3. Harry Gunnison Brown (1909). *Some Phases of Railroad Combination*. Diss. Yale University. (I should note that I have not examined the dissertation as it was deemed not suitable for copying. However, I am confident that his later book and articles capture its essential content.)

4. See Melvin Cross and Robert B. Eklund (1980). "A. T. Hadley on Monopoly Theory and Railroad Regulation: An American Contribution to Economic Analysis and Policy." *History of Political Economy* (Summer): 214–232.

5. Harry Gunnison Brown (1916). *Transportation Rates and Their Regulation*. New York: Macmillan & Co.

6. Harry Gunnison Brown (1925). "Railroad Valuation and Rate Regulation." *Journal of Political Economy* 33 (October): 505–530.

7. Alfred E. Kahn (1970). *The Economics of Regulation: Principles and Institutions*. Vol. 1. New York: John Ekelund & Sons: 111.

8. The term, then common, refers to economies of scale or decreasing average total costs.

9. Harry Gunnison Brown (1908). "Competitive and Monopolistic Price Making." *Quarterly Journal of Economics* 22: 626–639.

10. Brown (1907): 81.

11. Cross and Ekelund (1980): 227–229.

12. Harry Gunnison Brown (1915). "Review of C. Colson's *Railway Rates and Traffic*." *American Economic Review* 5 (September): 601–603.

13. Harry Gunnison Brown (1914). "The Competition of Transportation Companies." *American Economic Review* 4 (December): 771–792.

14. John Maurice Clark (1917). "Review of *Transportation Rates and Their Regulation*." *Journal of Political Economy* 25 (February): 208–209.

15. Maxwell Ferguson (1916). "Review of *Transportation Rates and Their Regulation*." *American Economic Review* 6 (September): 633.

16. C. F. Bickerdike (1916). "Review of *Transportation Rates and their Regulation*." *Economic Journal* 26 (103): 348–350.

17. *Ibid*.: 350.

18. Harry Gunnison Brown (1916). *Principles of Commerce*. Part 3. New York: Macmillan & Co.

19. D. Philip Locklin (1933). "The Literature on Railway Rate Theory." *Quarterly Journal of Economics* 47 (February): 167–230.

20. Frank Taussig (1891). "A Contribution to the Theory of Railway Rates." *Quarterly Journal of Economics* 5 (July): 438–465.

21. E. R. A. Seligman (1891). Discussant in the *Publications of the American Economics Association* 6: 56, 58.

22. A. C. Pigou and Frank Taussig (1913). "Railway Rates and Joint Costs." *Quarterly Journal of Economics* 27 (February, May and August): 378–384, 535–538 and 687–694 respectively.

23. Brown (1916): 9.

24. Irving Fisher (1911). *Elementary Principles of Economics.* New York: Macmillan & Co.: 297.

25. J. M. Clark (1917): 209.

26. See William Z. Ripley (1912). *Railroads, Rate and Regulation.* New York: Longmans, Green & Co.: 264–296.

27. Brown (1916): 47–49.

28. Kahn (1970): 166.

29. Alfred E. Kahn (September 5, 1984). Letter to author. Personal files, Iowa City, IA.

30. *Smyth* vs. *Ames* (1898). 169 U. S. 466: 546–547.

31. *Federal Power Commission* vs. *Hope Natural Gas Co.* (1944). 320 U. S.: 591, 601.

32. *Southwestern Bell Telephone* (1923). 262 U.S.: 276, 289–312.

33. Harry Gunnison Brown (1922). "Sharfman's *American Railroad Problem.*" *Quarterly Journal of Economics* 36 (February): 323–324.

34. *Ibid.*: 321.

35. Frederic G. Dorety (1923). "The Function of Reproduction Cost in Public Utility Valuation and Rate-Making." *Harvard Law Review* 37 (December): 505–530.

36. Brown (1925): 508.

37. *Ibid.*: 510.

38. *Ibid.*: 522.

39. *Ibid.*: 529–530.

40. James Bonbright (1926). "Progress and Poverty in Current Literature on Valuation." *Quarterly Journal of Economics* 40 (February): 295–328.

41. *Ibid.*: 205, n. 8.

42. John Bauer (1925). *Effective Regulation of Public Utilities.* New York: Macmillan & Co.

43. Bonbright (1926): 326.

44. John Bauer (1926). "Rate Base for Effective and Non-Speculative Railroad and Utility Regulation." *Journal of Political Economy* 34 (August): 470–500.

45. Ronald H. Coase described Bonbright in 1966 as an old master and a new master in the field of public utility pricing in *The Economics of Regulation of Public Utilities*, Conference at Northwestern University, Evanston, IL, July: 19–24.

46. Bauer (1926): 487.

47. Harry Gunnison Brown (1926). "Railroad Valuation Again: A Reply." *Journal of Political Economy* 34 (August): 500–508.

48. Bauer (1926): 487.

49. Brown (1926): 507–508.

50. John Bauer (1927). Chairman of Round Table Discussion, *American Economic Review* 17 (Supplement): 123–127.

51. *Ibid.*: 125.

52. *Ibid.*: 125–126.

53. *Ibid.*: 126.

54. James Bonbright (1928). "Railroad Valuation with Special Reference to the O'Fallon Decision." *American Economic Review* 18 (Supplement): 181–205.

Arthur T. Hadley (1928). "The Meaning of Valuation." *American Economic Review* 18 (Supplement): 173–180.

55. Bonbright (1928): 197.

56. Harry Gunnison Brown (1928). "Valuation of Public Utilities Discussion." *American Economic Review* 18 (Supplement): 213.

57. Harry Gunnison Brown (1928). "Economic Basis and Limits of Public Utility Regulation." *Reports of the American Bar Association* 53: 717–737.

58. Harry Gunnison Brown (1929). "Present Costs." *Public Utilities Fortnightly* 3: 237–246.

59. James Bonbright (1937). *The Valuation of Property*. Vol. II. New York: McGraw-Hill Book Company: 1086–1089 and 1104–1108.

60. James Bonbright (1940). "Major Controversies as to the Criteria of Reasonable Public Utility Rates." *American Economic Review* 30 (February): 382.

61. M. G. de Chazeau (1937). "The Nature of the 'Rate Base' in the Regulation of Public Utilities." *Quarterly Journal of Economics* 51 (February): 298–316.

62. Harold Hotelling (1938). "The General Welfare in Relation to Problems of Taxation and Railway and Public Utility Rates." *Econometrica* 6 (July): 242–269.

63. James C. Bonbright (1961). *Principles of Public Utility Rates*. New York: Columbia University Press: 226.

Chapter 8

International Trade and Finance

Introduction

IN THE AREA OF INTERNATIONAL TRADE AND FINANCE, Brown published articles and texts early in his career. Two of the influences on his thinking with regard to a theory of international trade were William Graham Sumner and, to a lesser extent, Henry George. Although Sumner and George were decided opponents on the issue of the single tax, they were uncompromising advocates of free trade in the classical tradition of Smith, Ricardo, Mill, et. al. Whether Brown actually studied with Sumner at Yale is uncertain as he never recorded that he had done so, although E. W. Kemmerer, in a review of one of Brown's text, mentioned that Brown had been Sumner's pupil.[1] Brown at least shared Sumner's fondness for Thomas Buckle's *The History of Civilization in England* and quoted from it on occasion.[2] Brown recommended George's *Protection and Free Trade* as a "very readable exposition."[3] In the area of foreign exchange he drew heavily from the works of Franklin Escher and George Goschen.[4]

International Trade and Exchange

BROWN'S *INTERNATIONAL TRADE AND EXCHANGE* was published first in 1914 and subsequently republished in two volumes in 1920 and 1921 as *Foreign Exchange* and *International Trade* respectively.[5] In 1916, he had combined a condensed version of these books with a section on transportation costs to make up his *Principles of Commerce*.[6] In addition to Kemmerer, Frank Taussig, Sumner Slichter and C. F. Bickerdike reviewed Brown's books.

Brown introduced his discussion in *Foreign Exchange* with chapters on the laws of money and the nature of bank credit along the lines of Fisher's interpretation of the quantity theory. Taussig objected that such an introduction was not necessary.[7] In the analysis of foreign exchange, exchange rate determination and specie flows, the reviewers found Brown to be fundamentally sound. However, they did not think he made any original contributions other than an emphasis on the possibilities of countries having different standards of value. A reviewer in the *Economic Journal*, Hartley Withers concurred and stressed its similarity to Escher's *Elements of Foreign Exchange*, but to be more abstract and theoretical and as a result was more "academic and *doctrinaire*."[8]

For his *International Trade* Brown was credited by Taussig and Bickerdike with having presented the orthodox or "British School" view of trade theory with consistency and precision. Taussig himself was considered heir to this line of thought, but he found fault with Brown's assumption that specie flow would take place quickly and would have a rapid effect on prices. Taussig did not doubt the conclusions of orthodox theory but felt it was poorly adapted to the problems of real, day-to-day trading situations. Taussig also mentioned that he did not agree with the contemporary criticisms of German economists of the comparative advantage approach. Bickerdike found Brown's analysis superior to that of J. S. Mill in its examination of the gains and losses from protective tariffs and similar to Edgeworth's more recent treatment, although lacking his graphical apparatus.[9]

A few years later Frank Graham attacked the comparative advantage rationale for free trade.[10] He specifically mentioned Brown's assertion (deduced from Mill's treatment) that the greater the variety of goods a country can offer for export, the better was the country's position in trade.[11] Graham argued that this was untrue and that greater variety was more likely to result in less favorable terms of trade unless totally new goods accounted for the variety. Brown, however, had argued that the statement was true only in general terms and that the greater variety of goods and services would imply a greater volume of trade, with all its attendant benefits.

Brown dedicated much of the text to question of free trade, which he advocated with little or no concession to protectionists' arguments. As mentioned by Kemmerer and Taussig, this view was the traditional one but had been challenged by economists both here and abroad for several years. For example, in 1890, Simon Patten had based a case for protection on dynamic considerations not treated in the classical approach. Taussig commented that

> there is more to be said on the workings of protective duties in detail, and on the conceivable advantages to be secured by them, than Professor Brown is ready to grant. The controversy between *Agrastaat* and *Industriestaat* is not to be dismissed so lightly as is done by Professor Brown; and the possible advantages from protection to young industries is underrated by him.[12]

Brown found the effect of a protective tariff on national wealth to be negative. He argued that in the long run export trade would be restricted by the tariff barrier to importation. A misallocation of resources was another consequence. He maintained that the gain to the protected industries would be more than balanced by the loss to others in the country. He found improbable but conceivable that a tariff would allow an industry to attain economies of scale so as to compete internationally. He recognized (following Mill and others) a possible indirect gain from improved terms of trade but concluded that this would only be temporary, as normally alternative outlets for the exports of the trading partners would be found. Citing the example of Great Britain, he showed that countries with low tariff barriers could compete successfully with countries with high tariffs and not be forced to raise their own rates.

Brown went on to discuss the distributional consequences of protective tariffs. Taussig complained in his review that too much emphasis was given to the effects on the distribution of wealth and especially on the development of economic rent.[13] Brown argued that the general result of a tariff would be to indirectly cause interest rates to rise as the degree of specialization in production fell; wages would fall as well. He differentiated cases where protected and unprotected goods were produced under various cost conditions. Where both types of goods were produced under conditions of substantially constant costs, the rise in the price of the protected goods would exceed the proportionate increase in money wages and prices, thus resulting in a lower real wage rate. Where the protected goods were produced under increasing cost conditions while the unprotected goods were produced under constant cost conditions, the effect would be a gain for landholders smaller than the loss to wage-earners. Brown found conceivable a case where wage-earners gained at the expense of landholders. This was where the protected goods' cost of production was constant and those of unprotected goods was increasing, and wage-earners as consumers were chiefly buyers of protected goods. Here, once again, the losses to the landholders would exceed the gains to wage-earners. He also argued that protection could benefit one area of the country at the expense of another and also may be conducive to the development of monopolies.

Brown next turned to special arguments for protection. He dismissed many arguments as fallacious or in need of exceptional circumstances to have any measure of validity. He felt that the current argument—then associated with Adolph Wagner[14]—for the protection of agriculture in "older," crowded European countries relied on the assumption that great restrictions would be placed upon trade in the future. Should trade prove to be no more restricted or freer, the country employing this policy would be damaged greatly because that country would have failed to take advantage of its comparative advantage in manufacturing products. His objections to the infant industry argument were primarily practical. He doubted especially that the political process could be relied upon to obtain the possible benefits of the strategy. He also argued that the benefits must somehow be compared to the losses to other less-favored industries before the strategy was adopted. He found military or self-sufficiency arguments for protection deserving of some consideration, but these were subject to reasonable objections as well.

Exchange with Thomas Nixon Carver

IN A 1919 NOTE TO THE *QUARTERLY JOURNAL OF ECONOMICS,* Brown criticized an argument made for protection by Thomas Nixon Carver in his *Principles of Political Economy.*[15] The note was titled, somewhat caustically, "An Eminent Economist Confused."[16]

Brown had noted earlier in his *Principles of Commerce* that Sidg-wick, Edgeworth and Carver held the opinion that in certain cir-cumstances protection could increase wages *and* increase na-tional wealth by "drawing labor out of lines of increasing cost."[17] Brown objected to the argument first made by Carver in 1902[18] that a move to freer trade could reduce national wealth. Carver had depicted a case where the removal of tariff barriers resulted in a switch from more to less labor-intensive cultivation. The dis-placed workers would find employment at lower wages, and the total product by assumption would be lower with landowners enjoying higher rents. Brown maintained that in this case there were two possibilities for the displaced workers. If they had no preferable alternative to their lines of work, they would be forced to accept wages low enough for the landlords to realize the same gain as would be forthcoming from the less labor-intensive pro-duction. Assuming the workers' productivity was unimpaired, the fall in wages would equal the rise in rent with no change in na-tional wealth. If a preferable alternative could be found by the workers, the landlords' rent would rise by more than the workers' wages fell. However, he conceded that although the "values" gen-erated in production would not fall, the "utilities" generated by it may. He hypothesized a case wherein the demand for a new product was largely by the wealthier classes as opposed to that of the old product.

Brown's point here, and the key point of his note, was that pro-tection in this hypothetical case was an inefficient means of ob-taining the desired results and that taxation of larger incomes—in particular, land income—was the preferable solution. Carver's re-joinder emphasized the different perspectives with regard to the question, international versus national.[19] He pointed out that the search for a preferred alternative may result in migration and, from the national standpoint, in a reduction in the national product. Brown's re-rejoinder pointed out that freer trade would increase per capita wealth of the hypothetical country except under highly unusual circumstances.

Book Reviews

IN THE 1920S, BROWN CONTINUED his interest in the international aspects of economics by reviewing books on the subject for the *American Economic Review*. He criticized John Henry Williams's explanation in *Argentine International Trade under Inconvertible Paper Money* for the rise in the gold premium.[20] He felt Williams's treatment tended to underestimate the effect of an over-issue of paper money. Williams had found instances in which increases in the gold premium took place concurrently with decreases in the volume of paper money. Brown noted that lagged effects may have been at work and that other temporary considerations, such as credit curtailment, business depression and falling prices in the rest of the world, may have contributed to the rise in the premium. Still, the principal cause may well have been previous over-issues of paper money. He objected to the author's "inductive verification" that there was a strong correlation between a high premium on gold with increased exports and diminished imports.[21] Brown maintained that the rise of the premium on gold relative to domestic prices of exported goods was the key factor and not the rise in the premium as such.

In his *Principles of International Trade*, Huntley M. Sinclair challenged the orthodox view that, under the gold standard, gold flows brought about adjustments for trade imbalances. Sinclair maintained "the adjustment would come in wages rather than through the influence of gold on prices."[22] Brown's reply was that this was too extreme a position; likewise, it was too extreme to assume that adjustment only could take place until the gold flow had been completed. He argued that it was not the gold flow per se but the decrease in demand for domestic goods or the increase in the demand for foreign goods that would lower domestic prices. He maintained that the question was essentially a monetary one.[23] Although Sinclair had found the quantity theory too simple a device for international finance, Brown defended the theory's usefulness. He recognized the postwar changes in international finance, such as the sterilization of gold by some countries, but he felt that the theory only needed to be further elaborated to account for these complications.

Finally, Brown reviewed Frank Taussig's *International Trade* in 1928.[24] He noted that Taussig's treatment conformed to the classical or orthodox approach. Although Brown concluded with a wholehearted recommendation of the work, he found objectionable Taussig's treatment of rent as a cost of production. Brown thought that Taussig's presentation slighted the importance of land as a price-determining factor and argued that rent was of equal importance in price determination. He cited the works of Jevons and Davenport in support of his view that the economic loss from the imposition of a tariff was the same whether labor, capital or land was diverted from its most effective use.

After 1930 Brown published sparsely in the field of international trade and finance. What little he did publish was primarily on international monetary policy.[25] Likewise, in his correspondence with Irving Fisher and James Harvey Rogers, Brown was concerned with price stability, recovery from the depression and the monetary standard. (His views in these areas were presented in Chapter 4.)

Conclusion

IN SUMMARY, BROWN DEMONSTRATED, as Taussig noted, a mastery of orthodox trade theory, but he did not make original contributions to the theory. He was an unyielding advocate and defender of free trade. Arguments made against free trade in Brown's early career would act as a catalyst for advances in trade theory, both strengthening and weakening the case for free trade. He defended the importance of the quantity theory of money as a key to the development of a more incisive view of international monetary relations. Without doubt, he would have supported the renaissance of the monetary approach to the balance of payments and exchange rates. He showed awareness that the theories of trade and finance had not reached the "final approximation" but felt that they stood "as a constant reproach to those who, through uneconomic interference with international trade, would line their pockets at the common expense."[26]

Notes

1. E. W. Kemmerer (1915). "Review of Brown's *International Trade and Exchange.*" *American Economic Review* 5 (June): 354–356.

2. Henry Thomas Buckle (1894). *The History of Civilization in England.* New York: Appleton.

3. Henry George (1891). *Protection or Free Trade.* New York: Henry George.

4. Franklin Escher (1911). *Elements of Foreign Exchange.* New York: Banking Publishing Co.
George J. Goschen (1896). *The Theory of Foreign Exchange.* London: Effingham, Wilson.

5. Harry Gunnison Brown (1914). *International Trade and Exchange: A Study in the Mechanisms and Advantages of Commerce.* New York: Macmillan Co.
Harry Gunnison Brown (1920). *Foreign Exchange: A Study in the Exchange Mechanisms of Commerce.* New York: Macmillan Co.
Harry Gunnison Brown (1921). *International Trade: A Study in the Economic Advantages of Commerce.* New York: Macmillan Co.

6. Harry Gunnison Brown (1916). *Principles of Commerce.* New York: Macmillan Co.

7. Frank Taussig (1915). "Review of *International Trade and Exchange.*" *Journal of Political Economy* 23 (June): 621–623.

8. Hartley Withers (1916). "Review of *Foreign Exchange: A Study in the Exchange Mechanism of Commerce* by H. G. Brown." *Economic Journal* 26 (103): 345–346.

9. C. F. Bickerdike (1916). "Review of *International Trade* by H. G. Brown." *Economic Journal* 26 (103): 346–347.

10. Frank Graham (1923–1924). "International Values Re-Examined." *Quarterly Journal of Economics* 38 (November): 54–86.

11. Brown (1916): 26–29.

12. Taussig (1915): 622.

13. *Ibid.*

14. Adolph Wagner (1901). *Agar- und Industriestaat.* Jena: Gustav Fisher.

15. Thomas Nixon Carver (1919). *Principles of Political Economy.* Boston: Ginn & Co.

16. Harry Gunnison Brown (1919). "An Eminent Economist Confused." *Quarterly Journal of Economics* 33 (May): 567–570.

17. Brown (1916) *Principles of Commerce:* 107.

18. Thomas Nixon Carver (1902). "Some Theoretical Possibilities of a Protective Tariff." *Publications of the American Economic Association* Series 3 (3): 167–182.

19. Thomas Nixon Carver (1919). "Rejoinder." *Quarterly Journal of Economics* 33 (May): 570–571.

20. Harry Gunnison Brown (1921). "Review of John Henry Williams' *Argentine International Trade Under Inconvertible Paper Money*." *American Economic Review* 11 (June): 308–313.

21. *Ibid.* : 311–312.

22. Harry Gunnison Brown (1933). "Review of Huntley M. Sinclair's *The Principles of International Trade*." *American Economic Review* 23 (March): 92–94.

23. *Ibid.*: 93.

24. Harry Gunnison Brown (1928). "Review of Frank Taussig's *International Trade*." *American Economic Review* 18 (December): 706–713.

25. Harry Gunnison Brown (1945). "Currency Devaluation and International Trade." *American Journal of Economics and Sociology* 5 (January): 227–237.

26. Brown (1923): 94

Chapter 9

Contributions as an Educator

Introduction

HARRY GUNNISON BROWN'S CONTRIBUTIONS as an educator are worthy of separate consideration. Beginning with an instructorship at Yale in 1909, he taught on a full-time basis for 51 years until retiring in 1960 at the age of 80. Even in retirement he gave guest lectures at the University of Missouri and elsewhere. David Kamerschen said of Brown: "I found him to be sharp as a tack analytically while still in his nineties."[1] At Missouri he carried a full load of classes while serving as departmental head for twenty-one years and as acting dean of the School of Business and Public Administration for six years. He evidently preferred not to take sabbaticals in order to keep his summers free for writing and relaxation. All this points to an exceptional dedication to the first requirement of his profession, instruction. Further evidence of his dedication and achievements in education may be found in the comments of his former students and colleagues. In addition to his various textbooks, Brown wrote several articles on teaching that reveal his approach to the teaching of economics.

Pinkney Walker, an ex-colleague during Brown's later years at Missouri, stated that "Dr. Brown was first and *foremost* a teacher."[2] Walker went on to expound on the qualities that made him an extraordinary lecturer. He reported that Brown was an "excellent speaker," "a masterful logician" and "a most effective and skillful debater." To these qualities Walker added that Brown exhibited "an unbounded enthusiasm and deep concern for and dedication to improve 'the common welfare.'"[3]

Walker's views find support in statements made by Brown's former students and by others who knew him. Alfred Kahn referred to Brown as a superb lecturer.[4] Lester Chandler, who studied and worked with Brown for four years, declared him to be a superb logician.[5] Joel Dirlam, a student, commented that Brown was an excellent debater "who welcomed challenge to his position."[6] Paul Junk referred to Brown as a master of the Socratic method in the classroom. Junk also noted that Brown would make use of parables, real world examples and rhetorical questions to make his points clearer.[7] Walker and others attest that Brown was not content that his students acquire technical competence alone in economic analysis but that they develop as well a philosophical framework in which economics is integrated into broader systems of thought. Walker and Chandler both noted that Brown believed that a more widespread understanding of economic principles could contribute to the advance of society and that he attempted to inculcate this spirit in his students from the introductory to the graduate levels of study. That Brown sought to give to students a basis on which to appraise economic institutions and proposals for economic reform also is clear. Finally, Walker declared Brown to be "far and away the best teacher I have ever known."[8]

DR Scott was a long time colleague and close friend of Brown. He was a professor of accounting and statistics and is best remembered for his *The Cultural Significance of Accounts*. Pinkney Walker reported that at a dinner in Brown's honor in 1951 Scott declared:

> The theoretical teaching for which he [Brown] has always stood has been the backbone of instruction in the School of Business and Public Administration during the first third of a century of its history. It has been the chief factor shaping the educational policy of the school. It has forced us all to think in terms of our economy as a whole. Thereby it has afforded a background against which to measure our several special interests.[9]

Methods and Concepts

BROWN WROTE A SERIES OF ARTICLES on the teaching of economics in the late 1940s.[10] One, "Objectives and Methods in Teaching the 'Principles' of Economics," listed economic fallacies to which students were likely to have been exposed. He recommended that special attention be given to the refutation of these fallacies. He saw the study of economics, as, in part, training in applied logic.

He felt that students should be shown "the usefulness of deductive reasoning from broad generalizations."[11] However, he did favor inductive verification of theories where possible. Quantitative expression of relationships, he maintained, would strengthen students' understanding and retention of concepts. Yet, he found unfair and unnecessary the use of calculus or complicated algebraic expressions or complicated graphs. For beginning students in most areas, he deemed simple arithmetic or simple algebra sufficient. Brown defended economic theory against the charge of inexactness by comparing the "given conditions" of the physicist to that of the economist, arguing that the methods of each were equally useful. He recommended that considerable class time be used for the examination of carefully chosen, illustrative examples following a discussion of the theoretical concepts involved. He further recommended that one to two class periods be given over to answering questions and altering examples to bring out their further ramifications until most, if not all, of the students demonstrate an understanding of the concepts. In this process, he suggested that hints be given in class that the examples might prove to be examination material.

Brown opposed the trend toward descriptive introductory courses that were burdened with definitions. He had found that the "facts" and definitions were likely to be soon forgotten and that emphasis on them would divert a student from gaining a basic understanding of cause and effect relationships in economics. However, social and political elements, where relevant, should be pointed out.

Brown encouraged student-teacher dialogue in the Socratic tradition. He maintained as a principle that no instructor should claim by his or any other authority the right to judge wrong any student's (well-intentioned) objections. If in dialogue the student's question could not be satisfied, then it was the instructor's duty to recognize his own error or deficiency in presentation.

As noted previously, Brown thought that courses in economics should not stop with the mastery of economic principles but should extend to the relationship of these principles to the welfare of society. He was aware that such an attempt could introduce subjective analysis, which in turn could become warped or biased. He warned:

> Nor is there any intention to suggest that the teacher should become a preacher or exhorter, even for so good an end as the general welfare. If the house, the playground, the school, the church, etc., have not given to the student any spark of altruism or any spirit of idealism, it is not likely that a college course in economics will do so.[12]

However, he felt that without exhortation the teacher could introduce such topics as exploitation or parasitism. Brown used such discussions to introduce his advocacy of land value taxation, free trade and regulation or elimination of monopolies. He was able to do this in an even-handed manner by welcoming objections to his views; if necessary, he introduced such objections himself. His evenhandedness may be seen in the reactions of his students. Their comments indicate that they were not always completely swayed by his arguments. Even his son Philips wrote that he was not convinced in the case of land value taxation that a separate assessment of land and improvements could be accomplished without great difficulty.[13] However, these same comments indicate that Brown was successful in eliciting a sympathetic understanding from his students on the principles of land value taxation. Brown ends this article on teaching in an optimistic fashion.

> The idealistic economist . . . must believe that his science contains the words—at any rate some of the words—of social salvation. Only so can his work continue to be inspired by the zest of anticipated usefulness.[14]

Principles Texts

AN EARLY PUBLICATION, *THE PRINCIPLES OF COMMERCE* (1916), was the nucleus of Brown's general textbook, *Economic Science and the Common Welfare*, which was first published in 1923. This text was revised five times and superseded in 1942 by *The Basic Principles of Economics*, which went through three editions. The 1946 edition was supplemented with a small companion volume, *A Postscript and Questions*. The number of revisions and editions would indicate that sales were at least adequate. Reviews of the text over the years, with few exceptions, found it praiseworthy.[15]

Reviewers were impressed with Brown's lucid style and his conciseness. *The Basic Principles of Economics* grew to 500 pages in length, but as one reviewer pointed out, competing texts of similar coverage frequently contained in excess of 800 pages.[16] Brown's text made very little use of graphs, charts or diagrams; thus, his writing style carried the burden of a clear exposition of relationships. The organization of the text would not be familiar to readers of contemporary texts in economics. The text, divided into two parts, dealt first with price determination, the general price level and trade while the second dealt with the distribution of the product. In this second part, chapters on the determination of utility, cost and value were indicative of Brown's early neoclassical approach. His organization was not drawn from that of other writers, although some influence of Fisher's *Elementary Principles of Economics* (1911), Taussig's *Principles of Economics* (1911) and Davenport's *Economics of Enterprise* (1913) may be discerned. (It seems odd to this author that Brown never recognized his general affinity with A. C. Pigou.) As noted in Chapter 4, Brown did not accept Keynesian analysis, and the later editions of his text did not mention directly this development. He dedicated a substantial portion of the text to questions of land value taxation; some reviewers found this excessive while other found that it added interest to the reading. Also controversial, the text implied his support for birth control. Later reviewers tended to find the text somewhat outdated, particularly because it was not as encyclopedic as the postwar textbooks.

Brown's political philosophy permeated the text. He lost no opportunity to make application of economic analysis to questions of public policy.

> I have attempted here to present a sort of philosophy or defense of the price system ("capitalism"),—not a defense of it as it is but an explanation of and defense of it as it might be.[17]

In a preliminary chapter ("Prejudice Versus Science"), he addressed the problem of bias in economic thinking from special or class interest or political affiliation.[18] He felt that these prejudices, in addition to ignorance and special bargaining, could lead a democracy to policies that were unwise for the general economic welfare. Although he found democracy deficient as a system in which to make economic decisions on the public level, he noted that the safeguards embodied in it made it superior to alternative systems. He found the growing influence of trained citizens to be a positive trend, if their training emphasized what he called "disinterested inquiry." He asked rhetorically:

> Why should we be so tremendously ashamed of an unimportant break in etiquette such as carrying to the mouth with a fork food supposed to carried by the hand, or appearance at a formal social function without the prescribed formal clothing, and be so little ashamed of a prejudice which controls our thinking? How is it that we look askance at the person whose pronunciation is provincial or whose sentences are ungrammatical yet fail to visit with disapproval the person whose emotions or class affiliations twist his reasoning processes out of all semblance of logical thinking?[19]

Brown counseled disinterested inquiry or a rigorous application of the scientific method coupled with concern for the common welfare.

Students and Legacy

MANY OF BROWN'S STUDENTS ACHIEVED PROMINENCE in the field of economics or in related areas. His students at either undergraduate or graduate level include Karl Bopp, Lester Chandler, L. Pao Cheng, Joel Dirlam, August Maffrey, Carl McGuire and Beryl Sprinkel.[20] Both of Brown's sons, Richmond and Phillips, studied economics under him at Missouri, and Phillips taught economics for many years at Southeastern Missouri State. Alfred Kahn, Russell Bauder, Mason Gaffney, and Paul Junk have indicated his influence on them through their association with him at Missouri without having been students. Brown's nephew, Milton Peers Brown, was a member and chairman of the Harvard Business School. Bopp commented in an essay written in honor of Elmer Wood, a longtime colleague and friend of Brown, on the environment he found at Missouri, which was one of intellectual ferment stimulated by DR Scott, Brown, J. H. Rogers and Myron Watkins.[21] At the University of Missouri for many years Brown was remembered through an annual memorial lecture given in his honor by the late Professor Walter L. Johnson in the introductory class Brown had taught for so many years The Department of Economics sponsors an annual lecture in topics of Brown's interest. Arnold Harberger, Mason Gaffney, Peter Mieszkowski, Daniel Holland and Alfred Kahn are among those who have given the lecture. Both an undergraduate and a graduate teaching award are given annually in Brown's name.

The true extent of Brown's legacy as an educator is impossible to measure. Beyond the thousands who heard him in the classroom and read his texts, many more heard him speak (gratis) to commercial, social and academic groups. Brown amply demonstrated the enthusiasm for economic education and reform that he wished to instill in his readers and listeners.

Notes

1. David R. Kamerschen (1987). "Some Surviving Elements in the Work of Henry George." *American Journal of Economics and Sociology* 46 (October): 490.

2. Pinkney Walker (1975). "In Memoriam." Memorial Service for Harry Gunnison Brown, March 23. Personal files, Iowa City, IA

3. *Ibid.*

4. Alfred Kahn (September 5, 1984). Letter to author. Personal files, Iowa City, IA.

5. Lester Chandler (December 17, 1978). Letter to Paul Junk as cited in *Selected Articles by Harry Gunnison Brown*. Ed. Paul Junk. New York: Robert Schalkenbach Foundation, 1980: xv.

6. Joel Dirlam (December 2, 1984). Letter to author. Personal files, Iowa City, IA.

7. Paul Junk (1980). Preface. *Selected Articles by Harry Gunnison Brown*. New York: Robert Schalkenbach Foundation: xii.

8. Walker (1975): 2.

9. *Ibid.*

10. Harry Gunnison Brown (1945). "Objectives and Methods in Teaching the 'Principles' of Economics." *American Journal of Economics and Sociology* 3 (October): 93–109.

———. (1946). "Rent Theory as a Teaching Problem on the Undergraduate Level." *American Journal of Economics and Sociology* 5 (January): 231–245.

———. (1946). "A Teaching Approach to the Incidence of Taxation of Capital."
American Journal of Economics and Sociology 4 (April): 389–401.

———. (1949). "Economic Fallacies and Economic Teaching." *American Journal of Economics and Sociology* 7 (January): 177–180.

11. Brown (1945): 95.

12. *Ibid.*: 107.

13. Phillips H. Brown (December 15, 1981). Letter to author. Personal files, Iowa City, IA.

14. Brown (1945): 110.

15. Reviews of Brown's books are listed in the bibliography.

16. George Sause (1958). "Economic Principles and Economic Analysis." *American Journal of Economics and Sociology* 17 (April): 333.

17. Harry Gunnison Brown (1942). *The Basic Principles of Economics.* Columbia, MO: Lucas Brothers: vii.

18. *Ibid.*: 3–8.

19. *Ibid.*: 7.

20. Karl Bopp was for many years the president of the Federal Reserve Bank of Philadelphia; Lester Chandler was Professor Emeritus at Princeton University; L. Pao Cheng taught at Simon Fraser University; Joel Dirlam taught at Connecticut University; August Maffrey was a widely known economist, banker and financial consultant; Carl McGuire was Professor Emeritus at the University of Colorado; and Beryl Sprinkel was the Undersecretary for Monetary Affairs at the Department of the Treasury.

21. Karl Bopp (1965) in *Essays in Monetary Theory in Honor of Elmer Wood.* Ed. Pinkney Walker. Columbia, MO: University of Missouri Press: 5.

Chapter 10

Conclusion

Introduction

A BROADER VIEW OF HARRY GUNNISON BROWN'S THOUGHT on political economy must include a consideration of his general philosophical and political views. In addition, his position with respect to Marxist, Institutionalist and Georgist thought are of interest. The effect of Brown's near heretical views on and advocacy of land value taxation on his professional reputation will be explored as well, and a summary reconsideration of his career as an economist will be offered.

As Lester Chandler has noted, Brown today would be considered a "conservative," yet he was very much a "liberal in the nineteenth century sense of the term."[1] Like many economists of the late nineteenth and early twentieth century, Brown championed causes for economic and social reform. Land value taxation, which became his primary interest, is not classified easily as liberal or conservative. He saw the political and economic system as flawed but amenable to improvement. He used the term "economic democracy" in his early writings to denote a goal to be sought. He subscribed to a "limited" faith in democracy to attain an "economic system fundamentally expedient and just."[2] Brown had trust in the functioning of competitive markets in which the proper regulation of natural monopolies and elimination of other monopolies were carried out. Yet he found the resulting distribution of income unjust due to the allowance of a return to the site value of land. Moreover, this allowance led to an inevitable reduction of economic incentive to labor and save.

Will Lissner, who was a journalist with the *New York Times* for much of his life as well as Brown's editor, saw his work as attempting to influence American liberalism. For Lissner classical liberalism contained a "heresy" in the form of a natural law that gave "divine sanction to the concentration of wealth and the impoverishment of its producers," and he reported that: "Brown struck at the very foundations of this heresy in *The Theory of Earned and Unearned Incomes....*"[3] Lissner concluded his article on Brown's contribution in the following manner:

> Through the Roaring Twenties, the Depressed Thirties, the War–Torn Forties and the Booming Fifties he has lambasted liberals, radicals and conservatives alike, seeking to make them confront the realities of economic logic.
>
> Our people run after nostrums of cartelization or socialization, though no theorist has succeeded in discovering how to make them work. Whether in the future we shall discover the unworkability of the alternatives to democratic capitalism the hard way, by trying them, or the easy way, by studying them and making rational choices, I would not care to predict. In any event Dr. Brown's democratic capitalism will have its day.[4]

Brown was not specific on the philosophical origins of his views. Evidently they were not religious in nature. As different as Henry George, Richard Ely and Irving Fisher were as political economists, they shared Christian underpinnings to the causes they promoted. In neither Brown's writings or preserved correspondence is there a clue as to his personal religious beliefs. His memorial service was conducted under the auspices of the Unitarian Church. He once stated that "more or less utilitarian grounds" were the basis of his belief that income should be classified as earned and unearned. He quoted Herbert Spencer:

> Briefly, then, the universal basis of cooperation is the proportioning of benefits received to services rendered.[5]

Reaction to Marxist, Institutionalist and Georgist Claims in Political Economy

BROWN REJECTED THE MARXIST CLAIM that interest was unearned or a surplus. He straightforwardly argued that capital's existence was due to abstinence or savings and that therefore the interest return was earned just as was the return to labor. Thus, for Brown the act of saving was potentially a service deserving of a fair return.

Should the "surplus" be taken by the state, economic incentives would be so impaired as to render the economy stagnant or worse.[6] He furthermore based his rejection of socialism on what he saw to be a necessarily coercive allocation of work or vocation.

Brown was familiar with economists whose thought was later to be labeled "institutionalist." He was a colleague of Thorstein Veblen for one year, yet Brown made only scattered references to Veblen and later responded to questions about him with a wry smile.[7] In one letter he recommended Veblen's *Theory of the Leisure Class* to an inquiring student as his best work.[8] When Paul Douglas was campaigning for Veblen's presidency of AEA in 1925, Brown chose to write a letter of support in lieu of signing the petition that had garnered 214 signatures. As reported by Joseph Dorfman, Brown expressed a fear that those with "radical proclivities" despite outstanding scholarship were being denied the presidency.[9] John Commons once wrote Brown asking for assistance for his presentation of arguments for a progressive land tax in the state of Wisconsin.[10] Horace M. Gray of the University of Illinois linked Brown with economists like Commons "who kept alive the spirit of democratic liberalism against the advancing tide of privileged, subsidized, monopoly capitalism."[11] However, when institutionalist economists tended to dismiss formal economic theory as a key guide to the understanding of the economy, Brown was sharply critical.

Although Brown came to be Henry George's most prominent academic proponent, he was also a critic of George. Brown clearly rejected George's "all-devouring rent thesis" and was critical of his interest and population theories. Brown found in George's interest theory an invalid distinction between "mechanical" and "biological" capital, which led George to an erroneous, productivity-of-nature explanation for interest. Brown found George's refutation of Malthusianism unconvincing and was himself an advocate of birth control. Also, he felt that George's theory of business depression was "hopelessly on the wrong track."[12] Despite these substantive differences with George on economic theory, Brown gave almost complete support to George's general proposal for tax reform and its ethical underpinning. Brown, of course, did not attempt to emphasize the "singleness" of the tax, nor did he form his ethical arguments in natural rights as did George. Yet Brown guments in natural rights as did George. Yet Brown considered George's errors to be dwarfed by his contributions to political, social and economic thought. Brown mentioned not only George's single-tax proposal but also his contributions to the theory of marginal productivity and his defense of free trade principles. Brown criticized George only when he felt his "errors" distracted from the fundamental message. Accordingly, these criticisms were presented only in Georgist publications. Brown found no inconsistency in transplanting the single-tax idea into neoclassical theory as he interpreted it.

Brown's Position in the Profession

BROWN'S OPEN ADVOCACY OF LAND VALUE TAXATION did not make him a pariah in the profession. He quickly attained his full professorship at Missouri and expressed in a letter his satisfaction with his position.[13] He never reported any infringement of his right to express his opinions. However, he did state in several articles (without mentioning names or institutions) that he had heard of cases where professors or graduate students were "razzed" for expressing an interest in land value taxation or advised—for their own good—not to pursue such an interest.[14] Paul Douglas, noted by Brown[15] to favor land value taxation, never brought up his views in professional journals or in the Senate.[16] In another instance, Russell Bauder, a former colleague of Brown's and graduate of the University of Wisconsin, wrote of his apprehension about his application to teach at another university because of his past association with Brown.[17] Bauder reported that he had been advised by John Commons, who expressed a high regard for Brown, to defend the professor should his interviewers raise the subject. When Bauder did so, he felt that he was not well received and was not offered the position he sought. Brown in several instances noted that he knew personally economists who were "definitely friendly to land value taxation," yet were reluctant to make this known and thereby lessen their influence.

Although Brown received several honors in his career,[18] he was never nominated for the presidency of the American Economics Association. Given the extensive nature of his contributions by the late 1930s, it is a question of some interest that he was not considered for this honor. An exchange of letters with Frank Knight in 1939 provides some insight into this matter. Brown wrote Knight on departmental matters but enclosed a copy of a letter he had sent to the members of the nominating committee of the Association. In it he proposed the candidacy of John Ise of the University of Kansas. In Knight's reply he said:

> The first thought that comes to mind is the name of another man who ought to be recognized in this connection, before too long, a man whom I have felt for years did not seem to get recognition in accord with his merits by the profession generally, and that is the man to whom this letter is addressed.[19]

Knight further stated that he would mention Brown as a possible candidate in his letter of support for Ise. Brown replied that he did not wish to be so mentioned for three reasons. First, he did not want his candidacy to rival that of Ise; second, he did not wish to be burdened with the responsibilities of the office, given his priorities; and third, he recently had failed to be elected to one of two vice-president posts of the Association and was asked to fill a temporary position on the executive committee, normally an elective position.

> It seems unlikely that I could be elected to any position in the Association despite the support of good friends like yourself. I am not unhappy about this, whatever may be the honor and distinction involved, because I am really more interested in persuading others of the logical justification for views I hold, than I am in filling any office and more so if the filling of an office would interfere in any way with my other purposes.[20]

Despite Brown's well-intentioned reservations, he would have accepted the presidency of the Association for the particular reason that he was most likely to have been denied it. The tradition of the presidential address presented those chosen with a unique opportunity to express their views. Brown would have utilized no small part of the address to state the case for land value taxation, and the nominating committee was likely to have made this a consideration of importance in its selection.

Brown's credentials, however evaluated, were comparable to those of many who served as president. Eccentricity as a criterion for denying the office to someone did not prevent the nomination of such economists as Irving Fisher (1918), Thorstein Veblen (declined), Herbert J. Davenport (1920) and Frank Knight (1950). Brown's occasionally caustic criticisms of other economists may have prompted disfavor, yet in 1939 Jacob Viner, a harsh critic, was selected. The denial of this honor also cannot easily be attributable to Brown's personality; he is reported to have been outgoing, courteous and friendly as evinced in his collegial friendship with Knight and longtime personal friendship with John Bauer despite their differences. In 1985 Martin Bronfenbrenner might have been thinking of Brown when he commented: "The popular picture of the single–taxer has however become the aged crank whose ideas have been refuted, who has outlived his usefulness, and who need not be taken seriously."[21] Yet Crauford Goodwin relates a story of Bronfenbrenner's chance encounter with Brown on a train ride from Chicago to Detroit to attend the American Economics Association annual meeting of 1938. According to Goodwin, Bronfenbrenner remembered: "With nothing better to do, Professor Brown spent several hours translating for my benefit the complexities of 'modern economics' into the simpler language of his own generation. . . . Much of my later floundering represents attempts, seldom successful, to apply the lessons of that one evening with Professor Brown."[22] Although several scholars of distinction were never chosen to be president of the Association, one may reasonably entertain the suspicion that Brown's views prevented him from attaining this esteemed position.

Comments and Conclusion

On Brown's economic thought, Alfred Kahn wrote:

> What impressed me more about his economic thinking was its coherence, its through internal consistency and its apparent sufficiency.[23]

He added:

It is an admirable system of economic thinking and Brown expounded it with grace, intellectual incisiveness and persistence.[24]

Although Kahn served only one year with Brown as a teaching assistant, his comments are remarkably insightful.

The neoclassical approach Brown adopted was not a precisely delimited model. He disliked the term "neoclassical," as he felt it signified too great a departure from classical thinking in economics. Although he made no signal, original contribution to the theory, his skill in its application allowed him to make many important contributions in several areas of thought. The consistent purpose in his writing was to make economic theory applicable to the perennial problems of a capitalistic economy. His studies in tax incidence are one example of his efforts. In them he strove to refine existing theory to form a sounder basis for tax policy decisions. The same was true of his careful and detailed work on finding principles for efficient regulatory practices. As a monetarist, he demonstrated flexibility and imagination quite outside of the usual caricature of pre–Keynesian monetary thought. His free trade advocacy was rooted in a concern for economic efficiency and growth.

Yet in all of these areas, as one may note in the preceding chapters, Brown found land value taxation to be a relevant and important consideration. Brown's espousal of the single tax idea was consistent with his theoretical position in economics. As more economists tended to merge land and capital, not infrequently for reasons of expediency, and thereby make more difficult his advocacy, he moved to justify the separation of land from capital on theoretical grounds. He saw economic rent as the marginal product of land space in the neoclassical manner, yet also as a surplus over interest and wages in the classical fashion. The return to land space was an absolute amount "measured and determined by the surplus over production at the extensive margin."[25] Brown differed with Fisher's view on capital and interest, arguing that the value of capital was in large part determined by its cost of production or reproduction. Thus, the situation value of land having no cost of production was determined by the capitalization of expected future rent at some previously determined rate of interest. Brown supported land value taxation as a tax that would not result in the distortion of market prices and that was in accord with distributive justice. Also, greater taxation of land values would to some extent reduce the taxation of labor effort and investment and thus further economic efficiency and growth.

One, as Alfred Kahn noted, may well question the sufficiency and lack of specificity of the neoclassical approach Brown employed. However, he himself often pointed to the need for further elaboration and refinement of the theory and consistently worked to this end.

Statements by M. Slade Kendrick in his 1951 *Public Finance* demonstrate an open–mindedness Brown felt was all–too–lacking in the profession. Kendrick commented:

> From Henry George in latter part of the nineteenth century, to Professor H. G. Brown, brilliant economic theorist of our day, the single tax has not lacked advocates whose views command respect. The clear logic with which the case for the single tax is presented, warmed by the fires of conviction, is ample reason for an examination of the issues.[26]

Despite the personal compliment, Brown would not have been pleased with Kendrick's subsequent rejection of the single tax. Kendrick's consideration of the single tax as opposed to more general arguments for land value taxation tended to bias his examination.

However, his fair and objective presentation of the arguments is due in large part to Brown's influence. In 1969 Dick Netzer responded to a letter from Brown complimenting Netzer's *Economics of the Property Tax* and stated: "I hope that my work, and what seems to be a growing body of work by other economists, so long after you had begun to write on land value taxation, can affect the climate of opinion sufficiently to lead to adoption of land value taxation by some major jurisdictions."[27] I was, in 1984–5, in the original version of this study, uncertain as to whether especially the "climate of opinion" had been much changed. Now I would venture to say that it has.

Robert Heilbroner commented that upon Henry George's death his reputation "went straight into the underworld of economics."[28] Whether Heilbroner's assessment of the fate of George's thought is correct or not, the reputation of Harry Gunnison Brown as an economist appears to have suffered as a result of his persistent espousal of George's cause. This, and Brown's other viewpoints which have waxed and waned in popularity over the course of the century, explain the present–day neglect of his contributions. However, the verdict of history is open–ended, and Brown's dedication to carry on with the "zest of anticipated usefulness" may yet find vindication.

Notes

1. Lester Chandler (December 17, 1978). Cited in Paul Junk's Preface to *Selected Articles by Harry Gunnison Brown*. New York: Robert Schalkenbach Foundation, 1980: xv.

2. Harry Gunnison Brown (1925). *The Taxation of Earned and Unearned Incomes*. Columbia, MO: Lucas Brothers: 49.

3. Will Lissner (1958). "Harry Gunnison Brown's Influence on American Liberalism." *Henry George News* (July).

4. *Ibid.*

5. Herbert Spencer (1942). Quoted by Harry Gunnison Brown in *The Basic Principles of Economics*. Columbia, MO: Lucas Brother: 220.

6. Harry Gunnison Brown. "Academic Freedom and the Defense of Capitalism." *American Journal of Economics and Sociology* 15 (January): 173–182.

7. Pinkney Walker (December, 1983). Interview by author. Personal files, Iowa City, IA.

8. Harry Gunnison Brown (October 22, 1928). Letter to Lung Chung. Joint Collection, University of Missouri Western Historical Manuscript Collection, Columbia, MO.

9. Thorstein Veblen (1973). *Essays, Reviews and Reports. Previously Uncollected Writings*. Ed. Joseph Dorfman. Clifton: Augustus M. Kelley: 272.

Joseph Dorfman quoted the following portion of the letter from Brown to J. M. Clark dated September 24, 1925: "So far as I am aware, no academic American economist of equal years and distinction, has ever failed of election to that office and a considerable number have been chosen whose distinction is far less. But there is another aspect of the problem, to which I believe attention should be directed; viz., the growth of the feeling, in the minds of many members, that the system of election throws control into the hands of an 'Old Guard' and that, under the circumstances, there is no chance of ever electing as president a person, no matter how distinguished for scholarship, of such radical proclivities as Veblen. It seems to me that the election of Veblen should do something to hearten those members who believe that scholarly contributions of importance should bring no less honor to radical than to conservatives."

10. Harry Gunnison Brown (June 10, 1926). Letter to John Commons. Joint Collection University of Missouri Western Historical Manuscript Collection–Columbia and State Historical Society of Missouri Manuscripts.

11. Horace M. Gray (April 2, 1975). Letter to Weld Carter. Cited in Paul Junk's Preface to *Selected Articles by Harry Gunnison Brown*. New York: Robert Schalkenbach Foundation, 1980: iv.

12. Harry Gunnison Brown (November 29, 1930). Letter to Walter Verity. Joint Collection University of Missouri Western Historical Manuscript Collection–Columbia and State Historical Society of Missouri Manuscripts.

13. Harry Gunnison Brown (October 13, 1927). Letter to John H. Sherman. Joint Collection University of Missouri Western Historical Manuscript Collection–Columbia and State Historical Society of Missouri Manuscripts.

14. Harry Gunnison Brown (1956). "Academic Freedom and the Defense of Capitalism." *American Journal of Economics and Sociology* 15 (January): 178–179.

15. Harry Gunnison Brown (1928). *Significant Paragraphs from Henry George's Progress and Poverty*. New York: Doubleday, Doran & Co.: 80.

16. Douglas, however, as Chairman of the National Commission on Urban Problems, did in its minority opinion support tax reforms. *Report of the National Commission on Urban Problems to the Congress and to the President of the United States*. Washington, DC: U. S. Printing Office, 1968.

17. Russell Bauder (February 18, 1930). Letter to Harry Gunnison Brown. Joint Collection University of Missouri Western Historical Manuscripts Collection–Columbia and State Historical Society of Missouri Manuscripts.

18. Brown was president of what is now the Midwestern Economics Association in 1942. Williams College awarded him an honorary doctorate.

19. Frank Knight (April 29, 1939). Letter to Harry Gunnison Brown. Joint Collection University of Missouri Western Historical Manuscript Collection–Columbia and State Historical Society of Missouri Manuscripts.

20. Harry Gunnison Brown (May 2, 1939). Letter to Frank Knight. Joint Collection University of Missouri Western Historical Manuscript Collection–Columbia and State Historical Society of Missouri Manuscripts.

21. Martin Bronfenbrenner (1985). "Early American Leaders—Institutional and Critical Traditions." *American Economic Review* 75 (December): 17.

22. Craufurd D. Goodwin (1998). "Martin Bronfenbrenner, 1914–1997." *Economic Journal* 108 (November): 1777–1778.

23. Alfred Kahn (September 5, 1984). Letter to author. Personal files, Iowa City, IA

24. *Ibid.*

25. Harry Gunnison Brown (1942). *The Basic Principles of Economics.* Columbia, MO: Lucas Brothers: 427.

26. M. Slade Kendrick (1951). *Public Finance.* Boston: Houghton Mifflin Co.: 233.

27. Dick Netzer (February 11, 1969). Letter to Harry Gunnison Brown. Personal files, Iowa City, IA.

28. Robert Heilbroner (1961). *The Worldly Philosophers.* New York: Simon and Schuster: 163.

Books, Articles and Letters by Harry Gunnison Brown

"The Basis of Rate-Making as Affected by Competition Versus Combination of Railroads." *Yale Review*, 16 (May 1907): 79–86.

"Competitive and Monopolistic Price Making." *Quarterly Journal of Economics* 22 (August 1908): 625–639.

"Review of *Gold, Prices and Wages under the Greenback Standard* by Wesley C. Mitchell." *Yale Review* 18 (May 1909): 99–101.

"A Problem in Deferred Payments and the Tabular Standard." *Quarterly Journal of Economics* 23 (August 1909): 714–718.

Some Phases of Railroad Combination. Diss. Yale University (1909).

"Review of *Railroad Freight Rates in Relation to Industry and Commerce* by Logan A. McPherson." *Yale Review* (February 1910): 331–433.

"Commercial Banking and the Rate of Interest." *Quarterly Journal of Economics* 24 (August 1910): 743–749.

"Typical Commercial Crises Versus a Money Panic." *Yale Review* 19 (August 1910): 168–176.

"Review of *The Diminished Purchasing Power of Railway Earnings* by C. C. McCain." *Yale Review* 19 (August 1910): 201–202.

"Review of *Gold Production and Future Prices* by Harrison H. Brace." *Yale Review* 19 (November 1910): 328–330.

"Rising Prices and Investments." Chapter III of *How To Invest When Prices Are Rising* by Irving Fisher, E. W. Kemmerer and Others. Scranton, PA: Sumner and Co. (1912): 33–52.

"Review of *Law of Wages. An Essay in Statistical Economics* by Henry Ludwell Moore." *American Economic Review* 2 (December 1912): 875–877.

"The Marginal Productivity Versus the Impatience Theory of Interest." *Quarterly Journal of Economics* 27 (August 1913): 630–650.

International Trade and Exchange: A Study in the Mechanisms and Advantages of Commerce. New York: Macmillan Company, 1914.

"The Discount Rate Versus the Cost of Production Theory of Capital Valuation." *American Economic Review* 4 (June 1914): 340–349.

"The Competition of Transportation Companies." *American Economic Review* 4 (December 1914): 771–792.

"Review of *The Case for Railway Nationalization* by E. Davies." *American Economic Review* 4 (December 1914): 948.

"Review of *Where and Why Public Ownership has Failed* by Yves Goyot." *American Economic Review* 5 (March 1915): 148–149.

"Review of *Railroads, Rates and Traffic* by C. Colson." *American Economic Review* 5 (September 1915): 601–603.

Principles of Commerce. New York: Macmillan Company, 1916.

Transportation Rates and Their Regulation. New York: Macmillan Company, 1916.

"Review of *On the Relation of Imports to Exports* by J. T. Peddie." *American Economic Review* 6 (March 1916): 124.

"Review of *Principles of Money and Banking* and *Exercises and Questions for Use with Principles of Money and Banking* by Harold G. Moulton." *Journal of Political Economy* 24 (December 1916): 1018–1019.

"The Ethics of Land Value Taxation." *Journal of Political Economy* 25 (May 1917): 464–492.

International Trade: A Study in the Advantages of Commerce. New York: Macmillan Company, 1917.

Foreign Exchange: A Study of the Exchange Mechanism of Commerce. New York: Macmillan Company, 1917.

The Theory of Earned and Unearned Incomes. Columbia, MO: Missouri Book Company, 1918.

"Review of *Modern Currency Reforms* by Edwin Walter Kemmerer." *Journal of Political Economy* 26 (February 1918): 208–210.

"An Eminent Economist Confused." *Quarterly Journal of Economics* 33 (May 1919): 567–570. ("A Re-Rejoinder": 571–572)

"An Oversight in the Theory of Incidence." *Quarterly Journal of Economics* 33 (August 1919): 734–736.

"A Balanced Industrial System: Discussion." *American Economic Association–Papers and Proceedings* 10 (March 1920): 78–88.

"Some Frequently Neglected Factors in the Incidence of Taxation." *Journal of Political Economy* 28 (June 1920): 499–504.

The Taxation of Unearned Incomes. Columbia, MO: Missouri Book Company, 1921.

"Review of *Argentine International Trade Under Inconvertible Paper Money* by John Henry Williams." *American Economic Review* 11 (June 1921): 308–313.

"The Shifting and Incidence on Sales of Land and Capital Goods and on Loans." *Journal of Political Economy* 29 (October 1921): 643–653.

"Review of *The American Railroad Problem* by I. Leo Sharfman." *Quarterly Journal of Economics* 36 (February 1922): 323–334.

"The Incidence of Compulsory Insurance of Workmen." *Journal of Political Economy* 30 (February 1922): 67–77.

"Review of *Outlines of Public Finance* by Merlin Hunter." *National Municipal Review* 2 (November 1922): 391.

"Review of *The Principles of International Trade* by Huntley M. Sinclair." *American Economic Review* 13 (March 1923): 92–94.

Economic Science and the Common Welfare. Columbia, MO: Lucas Brothers, 1923. (five subsequent editions in 1925, 1926, 1929, 1931 and 1936)

The Economics of Taxation. New York: Henry Holt & Company, 1924.

"The Single-Tax Complex of Some Contemporary Economists." *Journal of Political Economy* 32 (April 1924): 164–190.

"Is A Tax On Site Values Never Shifted?" *Journal of Political Economy* 32 (June 1924): 375–382.

The Taxation of Unearned Incomes. Columbia, MO: Lucas Brothers, 1925.

"Railroad Valuation and Rate Regulation." *Journal of Political Economy* 33 (October 1925): 505–530.

"Is American Liberalism a Betrayal of the Masses?" *Libertarian* (November 1925).

Relieving Business through Scientific Taxation: An Address Delivered May 28, 1926. New York: American Association of Scientific Taxation, 1926.

"Land Rent as a Function of Population Growth." *Journal of Political Economy* 34 (June 1926): 274–288.

Letter to John Commons, June 10, 1926. Joint Collection University of Missouri Western Historical Manuscript Collection Columbia-and State Historical Society of Missouri Manuscripts.

"Railroad Valuation Again: A Reply." *Journal of Political Economy* 34 (August 1926): 500–508.

"Land Speculation and Land Value Taxation." *Journal of Political Economy* 35 (June 1927): 390–402.

Letter to John H. Sherman, October 13, 1927. Joint Collection University of Missouri Western Historical Manuscript Collection-Columbia and State Historical Society of Missouri Manuscripts.

Significant Paragraphs from Henry George's Progress and Poverty. New York: Doubleday, Doran & Company, 1928.

"Economic Basis and Limits of Public Utility Regulation." *Reports of the American Bar Association* 53 (1928): 717–737.

"Taxing Rental versus Taxing Salable Value of Land." *Journal of Political Economy* 36 (February 1928): 164–168.

"Valuation of Public Utilities—Discussion." *American Economic Review* 18, Supplement (March 1928): 211–216.

"Honest Farm Relief and Fair Taxation." *Land and Freedom* (October 1928).

Letter to Lung Chung, October 22, 1928. Joint Collection University of Missouri Western Historical Manuscript Collection-Columbia and State Historical Society of Missouri Manuscripts.

"Should Bare Land Values be Taxed More Heavily?" *Journal of Land and Public Utility Economics* 4 (February–November 1928): 375–392.

"Review of *International Trade* by Frank Taussig." *American Economic Review* 18 (December 1928): 706–713.

"'Present Costs.'" *Public Utility Fortnightly* 3 (March 7 1929): 237–246.

"Capital Valuation and the 'Psychological School.'" *American Economic Review* 19 (September 1929): 357–362.

"Land, Capital and Opportunity Cost: A Reply." *American Economic Review* 20 (June 1930): 248–251.

"Tax Relief for Farmers versus Tax Relief for Real Estate." *Tax Facts* (July 1930).

"The Pretense About Intangibles Escaping Taxation." *Tax Facts* (August 1930).

Tax Relief for Real Estate. (pamphlet). 1930.

Letter to James Harvey Rogers, October 4, 1930. Rogers Papers, Yale University Library, New Haven, CT.

Letter to Walter Verity, November 29, 1930. Joint Collection University of Missouri Western Historical Manuscript Collection-Columbia and State Historical Society of Missouri Manuscripts.

A Talk to Businessmen, Workingmen and Farmers about Taxes. (pamphlet). New York: Robert Schalkenbach Foundation, 1930.

"Review of *Economic Fragments* by Dennis H. Robertson." *American Economic Review* (March 1931): 704–707.

"Opportunity Cost: Marshall's Criticism of Jevons." *American Economic Review* 21 (September 1931): 498–500.

Letter to James Harvey Rogers, May, 1932. Joint Collection University of Missouri Western Historical Manuscripts Collection-Columbia and State Historical Society of Missouri Manuscripts.

The Economic Basis of Tax Reform. Columbia MO: Lucas Brothers, 1932.

"Nonsense and Sense in Dealing with the Depression." *Beta Gamma Sigma Exchange* (Spring 1933): 97–107.

Letter to James Harvey Rogers, November 23, 1933. Rogers Papers, Yale University Library, New Haven, CT.

Letter to the Committee for the Nation, December 1933. Rogers Papers, Yale University Library, New Haven, CT.

"Review of *The Philosophy of Henry George* by George R. Geiger." *The Philosophical Review* 43 (1934): 215–217.

"A Story of Tax Relief for Land and of New Deal Prosperity: The Keynote Convention Speech by Hon. B. A. Partyman." *Land and Freedom* 35 (July–August and November–December 1935): 150–155 and 191–196.

"A Defense of the Single-Tax Principle." *Annals of the American Academy of Political and Social Sciences* 183 (January 1936): 63–69.

Tax Relief –Pretense and Reality. (pamphlet). London: International Union for Land Value Taxation and Free Trade (September 1936).

"Radical Literary Intelligentsia and Hard-Headed Propertied Conservatives: A Study in Similarities." *Land and Freedom* (December 1936):
171–175.

Letter to Irving Fisher, February 6, 1937. Fisher Papers, Yale University
Library, New Haven, CT.

"Triple A: Logic Plowed Under." *The Freeman* 1 (November 1937): 3.

"Why the Duke's in a Fog." *The Freeman* 1 (December 1937): 9–10.

"Economic Fundaments for the Utility Baiters: 1. Taxes Hit Bills or Pay
Envelopes, 2. Valuation: Economic, Not Punitive Job." *The Freeman*
1 (January 1938): 12–15.

"Taxes Go 'Round and 'Round." *The Freeman* 1 (January 1938): 19.

"The Diabolists Exorcise Monopoly." *The Freeman* 1 (February 1938): 7–
8.

"The Farm Act: 1. Only Farmers? Pension Everybody, 2. No 'Farm' Help?
That Heretic." *The Freeman* 1 (March 1938): 10, 9–10.

"Tax Relief – For Monkey Business." *The Freeman* 1 (April 1938): 3–4.

"Austria – Not Fascism's Last Victim." *The Freeman* 1 (May 1938): 5–6.

"Why States Go Totalitarian." *The Freeman* 1 (May 1938): 17–19.

"Coin Slogan, Dodge Tax." *The Freeman* 1 (June 1938): 5–6.

"How to Aid Croppers, Slummies." *The Freeman* 1 (July 1938): 3–4.

"This Road Leads to Collectivism." *The Freeman* 1 (August 1938): 6–7.

"The Clarions of the Battle Call." *The Freeman* 1 (September 1938): 3–4.

"The Land of 'Make Believe.'" *The Freeman* 1 (September 1938): 17.

"Getting Milk from Half-Starved Cows." *The Freeman* 1 (October 1938):
10–11.

"The Great Silence of Liberals." *The Freeman* 2 (November 1938): 12–13.

"Two-Timing Us with Two Prices." *The Freeman* 2 (December 1938): 6–7.

"Taxing Mortgages: Another Red Herring." *The Freeman* 2 (January 1939):
15–16.

"Democracy's Ideal: 'Let's Get Ours.'" *The Freeman* 2 (February 1939):
14–15.

"What is a 'Liberal'?" *The Freeman* 2 (March 1939): 14–15.

"New Scheme to Help Landowners." *The Freeman* 2 (April 1939): 15.

"The Incidence of a General Output or a General Sales Tax." *Journal of
Political Economy* 47 (April 1939): 254–262. (See also "A Correction."
Journal of Political Economy 46 [June 1939]: 418–420.)

"Machinery: A Senatorial Scapegoat." *The Freeman* 2 (May 1939): 17.

Letter to Frank Knight, May 2, 1939. Joint Collection University of Missouri
Western Historical Manuscripts Collection-Columbia and State Historical Society of Missouri Manuscripts.

" 'Liberals' Continue Great Silence." *The Freeman* 2 (June 1939): 10.

"How Sales Tax Hit Wages." *The Freeman* 2 (August 1939): 14.

"The Void in the College Curricula." *The Freeman* 2 (September 1939):
17–18.

"Textbooks Don't Tell." *The Freeman* 2 (October 1939): 17–18.

"An Academic Psychosis." *The Freeman* 3 (November 1939): 18–19.

"From Poland to Points West." *The Freeman* 3 (December 1939): 39–40.

"Beware the Haunting Spectre." *The Freeman* 3 (January 1940): 57–58.

"An Open Letter to Senator O'Mahoney." *The Freeman* 3 (February 1940): 82–83.

"The Single Tax Principle—'Crackpotism' or Commonsense." *Education* 60 (March 1940): 403–409.

"Impoverishing Our Friend, the Farmer." *The Freeman* 3 (April 1940): 137.

"Objections to the 100% Reserve Plan." *American Economic Review* 30 (June 1940): 309–314.

"For Predation There Must Be Production." *The Freeman* 3 (September 1940): 253–254.

"Society Cannot Live by Robbery." *The Freeman* 3 (October 1940): 278–279.

Letter to Lester Chandler, October 4, 1940. Joint Collection University of Missouri Western Historical Manuscripts Collection-Columbia and State Historical Society of Missouri Manuscripts.

"Review of *Democracy versus Socialism* by Max Hirsh." *Journal of Political Economy* 48 (December 1940): 928–929.

"Has the Black Cloud a Silver Lining?" *The Freeman* 4 (November 1941): 12–13.

"Economic Rent: In What Sense a Surplus?" *American Economic Review* 31 (December 1941): 833–835.

Progress and Poverty by Henry George. Rearranged and abridged by Harry Gunnison Brown. New York: Robert Schalkenbach Foundation, 1941.

Basic Principles of Economics and Their Significance for Public Policy. Columbia, MO: Lucas Brothers, 1942 (2nd ed., 1947).

"Can We Escape Communism?" *The Freeman* 5 (February 1942): 75.

"Taxes to Beat the Axis." *The Freeman* 5 (May 1942): 152–153.

"A Reply to Mr. Woodlock." *The Freeman* 5 (August 1942): 225, 230, 236.

"Russian Bravery & Russian Land." *The Freeman* 5 (September 1942): 250, 257–258.

"Review of *American Taxation: Its History as a Social Force in Democracy* by Sidney Ratner." *American Economic Review* 32 (September 1942): 602–604.

"Fiscal Policy and War-Time Price Control." *American Journal of Economics and Sociology* 2 (October 1942): 1–14.

"Twill Be Different after the War." *The Freeman* 6 (November 1942): 3.

"The Appeal of Communist Ideology." *American Journal of Economics and Sociology* 2 (January 1943): 161–174.

"Land Values in New York City." *The Freeman* 6 (January 1943): 19.

"Anticipation of an Increment and the 'Unearned Decrement' in Land Values: A Study in Some Irrelevant Theorizing." *American Journal of Economics and Sociology* 2 (April 1943): 343–357.

"Subsidies and War-Time Price Control." *American Journal of Economics and Sociology* 2 (July 1943): 453–457.

"The Danger in the Mounting National Debt." *American Journal of Economics and Sociology* 3 (October 1943): 1–14.

"The Conservative Program for Tax Reform." *American Journal of Economics and Sociology* 3 (October 1943): 129–132.

"Policies for Full Post-War Employment." *American Journal of Economics and Sociology* 3 (January 1944): 141–154.

"An Off-Line Switch in the Theory of Value and Distribution." *American Journal of Economics and Sociology* 3 (April 1944): 397–417.

"The System of Free Enterprise and Its Caricature." *American Journal of Economics and Sociology* 4 (October 1944): 87–98.

"Currency Devaluation and International Trade." *American Journal of Economics and Sociology* 4 (January 1945): 227–237.

"What are Profits?" *American Journal of Economics and Sociology* 4 (April 1945): 333–342.

"Financing Social Insurance." *American Journal of Economics and Sociology* 4 (July 1945): 440.

"Taxation According to 'Ability to Pay': What it Means and What is Wrong with It." *American Journal of Economics and Sociology* 4 (July 1945): 461–477.

"Objectives and Methods in Teaching the Principles of Economics." *American Journal of Economics and Sociology* 4 (October 1945): 93–109.

"A Teaching Approach to the Incidence of Taxation on Capital." *American Journal of Economics and Sociology* 5 (January 1946): 231–245.

"Rent Theory as a Teaching Problem on the Undergraduate Level." *American Journal of Economics and Sociology* 5 (April 1946): 389–401.

"The Alleged Injustice of Increasing Land Value Taxation Without Compensation." *American Journal of Economics and Sociology* 5 (April 1946): 327–350.

"Some Recent Academic Criticisms of Land Value Taxation: Are They Intellectually Respectable?" *American Journal of Economics and Sociology* 5 (July 1946): 521–532.

"The Perplexed Economists." *Henry George News* (October 1946).

A Postscript and Questions. Columbia, MO: Lucas Brothers, 1946. (A companion volume to *The Basic Principles of Economics.*)

"The Tariff Question." *The Westerner*. Record Stockman Inc. (June 1947).

"Taxation and Ability to Pay." *Labor and Labor Relations Yearbook and Directory*. New York and Washington: Industrial Relations Publishing Corporation, 1947.

"Two Decades of Decadence in Economic Theorizing." *American Journal of Economics and Sociology* 7 (January 1948): 145–172.

"Bourgeois Confusion and Proletarian Myopia." *American Journal of Economics and Sociology* 7 (October 1948): 38–48.

"Henry George and the Causation of Interest." *Henry George News* (October 1948): 1, 4–5, 8.

Objectives, Prejudices and Techniques in the Teaching of Economics. (pamphlet). New York: Schalkenbach Foundation, 1948.

"Economic Fallacies and Economic Teaching." *American Journal of Economics and Sociology* 8 (1949): 177–180.

"The Challenge of Australian Tax Policy." *American Journal of Economics and Sociology* 8 (July 1949): 377–400.

Some Disturbing Inhibitions and Fallacies in Current Academic Economics. (pamphlet). New York: Schalkenbach Foundation, 1949.

"Justice and Sense in Taxation." Chapter III of *Twentieth Century Economic Thought*. Ed. Glenn Hoover. New York: New York: Philosophical Library, 1950.

"A Dilemma of Contemporary Keynesism." *American Journal of Economics and Sociology* 10 (April 1951): 237–246.

"The Size of the National Debt." *American Journal of Economics and Sociology* 11 (October 1951): 55–60.

"Cost of Production, Price Control and Subsidies: An Economic Nightmare." *American Economic Review* 42 (March 1952): 126–134.

"The Prospector and Economic Rent." *American Journal of Economics and Sociology* 12 (April 1953): 301–304.

"Academic Freedom and the Defense of Capitalism." *American Journal of Economics and Sociology* 15 (January 1956): 172–182.

"Foundations, Professors and 'Economic Education.'" *American Journal of Economics and Sociology* 17 (January 1958): 148–152.

"Tax Policy and the Modern City." *American Journal of Economics and Sociology* 17 (April 1958): 279–282.

"Land Value Taxation and the Rights of Property." *American Journal of Economics and Sociology* 18 (October 1958): 35–48.

"The Keynes-Hansen 'Demand for Labor' Notion." *American Journal of Economics and Sociology* 19 (January 1959): 149–156.

"Monetary And Fiscal Counter-Depression Policy: An Analysis Correcting Keynes' Ignoring of Tax Burdens." *American Journal of Economics and Sociology* 18 (July 1959): 337–351.

"Criteria for a Rational Tax System." *American Journal of Economics and Sociology* 20 (July 1961): 443–447.

"An Oversight in the Dominant Theory of Interest." *American Journal of Economics and Sociology* 21 (April 1962): 203–207.

"The Communist Specter in Latin America." *American Journal of Economics and Sociology* 21 (July 1962): 307–308.

"Tax Policy for Optimal Production." *American Journal of Economics and Sociology* 24 (January 1965): 7–8.

"Capital Incentive Reform Beneficial to Labor." *American Journal of Economics and Sociology* 24 (January 1965): 69–70.

The Economics of Taxation. Chicago: University of Chicago Press (Midway Reprints), 1979.

Selected Articles by Harry Gunnison Brown: The Case for Land Value Taxation. Ed. Paul Junk. New York: Robert Schalkenbach Foundation, 1980.

Books and Articles Co-Authored or Co-Edited by Harry Gunnison Brown

The Purchasing Power of Money. Irving Fisher, assisted by Harry Gunnison Brown. New York: Macmillan Company, 1970.

"Plant Location and Community Tax Policy." With Elizabeth Read Brown. *American Journal of Economics and Sociology* 13 (October 1954): 55–58.

Land Value Taxation Around the World. Eds. Harry Gunnison Brown, Harold S. Buttenheim, Philip H. Cornick, and Glenn Hooover. New York: Robert Schalkenbach Foundation, 1955.

The Effective Answer to Communism and Why You Don't Get it in College. With Elizabeth Read Brown. New York: Robert Schalkenbach Foundation, 1958.

"Land Value Taxation's Incidence." With Elizabeth Read Brown. *Journal of Economics and Sociology* 25 (January 1966): 25–26.

"The City—Will It Be Revolutionized?" With Elizabeth Read Brown. *Journal of Economics and Sociology* 25 (July 1966): 335–336.

"Incentive Taxation in Australia." With Elizabeth Read Brown. *Journal of Economics and Sociology* 26 (October 1967): 416.

"Obstacles to Adoption of Land Value Taxation: The Story of Meadville." With Elizabeth Read Brown, *Journal of Economics and Sociology* 27 (October 1968): 387–392.

"Attack on Tax Reform in Hawaii." With Elizabeth Read Brown. *Journal of Economics and Sociology* 28 (January 1969): 106–108.

"Can We Avoid Communized Housing." With Elizabeth Read Brown. *The Diary of Alpha Kappa Psi* (Spring 1969): 7–8.

Secondary Sources

Adams, H. C. (1898). *The Science of Finance*. New York: Henry Holt & Company.

Adams, Thomas S. (1916). "Tax Exemption through Capitalization: A Fiscal Fallacy." *Americican Economic Review* 6 (June): 271–287.

American Economic Review. (1939). "Obituary for James Harvey Rogers." 29 (December): 913–914.

Andelson, Robert V., ed. (1979). *Critics of Henry George: A Centenary Appraisal of the Strictures on Progress and Poverty*. Rutherford, NJ: Fairleigh Dickinson University Press.

———, ed. (2000). "Land Value Taxation Around the World." *American Journal of Economics and Sociology* 59 (Supplement): 1–451. (Also *Land Value Taxation Around the World*. Boston: Blackwell Publishers, 2000).

Andelson, Robert V. and Mason Gaffney. (1979). "Seligman and His Critique from Social Utility." In *Critics of Henry George*. Rutherford NJ: Fairleigh Dickinson University Press.

Anonymous. (1920). "Book Notes on *The Theory of Earned and Unearned Incomes* by Harry Gunnison Brown." *Political Science Quarterly* 35 (December): 693–694.

———. (1932–33). "The Professor and The Single Tax." *Land and Freedom*: 206–207.

Back, Kenneth. (1970). "Land Value Taxation in Light of Current Assessment Theory and Practice." In *The Assessment of Land Value*. Ed. Daniel Holland. Madison, WI: University of Wisconsin Press.

Barber, William J., ed. (1997). *The Works of Irving Fisher*. Assisted by Robert W. Dimand and Kevin Foster. Consulting ed. James Tobin. London: Pickering & Chatto.

Barker, Charles Albro. (1955). *Henry George*. New York: Oxford University Press.

Bauder, Russell. (1930). Letter to Harry Gunnison Brown, 18 February. Joint Collection University of Missouri Western Historical Manuscript Collection-Columbia and State Historical Society of Missouri Manuscripts.

Bauer, John. (1925). *Effective Rate Regulation of Public Utilities*. New York: Macmillan Company.

———. (1926). "Rate Base for Effective and Non-Speculative Railroad and Public Utility Regulation." *Journal of Political Economy* 34 (August): 470–500.

———. (1927). Chairman of Round Table Conference, "The Problem of Effective Utility Regulation." *American Economic Review* 17 (March): 123–127.

Bickerdike, C. F. (1912). "The Principle of Land Value Taxation." *Economic Journal* 22: 1–15.

——. (1916a). "Review of *International Trade: A Study in the Economic Advantages of Commerce* by Harry Gunnison Brown." *Economic Journal* 26 (103): 346–347.

——. (1916b). "Review of *Transportation Rates and Their Regulation* by Harry Gunnison Brown." *Economic Journal* 26 (103): 348–350.

Bird, Richard M. (1960). "A National Tax on the Unimproved Value of Land: The Australian Experience 1910–1952." *National Tax Journal* 13 (December): 386–392.

Bishop, Ward. (1933). "Review of *The Economic Basis of Tax Reform* by Harry Gunnison Brown." *American Economic Review* 23 (December): 761–763.

Blaug, Mark. (1985). *Economic Theory in Retrospect,* 4th ed. Cambridge: Cambridge University Press.

——. (2000). "Henry George: Rebel with a Cause." *European Journal of the History of Economic Thought* 7 (Summer): 270–288.

Böhm-Bawerk, Eugen. (1923). *The Positive Theory of Capital.* New York: G.E. Strechert & Co.

——. (1959). *Capital and Interest,* 3 vols. South Holland, IL: Libertarian Press.

Bonbright, James C. (1926). "Progress and Poverty in Current Literature on Valuation." *Quarterly Journal of Economics* 40 (February): 295–328.

——. (1928). "Railroad Valuation with Special Reference to the O'Fallon Decision." *American Economic Review* 18, Supplement (March): 181–205.

——. (1937). *The Valuation of Property,* 2 vols., New York: McGraw-Hill Book Company.

——. (1941). "Major Controversies as to the Criteria of Reasonable Public Utility Rates." *American Economic Review* 31 (February): 379–389.

——. (1961). *Principles of Public Utility Rates.* New York: Columbia University Press.

Bopp, Karl. (1932). "Two Notes on the Federal Reserve System." *Journal of Political Economy* 40 (June): 379–391.

——. (1965). "Confessions of a Central Banker." *Essays in Monetary Economics in Honor of Elmer Wood.* Pinkney Walker, ed. Columbia, MO: University of Missouri Press.

Boulding, Kenneth. (1984). Letter to author, 6 October. Personal Files, Iowa City, IA.

Bowen, Howard. (1939). Letter to Harry Gunnison Brown, 19 May. Joint Collection University of Missouri Western Historical Manuscript Collection-Columbia and State Historical Society of Missouri Manuscripts.

Bradford, David F. (1978). "Factor Prices May Be Constant But Factor Returns Are Not." *Economic Letters* 1:199–203.

Breckenfield, Gurney. (1983). "Higher Taxes That Promote Development." *Fortune* 108 (18 August): 68–71.

Brittain, J. A. (1971). "The Incidence of Social Security Payroll Taxes." *American Economic Review* 61 (March): 110–125.

Bronfenbrenner, Martin. (1985). "Early American Leader—Institutional and Critical Traditions." *American Economic Review* 75 (December): 13–27.

Brown, Elizabeth Read. (1961). "How College Textbooks Treat Land Value Taxation." *American Journal of Economics and Sociology* 20 (January): 147–167.

Browning, Edgar K. (1978). "The Burden of Taxation." *Journal of Political Economy* 86 (April): 649–674.

———. (1986). "Reply to Professor Due." *National Tax Journal* 39 (December): 541–542.

Brown, Phillips Hamlin. (1981). Letter to author, 15 December. Personal files, Iowa City, IA.

Brueckner, Jan K. (1986). "A Modern Analysis of the Effects of Site Value Taxation." *National Tax Journal* 39 (March): 49–58.

Buchanan, James M. (1960). *Fiscal Theory and Political Economy: Selected Essays*. Chapel Hill: The University of North Carolina Press.

Buckle, Henry Thomas. (1894). *The History of the Civilization of England*. New York: Appleton.

Buehler, Alfred G. (1940). *Public Finance*. New York: McGraw-Hill Book Company.

Bye, Carl R. (1940). *Developments and Issues in the Theory of Rent*. Morningside Heights, NY: Columbia University Press.

Calvo, Guillermo A., Laurence J. Kotlikoff, and Carlos Alfredo Rodriguez. (1979). "The Incidence of a Tax on Pure Rent: A New (?) Reason for an Old Answer." *Journal of Political Economy* 87 (August): 254–262.

Cannan, Edwin. (1967[1894]). *A History of the Theories of Production and Distribution in English Political Economy 1776–1848*. London: Rivington; reprint ed., New York: Augustus Kelley.

———. (1907). "The Proposed Relief of Buildings from Local Rates." *Economic Journal* 17: 36–46.

———. (1964[1930]). *A Review of Economic Theory*. London: P.S. King & Son; reprint ed., New York: Augustus Kelley.

Carlton, Frank T. (1907/1908). "The Rent Concept, Narrowed and Broadened." *Quarterly Journal of Economics* 22 (November): 48–61.

Carver, Thomas Nixon. (1902). "Some Theoretical Possibilities of a Protective Tariff." *Publications of the American Economics Association*, Ser. 3, 3: 167–182.

———. (1915). *Essays in Social Justice*. Cambridge: Harvard University Press.

———. (1919a). *Principles of Political Economy*. Boston: Ginn & Company.

———. (1919b). "Rejoinder." *Quarterly Journal of Economics* 33 (May): 570–571.

Cassel, Gustav. (1928). Testimony Before the Banking and Currency Committee of the House of Representatives, May.

———. (1932). *The Theory of Social Economy*. New York: Harcourt Brace & Company.

Chandler, Lester. V. (1971). *American Monetary Policy 1928–1941*. New York: Harper & Row Publishers.

———. (1980[1978]). Letter to Paul Junk, 17 December, in *Selected Articles By Harry Gunnison Brown*. New York: Robert Schalkenbach Foundation.

Cirillo, Renato. (1984). "Leon Walras and Social Justice." *American Journal of Economics and Sociology* 43 (January): 53–60.

Clark, John Bates. (1890). "The Ethics of Land Tenure." *International Journal of Ethics* 1 (October): 298–316.

———. (1899). *The Distribution of Wealth*. New York: Macmillan Company.

Clark, John Maurice. (1917). "Review of *Transportation Rates and Their Regulation* by Harry Gunnison Brown." *Journal of Political Economy* 25 (February): 208–209.

Coase, Ronald H. (1966). *The Economics of Regulation of Public Utilities*. Conference at Northwestern University, 19–24 July.

Cobb, Charles and Paul H Douglas. (1928). "A Theory of Production." *American Economic Review* 18 (March): 139–195.

Cohen, Avi. (forthcoming). *A Century of Capital Controversy: Scarcity, Production, Equilibrium and Time from Böhm-Bawerk to Bliss*.

Commons, John. (1900). "Review of *The Economics of Distribution* by John Hobson." *Annals of the American Academy of Political and Social Sciences* 16 (July): 1333–137.

———. (1907). "Political Economy and Business Economy: Comments of Fisher's Capital and Income." *Quarterly Journal of Economics* 22 (November): 120–125.

———. (1922). "A Progressive Tax on Land Values." *Political Science Quarterly* 38 (March): 41–68.

———. (1925). "Review of *Economic Science and the Common Welfare*." *American Economic Review* 15 (September): 480–485.

———. (1934). *Institutional Economics*. New York: Macmillan & Company.

Cord, Steven. (1984[1965]). *Henry George: Dreamer or Realist?* Philadelphia: University of Pennsylvania Press; reprint ed., New York: Robert Schalkenbach Foundation.

———. (1986). "How Much Revenue Would a Full Land Value Tax Yield?" *American Journal of Economics and Sociology* 44 (July): 279–293.

Cord, Steven and Robert V. Andelson. (1979). "Ely, A Liberal Economist Defends Landlordism." In *Critics of Henry George*. Ed. Robert V. Andelson. Rutherford, NJ: Fairleigh Dickinson University Press.

Cross, Melvin, and Robert B. Ekelund. (1980). "A. T. Hadley on Monopoly Theory and Railway Regulation: An American Contribution to Economic Analysis and Policy." *History of Political Economy* 12 (Summer): 214–232.

da Empoli, Domenico. (1966). *Analisi critica di alcuni effetti dell'imposta generale sulle vendite.* Milan: Giuffrè.

Davenport, Herbert J. (1908). *Value and Distribution.* Chicago: University of Chicago Press.

———. (1910). "Social Productivity versus Private Acquisition." *Quarterly Journal of Economics* 25 (November): 96–118.

———. (1911). "The Extent and Significance of the Unearned Increment." *Publications of the American Economic Association* Ser. 4, 11: 322–31.

———. (1916). "Fetter's *Principles.*" *Journal of Political Economy* 24: 344–362.

———. (1917)."Theoretical Issues in the Single Tax." *American Economic Review* 7 (March): 1–30.

———. (1919)."The War Tax Paradox." *American Economic Review* 9 (March): 34–36.

de Chazeau, M. G. (1937). "The Nature of the 'Rate Base' in the Regulation of Public Utilities." *Quarterly Journal of Economics* 51 (February): 298–316.

de Kruif, Paul. (1926). *Microbe Hunters.* New York: Harcourt, Brace & Company.

Dewey, John. (1938). "Preface." *Significant Paragraphs from Henry George's* Progress and Poverty. New York: Doubleday, Doran & Company.

Dimand, Robert W. (1997). "Editorial Introduction." *The Works of Irving Fisher*, Vol. 7, *The Making of Index Numbers.* Ed. William Barber. London: Pickering & Chatto.

———. (1998). "The Fall and Rise of Irving Fisher's Macroeconomics." *Journal of the History of Economic Thought* 20 (June): 191–201.

———.(1999). "Irving Fisher's Monetary Economics." *The Economics of Irving Fisher: Reviewing the Scientific Work of a Great Economist.* Eds. Hans-E. Loef and Hans G. Monissen. Northampton, MA: Edward Elgar.

Dirlam, Joel B. (1939). Letter to Harry Gunnison Brown, 29 April. Joint Collection University of Missouri Western Historical Manuscript Collection-Columbia and State Historical Society of Missouri Manuscripts.

Dorety, Frederic C. (1923). "The Function of Reproduction Cost in Public Utility Valuation and Rate-making." *Harvard Law Review* 37 (December): 173–200.

Dorfman, Joseph. (1959). *The Economic Mind in American Civilization*. New York: Viking Press.

———, ed. (1973). *Thorstein Veblen, Essays, Reviews and Reports: Previously Uncollected Writings*. Clifton, NJ: Augustus Kelley.

Dorfman, Robert. (1959). "Waiting and the Period of Production." *Quarterly Journal of Economics* 73 (August): 351–368.

Dorn, James A. (1983). "An Introduction: A Historical Perspective on the Importance of Stable Money." *Cato Journal* 3 (Spring): 1–8.

Douglas, Paul. (1972). *In The Fullness of Time*. New York: Harcourt, Brace and Janovich.

Due, John F. (1942). *The Theory of Incidence of Sales Taxation*. Morningside Heights, NY: King Crown Press.

———. (1953). "Toward a General Theory of Sales Tax Incidence." *Quarterly Journal of Economics* 68 (May): 253–266.

———. (1986). "Tax Incidence, Indirect Taxes and Transfers—A Comment." *National Tax Journal* 39 (December): 539–540.

Dwyer, Terence M. (1980). *A History of Land-Value Taxation*. Diss. Harvard University. Ann Arbor: UMI, 1990.

Edgeworth, F. Y. (1897). "The Pure Theory of Taxation." *Economic Journal* 7 (June): 226–238.

———. (1899). "Professor Seligman On the Mathematical Method." *Economic Journal* 9 (June): 286–315.

———. (1925). *Collected Papers Relating to Political Economy*. 2 vols. New York: Burt Franklin.

Edwards, Mary. (1984). "Site Value Taxation in Australia: Where Land is Taxed More and Improvements Less, Average Housing Value and Stock are Higher." *American Journal of Economics and Sociology* 43 (October): 481–495.

Ely, Richard T. (1917). "Landed Property as an Economic Concept and as a Field of Research." *American Economic Review* 7, Supplement (March): 18–33.

———. (1928). "Land Income." *Political Science Quarterly* 43 (September): 408–427.

Ely, Richard T., Thomas S. Adams, Max O. Lorenz, and Allyn Young. (1930). *Outlines of Economics*, 5th ed. New York: Macmillan and Company.

Escher, Franklin. (1911). *Elements of Foreign Exchange*. New York: Banking Publishing Company.

Fairchild, Fred. (1911). *Essentials of Economics*. New York: American Book Company.

———. (1926). "Review of *The Economics of Taxation* by Harry Gunnison Brown." *American Economic Review* 19 (June): 343–344.

Feder, Kris A. (1993). *Issues in the Theory of Land Value Taxation*. Diss. Temple University.

Federal Power Commission vs. *Hope Natural Gas Co.*, 320 U.S. 591, 601 (1944).

Feldstein, Martin. (1977). "The Surprising Incidence of a Tax on Pure Rent: A New Answer to an Old Question." *Journal of Political Economy* 85 (April): 349–360.

Ferguson, Maxwell. (1916). "Review of *Transportation Rates and Their Regulation* by Harry Gunnison Brown." *American Economic Review* 6 (September): 632–633.

Fetter, Frank A. (1900). "Recent Discussion of the Capital Concept." *Quarterly Journal of Economics* 15 (November): 1–45.

———. (1901). "The Passing of the Old Rent Concept." *Quarterly Journal of Economics* 15 (May): 416–455.

———. (1904a). *The Principles of Economics*. New York: Century Company.

———. (1904b). "The Relations Between Rent and Interest." *Publications of the American Economics Association* Ser. 3, 5 (February): 176–240.

———. (1914a). "Interest Theories Old and New." *American Economic Review* 4 (March): 68–92.

———. (1914b). "Capitalization Versus Productivity Rejoinder." *American Economic Review* 4 (December): 856–859.

Fillebrown, Charles B. (1908). Chairman of Round Table Discussion, "Agreements in Political Economy." *Publications of the American Economics Association* Ser. 3. n. 5: 117–123.

———. (1909). *The A B C of Taxation*, 2nd ed. New York: Doubleday, Page & Company.

Fine, Ben. (1983). "The Historical Approach to Rent and Price Theory Reconsidered." *Australian Economic Papers* 22 (June): 137–143.

Fischel, William A. (1998). "The Ethics of Land Value Taxation Revisited: Has the Millennium Arrived Without Anyone Noticing?" in *Land Value Taxation: Can It and Will It Work Today?* Ed. Dick Netzer. Cambridge, MA: Lincoln Institute of Land Policy.

Fisher, Irving. (1909). "The Rate of Capital and Income and the Rate of Interest: A Reply to Critics. *Quarterly Journal of Economics* 23 (May):536–541.

———. (1911a). *Elementary Principles of Economics*. New York: Macmillan Company.

———. (1911b). *The Purchasing Power of Money*. With the assistance of H.G. Brown. New York: Macmillan Company.

———. (1911c). "The Impatience Theory of Interest." *Scientia* 9: 380–401.

———. (1913). "The Impatience Theory of Interest." *American Economic Review* 3 (September): 610–618.

———. (1920). *Stabilizing the Dollar*. New York: Macmillan Company.

———. (1928). Letter to Harry Gunnison Brown, 10 May. Joint Collection University of Missouri Western Historical Manuscript Collection-Columbia and State Historical Society of Missouri Manuscripts.

———. (1929). Letter to Harry Gunnison Brown, 1 October. Joint Collection University of Missouri Western Historical Manuscript Collection-Columbia and State Historical Society of Missouri Manuscripts.

———. (1997[1930a]). Letter to Dennis Robertson, 13 August. In *The Works of Irving Fisher*, Vol. 9. Ed. William Barber, London: Pickering & Chatto.

———. (1965[1930b]). *The Theory of Interest*. New York: Macmillan & Company; reprint ed., New York: Augustus Kelley.

———. (1932a). *Booms and Depressions*. New York: Adelphi Company.

———. (1932). "The Single Tax." *The International Musician*.

———. (1935). *100% Money*. New York: Adelphi Company.

———. (1942). *Constructive Income Taxation: A Proposal for Reform*. New York: Harper & Brothers.

Foster, Geoffrey A. (2000). "Australia." *Land Value Taxation Around the World*. Boston: Blackwell Publishers.

Fraser, L. M. (1937). *Economic Thought and Language*. London: A. & C. Black.

Freedman, Craig. (1995). "The Economist as Mythmaker—Stigler's Kinky Transformation." *Journal of Economic Issues* 24 (March): 175–209.

Friedman, Milton. (1969). Letter to David J. Byrnes, 19 February. Joint Collection University of Missouri Western Historical Manuscript Collection-Columbia and State Historical Society of Missouri Manuscripts.

Friedman, Milton. (1984). Letter to the author. 6 October. Personal files, Iowa City, IA.

Gaffney, Mason. (1970). "Adequacy of Land as a Tax Base." *The Assessment of Land Value*. Ed. Daniel Holland. Madison, WI: University of Wisconsin Press.

———. (1978). "Two Centuries of Thought on Taxation of Land Rents." *Land Value Taxation*. Ed. Richard Lindholm and Arthur Lynn, Jr. Madison, WI: University of Wisconsin Press.

———. (1994a). "Neo-classical Economics as a Stratagem against Henry George." *The Corruption of Economics*. Ed. Mason Gaffney and Fred Harrison. London: Shepheard-Walwyn.

———. (1994b). "Land as a Distinctive Factor of Production." *Land and Taxation*. Ed. Nicolaus Tideman. London: Shepheard-Walwyn.

———. (1997). Letter to the author. 26 November. Personal files, Iowa City, IA.

Garrison, F. W. (1913). "The Case for the Single Tax." *The Atlantic Monthly* (December):737–746.

Geiger, George R. (1933). *The Philosophy of Henry George*. New York: Macmillan Company.

———. (1936). *The Theory of the Land Question*. New York: Macmillan Company.

George, Henry. (1891). *Protection and Free Trade*. New York: Henry George.

Goodwin, Crauford D. (1998). "Martin Bronfenbrenner, 1914–1997." *Economic Journal* 108 (November): 1775–1780.

Goschen, George J. (1896). *The Theory of Foreign Exchange*. London: Effingham Wilson.

Graham, Frank. (1923). "International Values Re-Examined." *Quarterly Journal of Economics* 38 (November): 54–86.

———. (1941). "100 Per Cent Reserves: Comment." *American Economic Review* 31 (June): 338–340.

Gray, Horace M. (1980[1975]). Letter to Weld Carter, 2 April. In *Selected Articles by Harry Gunnison Brown*. Ed. Paul Junk. New York: Robert Schalkenbach Foundation.

Gunning, J. Patrick. (1997). "Herbert Davenport on the Single Tax." *American Journal of Economics and Sociology* 56 (October): 565–574.

Haberler, Gottfried. (1931). "Irving Fisher's *Theory of Interest*." *Quarterly Journal of Economics* 45 (May): 499–526.

Hadley, Arthur T. (1928). "The Meaning of Valuation." *American Economic Review* 18, Supplement (March): 173–180.

Hall, James K. (1940). "Round Table Discussion of Incidence of Taxation." *American Economic Review* 30 (March): 241–242.

Harberger, Arnold. (1979). Quoted on the back cover of the reprint of *The Economic of Taxation* by Harry Gunnison Brown. Chicago: University of Chicago.

———. (1984). Letter to author, 15 October. Personal files, Iowa City, IA.

Harris, C. Lowell. (1979). "Rothbard's Anarcho-Capitalist Critique." *Critics of Henry George*. Ed. Robert V. Andelson. Rutherford, NJ: Fairleigh Dickinson University Press.

———. (1986). Letter to Spencer Carr. Personal files, Iowa City, IA.

Hart, A. G. (1934/1935). "The Chicago Plan for Banking Reform." *Review of Economic Studies* 2: 104–117.

Hausman, Daniel. (1981). *Capital, Profits and Prices.* New York: Columbia University Press.

Heilbroner, Robert. (1961). *The Worldly Philosophers.* New York: Simon and Schuster.

Hewett, William W. (1929). "Capital Value Once More." *American Economic Review* 19 (December): 646–648.

Hicks, Ursula. "Can Land be Assessed for Purposes of Site Value Taxation?" *The Assessment of Land Value.* Ed. Daniel Holland. Madison, WI: University of Wisconsin Press.

Holland, Daniel, ed. (1970). *The Assessment of Land Value.* Madison, WI: University of Wisconsin Press.

Hotelling, Harold. (1938). "The General Welfare in Relation to the Problems of Taxation and Railway and Utility Rates." *Econometrica* 6 (July): 242–269.

Humphrey, Thomas M. (1971). "Role of Non-Chicago Economists in the Evolution of the Quantity Theory in America 1930–1950." *Southern Economic Journal* 38 (July): 12–19.

Hutt, W. W. (1979). *The Keynesian Episode.* Indianapolis, IN: Liberty Press.

Jenkins, H. P. B. (1955). "Excise Tax Shifting and Incidence: A Money Flows Approach." *Journal of Political Economy* 62 (April): 125–149.

Jensen, Jens Peter. (1931). *Property Taxation in the United States.* Chicago: University of Chicago Press.

Johnson, Alvin S. (1902). "Rent in Modern Economic Theory." *Publications of the American Economic Association* Ser. 3, 3 (February): 873–1007.

———. (1914). "The Case Against the Single Tax." *Atlantic Monthly* 113 (January): 27–37.

Jones, R. A. (1980). "Which Price Index for Escalating Debts?" *Economic Inquiry* 18 (April): 221–232.

Jorgenson, Emil O. (1925). *False Education in Our Colleges and Universities.* Chicago: Manufacturers and Merchants Federal Tax League.

Junk, Paul E., ed. (1980). *Selected Articles by Harry Gunnison Brown.* New York: Robert Schalkenbach Foundation.

Kahn, Alfred E. (1970). *The Economics of Regulation: Principles and Institutions,* 2 vols. New York: John Wiley & Sons.

———. (1984). Letter to author, 5 September. Personal files, Iowa City, IA.

Kaldor, Nicolas. (1960). *Essays on Value and Distribution.* Glencoe, IL: The Free Press of Glencoe, Illinois.

Kamerschen, David R. (1987). "Some Surviving Elements in the Work of Henry George." *American Journal of Economics and Sociology* 46 (October): 489–493.

Kemmerer, E. W. (1915). "Review of *International Trade and Exchange* by Harry Gunnison Brown." *American Economic Review* 5 (June): 354–356.

Kendrick, M. Slade. (1951). *Public Finance.* Boston: Houghton Mifflin Co.

Keynes, John Maynard. (1926). *The Official Papers of Alfred Marshall.* London: Macmillan.

———. (1936). *The General Theory of Employment, Interest and Money.* New York: Harcourt Brace & Company.

Kindleberger, Charles. (1978). *Manias, Panics and Crashes.* New York: Basic Books.

King, W. I. (1915). *The Wealth and Income of the People of the United States.* New York: Macmillan Company.

———. (1921). "Earned and Unearned Income." *Annals of the American Academy of Political and Social Sciences* 95 (May): 251–259.

———. (1924). "The Single-Tax Complex Analyzed." *Journal of Political Economy* 32 (October): 604–612.

Kirzner, Israel. (1993). "The Pure Time-Preference Theory of Interest: An Attempt at Clarification." *The Meaning of Ludwig von Mises.* Ed. Jeffrey M. Herbener. Norwell, MA: Kluwer Academic Publishers.

Kleiman, Ephriam. (2000). "Early Inflation Tax Theory and Estimates." *History of Political Economy* 32 (Summer): 233–265.

Knight, Frank. (1925a). "Review of *The Economics of Taxation* by Harry Gunnison Brown." *National Municipal Review* 14 (April): 377–338.

———. (1925b). "Review of *The Taxation of Unearned Incomes* by Harry Gunnison Brown." *National Municipal Review* 14 (April): 378.

———. (1933). "Review of *The Philosophy of Henry George* by George R. Geiger." *Journal of Political Economy* 41 (October): 687–690.

———. (1939). Letter to Harry Gunnison Brown, 29 April. Joint Collection University of Missouri Western Historical Manuscript Collection-Columbia and State Historical Society Manuscripts.

———. (1953). "The Fallacies in the Single Tax." *The Freeman* 3 (August): 809–811.

———. (1956). *On the History and Method of Economics: Selected Essays.* Chicago: University of Chicago Press.

Kolko, Gabriel. (1965). *Railroads and Regulation 1877–1975.* Princeton, NJ: Princeton University Press.

Lee, Susan Previant, and Peter Passel. (1979). *A New Economic View of American History.* New York: W.W. Norton & Company.

Lissner, Will. (1951). "Pennsylvania's New Optimal Graded Tax Law." *American Journal of Economics and Sociology* 10 (October): 41–43.

———. (1958). "Harry Gunnison Brown on American Liberalism." *Henry George News* (July).

———. (1975). "In Memoriam: H. G. Brown 1880–1975." *American Journal of Economics and Sociology* 34 (July): 246–248.

——. (1987). "In Memoriam: Elizabeth Read Brown." *American Journal of Economics and Sociology* 46 (July): 383–384.

Locklin, D. Philip. (1933). "The Literature on Railway Rate Theory." *Quarterly Journal of Economics* 47 (February): 167–230.

Loucks, William N. (1930). "The Unearned Increment in Land Values and Its Social Implication." *Annals of the American Academy of Political and Social Sciences* 148 (March): 67–81.

Mair, Douglas and Richard Damania. (1988). "The Ricardian Tradition and Local Property Taxation." *Cambridge Journal of Economics* 12: 435–449.

Marshall, Alfred. (1893). "On Rent." *Economic Journal* 3: 74–90.

——. (1907). *Principles of Economics,* 8th ed. New York: Macmillan and Company.

McCann, Jr., C. R., and Mark Perlman. (1993). "On Thinking About George Stigler." *Economic Journal* 103 (July): 994–1014.

Mering, Otto von. (1942). *The Shifting and Incidence of Taxation.* Philadelphia: The Blakiston Company.

Mieszkowski, Peter. (1969). "Tax Incidence Theory: The Effects of Taxes on the Distribution of Income." *Journal of Economic Literature* 7: 1103–1124.

——. (1972). "The Property Tax: An Excise Tax or Profits Tax?" *Journal of Public Economics* 1 (April): 73–96.

Mieszkowski, Peter and Zodrow, George R. (1985). "The Incidence of a Partial State Corporate Income Tax." *National Tax Journal* 38 (December): 489–496.

——. (1989). "Taxation and the Tiebout Model: The Differential Effects of Head Taxes, Taxes on Land Rents, Property Taxes." *Journal of Economic Literature* 27 (September): 1098–1146.

Mill, John Stuart. (1909). *Principles of Political Economy.* London: Longmans, Green & Company.

Millis, H. A. (1916). "Review of *The Principles of Economics* by Frank A. Fetter." *Quarterly Journal of Economics* 30 (May): 559–565.

Moss, Laurence S. (forthcoming). "The Seligman-Edgeworth Controversy about Tax Incidence: An Interpretation." *History of Political Economy.*

Musgrave, Richard. (1939). Letter to Harry Gunnison Brown, 21 November. Joint Collection University of Missouri Western Historical Manuscript Collection-Columbia and State Historical Society Manuscripts.

——. (1953). "On Incidence." *Journal of Political Economy* 61 (August): 306–323.

——. (1959). *The Theory of Public Finance.* New York: McGraw-Hill Company.

The National Cyclopedia of American Biography. (1979) 58: 43–44. Clifton, NJ: James T. White & Company.

Mussey, Henry Raymond. (1925). "Talking Taxes." *The Nation* (7 October): 389.

Netzer, Dick. (1969). Letter to Harry Gunnison Brown, 11 February. Personal files, Iowa City, IA.

———. (2001). "What Do We Need to Know about Land Value Taxation." *American Journal of Economics and Sociology* 60 (Supplement): 97–118.

Nicholson, J. S. (1893). "Address to the Economic Science and Statistics Section of the British Association." *Journal of Political Economy* 2 (December): 119–132.

Oates, Wallace E., and Robert M. Schwab. (1997). "The Impact of Urban Land Value Taxation: The Pittsburgh Experience." *National Tax Journal* 50 (March): 1–21.

Ogilvie, F. W. (1930). "Marshall on Rent." *Economic Journal* 40 (March): 1–24.

Pantaleoni, Maffeo. (1898). *Pure Economics.* London: Macmillan and Company.

Pareto, Vilfredo. (1971). *Manual of Political Economy.* New York: Augustus Kelley.

Parrish, John. (1967). "The Rise of Economics as an Academic Discipline: The Formative Years to 1900." *Southern Economic Journal* 34 (July): 1–17.

Patten, Simon Nelson. (1891). "Another View of the Ethics of Land Tenure." *International Journal of Ethics* 1 (April): 357–360.

———. (1902). *Theory of Prosperity.* New York: Macmillan Company.

Peckman, Joseph A. (1985). *Who Paid the Taxes, 1966–1985?* Washington DC: The Brookings Institution.

Pellengahr, Ingo. (1986). "Austrians Versus Austrians II, Functionalist Versus Essentialist Theories of Interest." *Lecture Notes in Economics and Mathematical Systems: Studies in Austrian Capital Theory, Investment and Time.* Ed. Malte Faber. Berlin: Springer-Verlag.

Peretz, Paul. (1997). "Social Security and Political Investment." *Polity* 30 (Fall): 79–106.

Pigou, A. C., ed. (1925). *Memorials of Alfred Marshall.* London: Macmillan and Company.

Pigou, A. C. and Frank Taussig. (1913). "Railway Rates and Joint Costs." *Quarterly Journal of Economics* 27 (May and August): 535–538, 687–694.

Post, Louis. (1926). *What is the Single Tax?* New York: Vanguard Press.

Price, L. L. (1893). "Review of *The Unseen Foundations of Society* by the Duke of Argyll." *Economic Journal* 3: 264–271.

Ricardo, David. (1951–1971). *Principles. Works of David Ricardo, Vol. 1, Principles of Political Economy.* Ed. P. Scraffa. Cambridge: Cambridge University Press.

Recktenwald, Horst Claus. (1971). *Tax Incidence and Income Redistribution: An Introduction.* Detroit, MI: Wayne State University Press.

Reichardt, William. (1997)."Tax the Land, Not Improvements, and Renew Our Cities." *Des Moines Sunday Register* (24 August): Section C: 1–2.

Reid, Gavin C. (1981). *The Kinked Demand Curve Analysis of Oligopoly.* Edinburgh: Edinburgh University Press.

———. (1990). Letter to author, 21 November. Personal files, Iowa City, IA.

Ripley, William Z. (1912). *Railroads, Rates and Regulation.* New York: Longmans, Green & Co.

Robbins, Lionel. (1930). "On a Certain Ambiguity in the Conception of Stationary Equilibrium." *Economic Journal* 40 (June): 194–214.

———. (1967[1933]). Introduction. *The Common Sense of Political Economy,* v. 1 by Philip H. Wicksteed. New York: Augustus Kelley.

Robinson, James Harvey. (1921). *The Mind in the Making.* New York: Harpers.

Robinson, Joan. (1933). *The Economics of Imperfect Competition.* London: Macmillan and Company.

Rogers, James Harvey. (1931). *American Weighs Its Gold.* New Haven: Yale University Press.

———. (1932). Letter to Harry Gunnison Brown, 21 May. Rogers Papers, Yale University Library, New Haven, CT.

———. (1933). Letter to Harry Gunnison Brown, 27 November. Rogers Papers, Yale University Library, New Haven, CT.

Rolph, Earl R. (1952). "A Proposed Revision of Excise-Tax Theory." *Journal of Political Economy* 55 (April): 102–117.

Rolph, Earl R. and George Break. (1961). *Public Finance.* New York: Ronald Press.

Rothbard, Murray. (1970). *Power and Markets.* Menlo Park, CA: Institute for Humane Studies,.

———. (1977). Introduction. *Capital, Interest and Rent: Essays in the Theory of Distribution by Frank A. Fetter.* Kansas City, MO: Sheed Andrews and McNeel Inc.

Ryan, Christopher K. (2000). "Elizabeth Read Brown." *A Biographical Dictionary of Women Economists.* Eds. Robert W. Dimand, Mary Ann Dimand, and Evelyn L. Forget. Northampton, MA: Edward Elgar.

Ryan, Christopher K. and Helen B. Ryan. (1999). "Remembrance and Appreciation Feature: George Raymond Geiger (1903–1998)." *American Journal of Economics and Sociology* 58 (January): 7–15.

Samuels, Warren J. (2000). Foreword. "Land Value Taxation Around the World." *American Journal of Economics and Sociology* (Supplement): ix–xii.

Samuelson, Paul. (1967). *Ten Studies in the Tradition of Irving Fisher.* New York: John Wiley & Sons.

———. (1979). "Land and the Rate of Interest." In *Theory for Economic Efficiency: Essays in Honor of Abba Lerner.* Eds. B. I. Greenfield, A. M. Levenson, W. Hamovitch, and E. Rotwein. Cambridge: MIT Press.

———. (2001). "A Modern Post-Mortem on Böhm's Capital Theory: Its Vital Normative Flaw Shared by Pre-Scraffian Mainstream Capital Theory." *Journal of the History of Economic Thought* 23 (September): 301–317.

Santayana, George. (1905). *Life of Reason.* New York: Charles Scribner's Sons.

Sause, George. (1958). "Economic Principles and Economic Analysis." *American Journal of Economics and Sociology* 17 (April): 33–36.

Schumpeter, J. A. (1928). "Wen trifft die Umsatzsteuer?" *Der Deutche Volkwirt* (16 November): 207–209;

Scitovsky, Tibor. (1950). *Welfare and Competition: The Economics of a Fully Employed Economy.* Chicago: Richard D. Irwin.

Seager, Henry C. (1900). "Review of J. B. Clark's *The Distribution of Wealth.*" *Annals of the American Academy of Political and Social Sciences* 16 (September):297–303.

———. (1912). "The Impatience Theory of Interest." *American Economic Review* 2 (December): 834–851.

———. (1913). "Comment on the Impatience Theory of Interest." *American Economic Review* 3 (September): 618–619.

———. (1931). *Labor and Other Economic Essays.* New York: Harpers & Brothers.

Seligman, E. R. A. (1891). Discussant in the *Publications of the American Economic Association* 6: 56–58.

———. (1892). "The Shifting and Incidence of Taxation." *Publications of the American Economics Association* 7 (March–May): 5–191.

———. (1912). "Recent Tax Reforms Abroad." *Political Science Quarterly* 27 (March): 454–469.

———. (1925). *Essays in Taxation,* 10th ed. New York: Macmillan Company.

———. (1926). *Principles of Economics.* New York: Longman, Green & Company.

Shoup, Carl. (1960). *Ricardo on Taxation.* New York: Columbia University Press.

Simon, Herbert A. (1943). "The Incidence of a Tax on Urban Real Property." *Quarterly Journal of Economics* 57 (May): 416–429.

Simons, Henry C. (1926). "Review of *The Economics of Taxation* by Harry Gunnison Brown." *Journal of Political Economy* 34 (February): 134–136.

———. (1936). "Rules Versus Authorities in Monetary Policy." *Journal of Political Economy* 44 (February): 1–30.

———. (1940). "Round Table on the Incidence of Taxation." *American Economic Review* 30 (March): 242–246.

Skouras, Athanassios. (1980). "Land and Taxation as Issues in Economic Theory." *American Journal of Economics and Sociology* 39 (October): 373–382.

Slemrod, Joel. (1994). "Professional Opinions about Tax Policy: 1994 and 1934." *National Tax Journal* 48 (March): 121–145.

Smyth vs. Ames, 169 U.S. 466, 546–547 (1898).

Souter, R. W. (1932). "Land, Capital and Opportunity Cost." *American Economic Review* 22 (June): 203–207.

Southwestern Bell Telephone. 262 U.S. 276, 289–312 (1923).

Spahr, Charles B. (1891). "The Single Tax." *Political Science Quarterly* 6 (December): 625–634.

Spengler, Joseph J. (1965). "Kinked Demand Curves: By Whom First Used?" *Sourthern Economic Journal* 32 (July): 81–84.

Sprinkel, Beryl W. (1981). Letter to author, 16 December. Personal files, Iowa City, IA.

Steindl, Frank G. (1995). *Monetary Interpretations of the Great Depression: A Review Study.* Ann Arbor, MI: University of Michigan Press.

Stevans, Frank Fletcher. (1962). *A History of the University of Missouri.* Columbia, MO: University of Missouri Press.

Stigler, George J. (1968). *Production and Distribution Theories.* New York: Agathon Press.

———. (1978). "The Literature of Economics: The Case of the Kinked Oligopoly Demand Curve." *Economic Inquiry* 16 (April): 185–204.

———. (1982). *The Economist as Preacher and Other Essays.* Chicago: University of Chicago Press.

[Sumner, William Graham.] (1881). "Review of *Progress and Poverty* by Henry George." *Scribner's Monthly* 28 (June): 312–313.

Taussig, Frank. (1891). "A Contribution to the Theory of Railway Rates." *Quarterly Journal of Economic* 5 (July): 438–465.

———. (1913). "Railway Rates and Joint Costs Once More." *Quarterly Journal of Economics* 27 (February): 378–384.

———. (1915). "Review of *International Trade and Exchange* by Harry Gunnison Brown." *Journal of Political Economy* 23 (June): 621–623.

———. (1926). *Principles of Economics,* 2 vols., 3rd ed. New York: Macmillan Company.

Tideman, Nicolaus, ed. (1994). *Land and Taxation.* London: Shepheard-Walwyn in association with the Centre for Incentive Taxation.

Trevelyn, Charles. (1907). "Land Value Taxation and the Use of Land." *Economic Journal* 17: 30–35.

Turner, John Roscoe. (1921). *The Ricardian Rent Theory in Early American Economics.* New York: New York University Press.

Tuttle, Charles. (1902). "Clark's *Distribution of Wealth.*" *Yale Review* 11 (August): 179–187.

Twerdocleboff, W. (1929). "Die Theorie der Steurerüberwälzung in der nuestern Literatur." *Zeitschrift für die gesamte Staatwissenschaft* Band 86, Heft 3: 513–543.

Viner, Jacob. (1922). "Textbooks in Government Finance." *Journal of Political Economy* 30 (April): 241–256.

Wagner, Adoph. (1901). *Agar- und Industreistaat.* Jena: Gustav Fischel.

Walker, Francis A. (1883). *Land and Its Rent.* Boston: Little, Brown & Company.

———. (1888). *Political Economy.* New York: Henry Holt & Company.

Walker, Pinkney C. (1952a). Preface. "Essays in Honor of Harry Gunnison Brown, Ph.D., L.H.D.; On the Occasion of His Retirement from the University of Missouri." *American Journal of Economics and Sociology* 11 (April): 227–228.

———. (1952b). "Publications of Harry Gunnison Brown, 1907–1951." *American Journal of Economics and Sociology* 11 (April): 357–359.

———. (1975). "In Memoriam." Memorial service for Harry Gunnison Brown, 23 March. Personal files, Iowa City, IA.

———. (1983). Taped interview with Pinkney Walker, Columbia, MO, December. Personal files, Iowa City, IA.

Walras, Léon. (1954). *Elements of Pure Economics.* Tr. William Jaffe. London: George Allen & Unwin.

Walsh, Correa. (1901). *The Measurement of General Exchange-Value.* New York: Macmillan & Company.

Warburton, Clark. (1928). "Economic Terminology: Factors of Production and Distributive Shares." *American Economic Review* 18 (March): 65–74.

———. (1948a). "Monetary Velocity and Monetary Policy." *Review of Economics and Statistics* 30 (November): 304–314.

———. (1948b). "Bank Reserves and Business Fluctuations." *Journal of the American Statistical Association* 3 (December): 542–558.

Wedgewood, Joseph. (1912). "The Principle of Land Value Taxation." *Economic Journal* 22: 388–397.

Wenzer, Kenneth C., ed. (1997). *The Henry George Centennial Trilogy.* Vols. I–III. Rochester, NY: University of Rochester Press.

———, ed. (1999). *Land Value Taxation: The Equitable and Efficient Source of Public Finance.* Armonk, NY: M. E. Sharpe and London: Shepheard Walwyn.

Wheaton, William C. (2000). "Decentralized Welfare: Will There Be Underprovision?" *Journal of Urban Economics* 48 (3): 526–555.

Wicksell, Knut. (1897). "Der Bankzins als Regulator der Warenpreise." *Jahrbucher fur National-Okonomie und Statistik* 13 (February): 228–243.

————. (1967[1934]). *Lectures on Political Economy*, Vol. 1. New York: Macmillan & Company; reprint ed., New York: Augustus Kelley.

————. (1958). "A New Principle of Just Taxation." *Classics in the Theory of Public Finance*. Eds. Richard Musgrave and Alan Peacock. London: Macmillan & Company.

Wieser, Frederich von. (1927). *Social Economics*. New York: Greenburg.

Wildasin, David E. (1988). "Indirect Distributional Effects in Benefit-cost Analysis of Small Projects." *Economic Journal* 98 (September): 801–807.

————. (2000). "Factor Mobility and Fiscal Policy in the EU: Policy Issues and Analytical Approaches." *Fiscal Policy* 31 (October): 339–378.

Withers, Hartley. (1916). "Review of *Foreign Exchange: A Study in the Exchange Mechanisms of Commerce* by Harry Gunnison Brown." *Economic Journal* 26 (103): 345–346.

Worcester, Dean A. (1946). "A Reconsideration of Rent Theory." *American Economic Journal* 36 (June): 258–277.

Yeager, Leland. (1973). "The Keynesian Diversion." *Western Economic Journal* 11 (June): 150–163.

————. (1979). "Capital Paradoxes and the Concept of Waiting." *Time, Uncertainty and Disequilibrium*. Ed. Mario J. Rizzo. Lexington, MA: Lexington Books.

Yoder, Dale. (1931). "Some Economic Implications of Unemployment Insurance." *Quarterly Journal of Economics* 45 (August): 622–639.

Young, Allyn A. (1916). "Nearing's Income; King's Wealth and Income." *Quarterly Journal of Economics* 30 (May): 575–587.

Young, Arthur Nichols. (1916). *The Single Tax Movement in the United States*. Princeton, NJ: Princeton University Press.

Zodrow, George R. (2001). "The Property Tax as a Capital Tax: A Room with Three Views." *National Tax Journal* 54 (March): 139–156.

Index

M

S